Visits to Bedlam

FRONTISPIECE. *Sixteenth-century engraving by Matthaus Greuter of Doctor Wurmbrandt curing insanity. A good example of the demonic theory of madness, it depicts a Renaissance psychiatrist at work. The shelves overhead are filled with medicines like "reason," "finesse," and "sense"; the poem underfoot is an advertisement for the doctor.*

Visits to Bedlam

Madness and Literature in the Eighteenth Century

by Max Byrd

UNIVERSITY OF
SOUTH CAROLINA PRESS
Columbia, South Carolina

First printing, 1974
Second printing, 1975

Published in Columbia, South Carolina, by the
University of South Carolina Press, 1974

Manufactured in the United States of America

Library of Congress Cataloging in Publication Data
Byrd, Max.
Visits to Bedlam.

Includes bibliographical references.
1. English literature—18th century—History and criticism. 2. Mental illness in
literature.
I. Title.
PR449.M4B9   820'.9'353   73-19855
ISBN 0-87249-312-1

For Brookes

Contents

Illustrations

Frontispiece. Sixteenth-century engraving by Matthaus Greuter of Doctor Wurmbrandt curing insanity

(following page 45)

Plate 1. William Hogarth's *Credulity, Superstition and Fanaticism: A Medley* (1762)

Plate 2. William Hogarth's last engraving in the series *Rake's Progress* (1735)

Plate 3. Richard Newton's *A Visit to Bedlam* (1794)

Plate 4. *The Mad Artist in Chains*, an eighteenth-century etching by an anonymous artist

(following page 77)

Plate 5. Wash drawing by Thomas Rowlandson of a doctor and a lunatic

Plate 6. *St. Luke's Hospital* (1809), a colored aquatint and etching by Thomas Rowlandson and Augustus Pugin

Plate 7. *Madness*, an eighteenth-century mezzotint by an anonymous artist

Plate 8. *Crazey Kate* (1815), a colored aquatint by G. M. Brighty after George Shepheard

All illustrations are from the Fry Print Collection, Yale Medical Library.

Preface

No one, then, was ever a great man without some touch of divine inspiration" *(Nemo igitur vir magnus sine aliquo adflatu divino umquam fuit).*[1] The observation was commonplace when Cicero made it, an idea far too ancient to be dated—ancient enough, in fact, to be regarded as one of those instinctual truths that civilizations simply assume and possess. Men who become great in some way, who extend themselves beyond the ordinary, do so, not through their own powers, but by means of supernatural powers. And yet the fear of supernatural powers is at least as old as the reverence for them: the gods who breathe into a human vessel may as easily be demonic as benevolent, their purposes may as easily be malicious. Athena inspires Teiresias to see the future, but Euripides presents Dionysus as a cruel, capricious divinity whose worshipers become his victims, symbols to other men of meaningless irrationality. For good reasons the ordinary response of men to the sight of inspiration is ambiguous, a curse or a blessing; and the name commonly given it is madness.

The chapters that follow examine this universal ambiguity of response to madness in the historical setting of eighteenth-century England. A few introductory pages seem appropriate here, however, for the remarkable interest of the eighteenth-century experience can be felt only partially without some reminder of the classical view. It is also important to make clear at the start that the kind of great man this study concerns is in general the literary man or the man of imagination, and the kind of greatness he represents, whether for good or evil, is a greatness of vision or, even less precisely, a greatness of soul. A man speaks the truth, Oscar Wilde says, only when he puts aside his ordinary self and speaks from behind a mask. Madness is the earliest, the most primitive, and the most enduring of such masks, and it is the relationship between mask and self, sane self, that I shall primarily consider. Seneca refines Cicero's words to suit our purposes: *Nullum magnum ingenium sine mixtura dementiae fuit* ("There has been no great genius without a touch of insanity").² The Platonic and Aristotelian statements are the *loci classici* of these balanced contradictions.

Plato expresses mythologically man's willingness to believe that madness gives its victims access to truths denied the normal man. In two dialogues, *Phaedrus* and *Ion*, he arranges different kinds of madness hierarchically and sets forth the special virtue of each type. Simple insanity—lunacy, idiocy, etc.—he calls purely evil, one of many human burdens. But there is another madness, he says, "which is a divine gift, and the source of the chiefest blessings granted to men."³ And this divine madness he breaks down into prophecy, poetry, and love. The truths these states of madness tender are notoriously difficult to communicate or prove; worse still, they may intoxicate their possessors, disfiguring them and driving them to a frenzy that shatters all conventional boundaries and isolates the madman from his audience. Bewildered and fearful, the normal man backs helplessly away from such a madman. Yet the cause of that disfiguring rapture is a beautiful one. As Socrates relates in a long myth to Phaedrus, the lover (as madman) recognizes in his beloved an image of a truth that in its migrations the lover's soul has known before; and the rediscovery of that truth brings the lover unspeakable joy, carrying him far from the everyday world of other men. Powerful in numbers but impotent in some spiritual way, normal men see these ecstasies warily from a distance, and what they do not approve in them as miraculous or divine they reject or ignore, if they safely can; what seems threatening to their everyday world they suppress. Nor is the divine afflatus always recognized for what it is. The man who returns to the cave in *The Republic*, having seen the sun, will be ridiculed or even put to death by those who remained in darkness. Even those men who recognize the divinity of madness must fight back the envious hostility born of their own acknowledged inferiority. "He who, having no touch of the Muses' madness in his soul," Plato declares, "comes to the door and thinks that he will get into the temple by the help of art—he, I say, and his poetry are not admitted; the sane man disappears and is nowhere when he enters into rivalry with the madman."[4] It is in this sense of threat and also inadequacy that the ambiguous response to madness takes its roots.

Indispensable authority was given to the authenticity of the madman's inspiration by Aristotle's famous Problem XXX, which begins with this question: "Why is it that all men who are outstanding in philosophy, poetry or the arts are melancholic, and some to such an extent that they are infected by the diseases arising from black bile, as the story of Heracles among the heroes tells?"[5] (The words *melancholic* and *mad* were for all practical purposes synonymous in Aristotle's time.) In the habitual manner of his age he took Plato's poetical or mythical insight and translated it into rational medical terms—terms of bile and body heat and so forth—but the basic conception that madness and greatness exist in a necessary and mysterious relationship continued as firmly as ever.

So long as the prophet and the poet are both familiar faces of madness—so long, that is, as madness erupts in a religious or mythmaking society—the possibilities of mere madness or demonic madness will be evenly weighed with the possibilities of inspiration. But one religious society at least could not fully support the implications of Aristotle's brilliant madman. "In the Middle Ages," asserts Professor Klibansky in *Saturn and Melancholy*, "which assessed the worth of an individual not according to his intellectual gifts and capacities but according to his virtues in which God's grace enabled him to persevere, such an idea was . . . less acceptable; indeed, wherever it raised its head, it came into conflict with certain basic principles. During the first twelve hundred years after Christ the idea of the highly gifted melancholic had apparently been forgotten."[6] The Middle Ages denied that madness might signify divine favor or privilege and declared instead that it signified divine punishment, thus drawing on that other very ancient saying, *Quos Deus vult perdere, prius dementat* ("Whom God would destroy, he first makes mad"). In the medieval view madness is punishment visited upon all men for Adam's sin or sometimes visited particularly upon the proud or rebellious man, frequently through the agency of devils. Professor Klibansky pursues the history of the inspired madman into the Renaissance, when with many complications the traditional balance was restored. And yet even in Renaissance representations we are still far from our modern figure of the alienated genius, a discarded seer like Melville or a tormented and splenetic poet like Baudelaire. The distance between such modern outcasts and earlier mad figures is to be understood chiefly by reference to the customary response of a culture on the broadest possible scale; today we might say by reference to questions of tolerance and deviancy.

The focus of these essays falls upon another period like the Middle Ages in which the claims of madness were denied. For approximately a hundred years, from the late seventeenth to the late eighteenth century in England, we find that with astonishing energy and vehemence English society assaulted the ancient idea of the extraordinary madman—indeed, it assaulted the person of the madman himself. It is from the beginning of this period that we date the widespread practice of incarceration of the insane. And it is in the literature of this period, the Age of Reason so-called, that we encounter the most complex and negative uses of the metaphor of the mask of madness. No one would dispute that the traditional perception of madness was present and was often articulated in the period; but similarly it seems indisputable that the thrust of the period, the overwhelming consensus, was as I have described it. My purpose in what follows is to describe the Augustan response to madness, to distinguish it from what we have been calling the traditional view, and to suggest how the Augustan response, which was a denial, evolved into the Romantic response, which was an embracing. I draw largely upon the imaginative literature of the eighteenth century for examples, for here we find the response at its most intense and complex, but I turn whenever possible to medical and social history for support. What I am attempting to set down, however, is not a chronological history of madness in the eighteenth century, but rather what Perry Miller has called a "rank of spotlights" upon a larger drama. When Edward Young quoted approvingly in 1759 those words of Cicero's that preface these pages,[7] a new movement in modern thought had begun, a movement that our own time has not yet exhausted. But such a movement gained its initial momentum by the force of its reaction against what stood solidly and immediately before.

Acknowledgments

A GREAT MANY FRIENDS HAVE HELPED ME AT ONE OR ANOTHER stage of writing, and although it is impossible to name them all here, I am very grateful.

In its original form this book profited enormously from the direction of two men: Walter Jackson Bate, rarest of humanists, has never failed to give me encouragement, help, and, if I could claim it, inspiration. And Alan Heimert, my teacher and friend for more than a decade, has shown me, as much by example as by precept, how to proceed in more than merely scholarly matters.

Brooke Hopkins and Charles E. Pierce, Jr., have been important critics and supporters at crucial points. And Mark Rose has been patience and warmth themselves.

A grant from Harvard University's Hyder Rollins Fund has aided publication. Illustrations are here reproduced through the courtesy of the Historical Library of the Yale Medical School. A version of the introduction was awarded the Winthrop Sargeant Prize at Harvard in 1970.

Only those who know my wife will understand how sincere—and how inadequate—the dedication is.

MAX BYRD
Yale University
New Haven, Conn.

Visits to Bedlam

CHAPTER ONE

Reason in Madness

In a memorable scene in the fourth act of *King Lear*, in the country near Dover, Edgar cries out in sudden anguish at the old king's raving,

> O! matter and impertinency mix'd;
> Reason in madness.[1]

Edgar is responding to Lear's shrewd declamations on social injustice, but his phrase inevitably suggests other, more general meanings of both madness and reason; it opens the way to associations that are traditional and familiar and that seem to apply to our experience of the play itself as well as of this single moment. For along with his contemporary from La Mancha, King Lear marks the culmination—and the disappearance—of what we may call classical madness. Lear's voice recalls countless other madmen's voices, and as he paces back and forth in frenzy, dressed, the stage directions tell us, "fantastically with wild flowers," Edgar's sane voice reminds us that what appears to be senseless suffering may be in fact what Plato thought it, a divine gift or even a blessing.

Three different examples of insanity appear in the play: Lear, Edgar, and the Fool. Two of them, however, we may consider not genuine: the madness of Edgar is entirely pretended, a simple disguise, and that of the Fool is problematic. That the Fool is actually mad is not likely to be granted easily by modern readers;

1

yet to a Renaissance audience neither was he quite sane. The tradition of the jester in European literature has been exhaustively studied (notably by Enid Welsford and, more recently, Walter Kaiser),[2] and his connections with the madman are both obvious and imprecise. But as William Empson has shown in *The Structure of Complex Words,* the concept of one generally involves the concept of the other. The clown who praises folly and the madman who embodies it both *seem* to be mad, both behave madly, and both are possible voices for dark truths. In the face of dark possibilities, however, Lear's Fool ironically embodies, not mysterious or heavenly truths, but simple shrewdness. We must be careful to understand the quality of his common sense and its place in the play. For this fool, like so many others, is worldly-wise, cynical; he distrusts, and his view of things is at heart satirical. His prophecy to the audience is typical:

> . . . When every case in law is right;
> No squire in debt, nor no poor knight;
> When slanders do not live in tongues;
> Nor cut-purses come not to throngs;
> When usurers tell their gold i' th' field;
> And bawds and whores do churches build;
> Then shall the realm of Albion
> Come to great confusion:
> Then comes the time, who lives to see't,
> That going shall be us'd with feet.
>
> [III.ii.85—94]

In Act IV Lear re-creates the Fool's tone and posture to such an extent that one could almost say he has replaced him. All along, for example, the Fool's bawdy has carried suggestions of that disgust with sex that Shakespeare sometimes so powerfully expresses—the Fool's language is riddled with images of disease and perversity. And during the storm in Act III Lear's bitterness toward his elder daughters has begun to grow toward its present full, mad misogyny:

> The wren goes to't, and the small gilded fly
> Does lecher in my sight.
> Let copulation thrive . . .
> . . . Behold yond simp'ring dame,

Whose face between her forks presages snow;
That minces virtue, and does shake the head
To hear of pleasure's name;
The fitchew nor the soiled horse goes to't
With a more riotous appetite.
Down from the waist they are Centaurs,
Though women all above:
But to the girdle do the Gods inherit,
Beneath is all the fiend's: there's hell, there's darkness,
There is the sulphurous pit—burning, scalding,
Stench, consumption; fie, fie, fie! pah, pah!

[IV.vi.115—31]

When Gloucester confesses his blindness, the mad Lear thunders,
"What! art mad? A man may see how this world goes with no
eyes." And he begins to expound like a violent and impatient
teacher. Sexual disgust plays a part in his initial attack on political
authority:

Thou rascal beadle, hold thy bloody hand!
Why dost thou lash that whore? Strip thine own back;
Thou hotly lusts to use her in that kind
For which thou whipp'st her.

But he moves quickly to the related theme of poverty and social
injustice:

The usurer hangs the cozener.
Thorough tatter'd clothes small vices do appear;
Robes and furr'd gowns hide all. Plate sin with gold,
And the strong lance of justice hurtless breaks;
Arm it in rags, a pigmy's straw does pierce it.
None does offend, none, I say, none; I'll able 'em:
Take that of me, my friend, who have the power
To seal th' accuser's lips. Get thee glass eyes;
And, like a scurvy politician, seem
To see the things thou dost not.

It is at this point that Edgar, who has been witnessing this
meeting, speaks his famous lines. And as if to uphold him, Lear
then quietly acknowledges Gloucester's identity and speaks elo-
quently to him of patience, expressing the Elizabethan

commonplace that a man begins to cry at the moment of his birth, repeating himself then, with a significant addition:

> When we are born, we cry that we are come
> To this great stage of fools.

Moments later he tells the guards who have come after him: "I am even / The natural fool of Fortune."

In these great speeches Lear has outdone the Fool, and he seems to know it. He has equaled him in range of reference and allusion, and he has surpassed him in the darkness and extremity of his vision—for his declaration carries the force of context. This new assessment of the tragic nature of life has come to him only after he has suffered in the storm what wretches feel, after he has begun to understand "unaccommodated man." To be foolish, as Lear is now, implies not knavery but rather self-punishing folly. The fool is his own victim, suffers his own consequences.

The idea that Lear has taken over the role of the Fool means that he has also taken over both the exile and the license of the fool: an outcast, he is now free to talk in ways normally forbidden; he has the license to criticize with impunity. Such license has always been the prerogative of the fool, but it has been the prerogative of the madman as well. Indeed, one of the fascinating things about the madman to ordinary men is the leave he has to speak his mind. English legal history—and our own practice today—formalizes this separation of responsibility from insanity. A vivid eighteenth-century statement of this privilege occurs in the course of a description of Bedlam in Ned Ward's *London Spy* (1703):

> Another was holding forth with as much Vehemence against Kingly Government, as a Brother of Commonwealth Doctrine, rails against Plurality of Livings: I told him he deserv'd to be Hang'd for talking of Treason. Now, says he, You're a Fool, we Madmen have as much Privilege of speaking our Minds, within these Walls, as an Ignorant Dictator, when he spews out his Nonsense to a whole Parish. Prithee come and Live here, and you may talk what you will, and no Body will call you in Question for it: Truth is Persecuted every where Abroad, and flies hither for

Sanctuary. . . . I can tell Great Men such bold Truths as they don't love to hear, without the danger of a Whipping-Post, and that you can't do: For if ever you see a Madman Hanged for speaking the Truth, or a Lawyer Whipp'd for Lying, I'll be bound to prove my Cap a Wheel-Barrow.[3]

Wisdom in madness, in other words, may be the result of freedom in madness; but the consequence of that wisdom and freedom is to be driven into exile by society or, alternatively, locked out of its sight.

Herman Melville makes the point more positively about Lear: "Through the mouths of the dark characters of Hamlet, Timon, Lear, and Iago, he [Shakespeare] craftily says, or sometimes insinuates, the things which we feel to be so terrifically true that it were all but madness for any good man, in his own proper character, to utter, or even hint of them. Tormented into desperation, Lear the frantic king tears off the mask, and speaks the sane madness of vital truth."[4] Yet when we consider those moments in *King Lear* of which Melville must be speaking—the mad scene of Act IV—we may find little that seems worthy of such grandiose praise. In fact, powerful though such scenes may be for us, to the Elizabethan audience that first witnessed them they were perhaps first of all—amusing. Madness was part of the entertainment. "Shakespeare's England," says G. Wilson Knight, "delighted in watching both physical torment and the comic ravings of actual lunacy."[5] It is a familiar point, but it is also another point of similarity between the madman and the fool.

The real nature of those vital truths that Lear utters is not mysterious, not mystical: it is satirical. His speeches to Gloucester and Edgar, as readers have long recognized, like Hamlet's "mad" speeches satirize human hypocrisy. It is his slashing attack on unequal wealth and unequal justice, after all, that makes Edgar cry out, "Reason in madness." And we might characterize that reason as penetrating rather than elevating: Lear sees through pretenses to practices. His command to the "rascal beadle," for example, may remind us of the section in Swift's *A Tale of a Tub* (narrated by a kind of madman) that begins, "I saw a woman flayed the other day. . . ."[6] In Lear's curses, moreover, we hear the accents of the ancient figure of the satirist-railer, the priest in primitive fertility rites who cursed the agents of infertility and exorcised them.[7] That figure, who enters literature as the Greek satirist Archilochus, wielded his curses like weapons, and his words were believed to have the power literally to sting, to wound, and to kill. Something of that magical satiric power survives here in Lear's attacks upon an offending world, already foreshadowed in the storm scene and earlier.

It may seem discordant—in theory if not in fact—to think of satire in the midst of tragedy. Yet essentially madness exists in literature and in culture as two metaphors, which are in fact names for each other: as inspiration and as folly. And categories are considerably more supple than we may sometimes imagine; and they are remarkably interdependent. Maynard Mack crystallizes the issue:

> Tragedy and satire, I suspect, are two ends of a literary spectrum. Tragedy tends to exhibit the inadequacy of norms, to dissolve systematic values, to precipitate a meaning containing—but not necessarily contained by—recognizable ethical codes. Satire, on the contrary, asserts the validity and necessity of norms, systematic values, and meanings that *are* contained by recognizable codes. Where tragedy . . . presents us a world in which man is more victim than agent, in which our commodities prove to be our defects (and vice versa), and in which blindness and madness are likely to be symbols of insight, satire tends to fortify our feeling that life makes more immediate moral sense. In the world it offers us, madness and blindness are usually the emblems of vice and folly. . . .[8]

It is not distorting this argument, I think, to claim that madness is the conclusive, the ultimate, metaphor of both tragedy and satire—the state in which both possibilities are present at once and neither can be enacted without somehow implying the other. (In a less complicated way, the same thing is true of blindness. In examining the eighteenth-century literature of madness we shall see both images in their full satiric implications.) Tragedy and satire form two ends of a literary spectrum because at bottom both are responses to discoveries of disorder. The tragic moment begins with the perception that the world makes no sense, that its order is illusory, that there is no order at all. In one sense all religions (and most philosophies) are also responses to the instinctive fear that disorder may be the nature of the world; religion is the conviction that God is not mad. When conviction becomes prayer, tragedy begins. We align satire with religion in this regard: although Lear's satirical speeches are all discoveries of disorder in this world, of senseless injustice and senseless human relations, in ordinary satire the disorder of folly may nonetheless be explained, perhaps corrected. But in tragic disorder—when Lear's world falls apart, from kingdom to family to self, its hierarchies shattered—explanations falter, standards waver. And yet the satirist has always the taste of fear about him too, and the tragic hero may sometimes be permitted hope, if not conviction.

It is the presence of this note of hope that has led critics (modern critics in particular) to see not only vital truths—that is, perceptions of disorder—in Lear's madness but also a kind of healing wisdom: Lear's experience is purgatorial; madness is both punishment and insight.[9] Religious doctrine sometimes clouds the matter—in effect pitting the optimistic against the pessimistic temperament—but most readers, I think, do feel that the king's insanity effects somehow a radical cure for him. Since Aeschylus at least, Western men have found it possible to believe that suffering leads finally to wisdom (we see a version of the same idea in the Book of Job). Indeed, most cultures accept the idea that a deformed or mutilated person—madness is only an extraordinary example—sometimes possesses a compensatory magical power. Conversely, to gain such power a man might have to surrender himself to mutilation or pain: hence the myth of Philoctetes, who carries both a magical bow and a stinking wound; hence too the story of Faust, who exchanges his soul for knowledge and power. Lear's madness is an extreme and complete representation of such compensated suffering.

For the eighteenth century Lear's compensation became Lear's reformation. The Renaissance had been fully conscious of the affirmative side of madness, but to the eighteenth century madness did not make Lear holy or bring him face-to-face with higher truth. In this view it is a disaster from which he recovers only providentially; it is a degradation, and it does not specifically teach him anything that any reasonable man might not already know. One clear example of this diminished stature is the century's favorite version of the play, Nahum Tate's adaptation (first acted in 1681), which features a happy ending and a crowd-pleasing marriage between Edgar and Cordelia: only the villains die. For most of us such a mawkish revision relaxes the great force of the play; it permits Lear to return to his throne and thereby implies that for a given amount of suffering in payment Lear can both have and eat his cake. The death of Lear, that "terrible scene," Johnson calls it, confirms our sense of transformation; it says that after what he has experienced—after what he has gained and lost—Lear cannot simply return to ordinary life. His death is a release from suffering, but also testimony of what he has become.

Yet it is difficult to imagine a critic in the eighteenth century who would endorse such a reading. A representative figure, William Richardson, regards Lear primarily as a man of "ungoverned sensibility."[10] A man, Richardson says, "in danger of becoming morose or inhuman. He entertains sanguine hopes; he allows every feeling to reign in his breast uncontrolled; his judgment is dazzled; and his imagination riots in rapturous dreams of enjoyment." To this undisciplined mind madness is inevitable, in fact, "natural." "Shakespeare has exhibited the madness of Lear, as the natural effect of such suffering on such a character. It was an event in the progress of Lear's mind, driven by such feelings, desires, and passions as the poet ascribes to him, as could not be avoided." Lear's case, however, is not hopeless. Richardson argues that slowly the chastisements of his sufferings take effect: "His misfortunes correct his conduct; they rouse reflection, and lead him to that reformation which we approve." In short, "As his misfortunes increase, we find him still more inclined to reflect on his situation. . . . He seems rational and modest." Though he reads like a parody of his age, nonetheless Richardson seems to me typical. Another critic, for example, Thomas Davies, approaches the play from approximately the same coordinates. "One great design of Shakespeare, in the choice of this fable," Davies writes, was to "hold forth to mankind the unhappy consequences of yielding to the sudden and impetuous impressions of anger."[11] Like Richardson, he regards Lear from a moralistic point of view: "We see Shakespeare introduce a character, amiable in many respects, brave, generous, frank, and benevolent; but at the same time, wilful, rash, violent, and headstrong. . . . Agony and distress lead him to the door of madness. Reason is at length dethroned, and a high paroxysm of frenzy succeeds. Nature affords some relief by a deliquium. Repose and medicinal application gently restore reason to her proper seat." For these critics Lear is a kind of Everyman who falls by his own defects from normality, but who at length and in the course of things recovers. "Every spectator," says Davies, "feels for himself and common humanity, when he perceives man, while living, degraded to the deprivation of sense and loss of memory! Who does not rejoice, when the creative hand of the poet, in the great actor, restores him to the use of his faculties!" Admirable and sympathetic though Davies's words be, it is important not to overlook where his emphasis falls. Lear's madness is a logical step in a sequence ("anger," "resentment," "Furious indignation," "violent rage," "agony and distress," "madness"). But the meaning of that step is degradation—"the deprivation of sense and loss of memory"—and our cause for rejoicing is not Lear's reconciliation with Cordelia, but rather the restoration of his faculties.

When Edgar, Gloucester's "good" son, pretends to be Tom o' Bedlam, his madness, it is clear from the beginning, has nothing of the fool or clown. He himself describes the character he assumes:

> . . . Whiles I may 'scape,
> I will preserve myself; and am bethought
> To take the basest and most poorest shape
> That ever penury, in contempt of man,
> Brought near to beast; my face I'll grime with filth,
> Blanket my loins, elf all my hairs in knots,
> And with presented nakedness outface
> The winds and persecutions of the sky.
> The country gives me proof and precedent
> Of Bedlam beggars, who, with roaring voices,
> Strike in their numb'd and mortified bare arms
> Pins, wooden pricks, nails, sprigs of rosemary;
> And with this horrible object, from low farms,

Poor pelting villages, sheep-cotes, and mills,
Sometime with lunatic bans, sometime with prayers,
Enforce their charity.

[II.iii.5—20]

We are here no longer in the presence of Plato's inspired madman. We see instead in Edgar's disguise an excruciating
metamorphosis and also a palpable alienation; like Lear in his
madness, Edgar will become an exile, thrust out of society as Lear
has been, one of those ritual exiles like lepers or convicts that
societies seem always to need. And Tom o' Bedlam is a historical
phenomenon, a good likeness of actual men who roamed the
Elizabethan countryside begging. His appalling poverty should
not go unnoticed—in the eighteenth century it would become a
badge of madness—but more immediately important for the
drama is the stark misery of his situation, how closely he is
"Brought near to beast." King Lear responds passionately to this
abjectness. Only moments before Tom appears, in the storm
scene of Act III, Lear begins to pity the "Poor naked wretches" of
his kingdom and denounces himself for his indifference:

. . . O! I have ta'en
Too little care of this. Take physic, Pomp;
Expose thyself to feel what wretches feel,
That thou mayst shake the superflux to them,
And show the Heavens more just.

[III.iv.32—36]

Exactly at this point Tom o' Bedlam appears, discovered by
Lear's Fool in a hovel. In his growing madness the king insists
that the treachery of daughters has reduced the lunatic to what he
is. And the sight of him urges Lear to a new insight. To Regan he
had earlier cried out in real anguish over the loss of his
attendants:

O! reason not the need; our basest beggars
Are in the poorest thing superfluous:
Allow not nature more than nature needs,
Man's life is cheap as beast's.

[II.iv.266—69]

Now in lines that make us think ironically of Hamlet he reconsiders: "Is man no more than this? Consider him well. . . . Unaccommodated man is no more but such a poor, bare, forked animal as thou art." And in his rage tears off his clothes to unaccommodate himself.

Tom's meaning for Lear, then, is as a stimulus to Lear's growing sense of relation, his perception of kinship with the wider world. The king's madness drives him to such company, and from the humiliation of it, after a long time, will come his reconciliation with Cordelia. But there is another phase in his response to Tom. By the time Kent finds them all in the storm, Lear has begun to take Tom not as a representative of human unhappiness, but in fact as a "philosopher"! He calls him "learned Theban" and "Athenian"; he asks him questions only a wise man can answer ("What is the cause of the thunder?"). And most significantly, when he sets up his mad trial of his daughters, he makes Tom the judge, a "robed man of justice," and places him beside "his yoke-fellow of equity," the Fool. This Tom o' Bedlam represents wisdom in madness and also wisdom in wretchedness. And in a strange kind of mirror effect, he recognizes madness, misery, and reason all in the figure of the mad king at Dover in Act IV.

The meanings of reason in madness are formidably complex here. On the one hand, the truths that Lear and the Fool speak in their insanity are social truths; their nature is corrosive and, above all, satirical. On the other hand, the lessons of madness for Lear can be called spiritual: he has learned and grown; more than any other Shakesperean hero he has *changed*. Tom o' Bedlam offers a less obvious example—one more directly relevant to the eighteenth century—but in his dual role as Edgar and as the Bedlam beggar he suggests both the authentic meaning of insanity, which is human desolation, and the precarious relationship all of us bear to it. Lear's response to Tom's madness is also a response to his own. The themes of madness and wisdom, madness and blindness, madness and misery reappear in altered and dogmatic form in the age of Pope and Swift—in *King Lear* they stand perfectly suspended.

CHAPTER TWO

The Dunciad
and *Augustan Madness*

By the end of the seventeenth century the world that created King Lear had disappeared. Speculative historians, it is true, sometimes extend the conventional boundaries of the Renaissance in England seventy years or more to include the age of Swift and Pope, so that the Augustan Age then marks only a subsiding of that vast intellectual tide. The forms and preoccupations of the Renaissance persist, after all, in the great Augustans: the values of what is often called Christian humanism, especially the sovereignty of reason, the insistence that the community as well as the individual be virtuous, and the nervous, muted fear that order and intelligibility may collapse at any moment. But these lines from *The Dunciad* sound the Augustan note, a note whose literary allusiveness serves to express loss as well as continuity:

> Yet, yet a moment, one dim Ray of Light
> Indulge, dread Chaos, and eternal Night!
> Of darkness visible so much be lent,
> As half to shew, half veil the deep Intent.
> Ye Pow'rs! whose Mysteries restor'd I sing,
> To whom Time bears me on his rapid wing,
> Suspend a while your Force inertly strong,
> Then take at once the Poet and the Song.
> Now flam'd the Dog-star's -unpropitious ray,
> Smote ev'ry Brain, and wither'd ev'ry Bay;

Sick was the Sun, the Owl forsook his bow'r,
The moon-struck Prophet felt the madding hour:
Then rose the Seed of Chaos, and of Night,
To blot out Order, and extinguish Light,
Of dull and venal a new World to mold,
And bring Saturnian days of Lead and Gold.

[IV.1−16][1]

No reader requires a footnote to tell him that the "Dog-star's unpropitious ray" traditionally sends madness. Here an unmistakable madness, universal and sterile, withers the humanistic landscape, and the poet's tone by itself says that the eclipse of reason is permanent and unambiguous; we expect no truths from this moonstruck prophet, no supernatural insight to compensate for this extinguished light. Madness, Chaos, and Night have dethroned Reason, and now they alone figure in the altered representations of madness that inform Alexander Pope's great masterpiece. For us the poem may best be seen as a *Narrenschiff*, one more ship of fools in a venerable and enormous fleet. Like his predecessors, Pope creates and sets in motion an entire world of folly—folly that is called "madness" time and again—but his selections, perceptions, and judgments of human irrationality differ in the most fundamental ways from the classical vision that we have already traced. It should become clear in what follows that to turn from *King Lear* to *The Dunciad*, from high tragedy to mock heroic, is not only to step from one end of the literary spectrum to the other; it is also unmistakably to step from one historical era to another.

What we sense first as different in Pope's representation of madness is the loss of spiritual value that it has suffered. Madness had meant both punishment and insight for Lear, as it nearly always does in tragedy. For tragic madness carries us upwards beyond the bounds of the ordinary, toward the heroic or toward the charitable gods. Lear's mad satiric speeches, for example, form only one part of the play, and not the last part. His attacks on a newly discovered social disorder are balanced by the recovery at the end of the drama, by reconciliation if not re-

"Come, let's away to prison," Lear tells Cordelia,
blessings, forgiveness, and a new beginning. But in
of insane, nightmarish Dunces, madness is not

illuminated by the possibilities of recovery. It means not punishment and insight, but only punishment, as it nearly always does in satire; and though it too carries us beyond the bounds of the normal world, it seems to carry the normal world with it, and its direction is downwards toward folly and catastrophe.

It ought to be emphasized at once, however, that madness in Pope's poetry is metaphorical, not literal; he uses the image of madness to attack supposedly sane people, to pillory corrupt political and social leaders, not to attack actual insanity. This aggressive purposefulness, inevitably limited in comparison with the less-specific intentions (and effects) of *King Lear*, goes far toward creating *The Dunciad*'s negative vision of madness. The Dunces are no visionary satirists like Lear on the heath or like Stultitia in Erasmus's *Praise of Folly*; they belong instead to the grim Juvenalian tradition in which a brutalized lunacy serves to express the satirist's outrage. In their narrow madness the Dunces merely embody folly; they cannot attack it, as Lear and Stultitia do, through reason in madness. Lost from the Augustan representation, in other words, is a certain complexity of plot, compensated by a ferocious (and usually justified) clarity of purpose. But it is a highly significant loss all the same. The movement of Shakespeare's plot allows King Lear to travel both into and out of madness; it allows him to recover; it grants him perspective on both madness and sanity; and it even permits a kind of dialogue between the two. *The Dunciad*'s purposes eliminate this more complicated structure and its various shiftings of perspective; its plot runs directly along a single curve, magnifying or shrinking its victims until they burst or disappear. In works like *King Lear* we see madness as part of a world where real sanity also exists and is sought; a countering image to Lear's madness is always accessible, if not actually present: Cordelia stands ready to return whenever he calls her—indeed, she returns in love before she is called. But in *The Dunciad* there simply are no sane figures: the nightmarish distortions, the relentless anger we feel in the poem are inescapable consequences of transforming the supposedly sane world into Bedlam. The Dunces enter into no relationships with sanity, as Lear's Fool does with Lear. In other poems Pope does contrast sane and lunatic characters—the *Epistle to Bathurst* is a good example—but they merely stand beside each other, signposts to virtue or folly; they establish no dialogue, and the simplicity of the satiric plot' prevents their exchanging roles, however briefly. The value of madness plunges downwards in *The Dunciad* initially, then, because Pope's purpose is satiric, satiric in the primitive sense. Like any ritualistic railer, like any Archilochus, Pope lisps in savage numbers in order to punish and to drive away agents of moral infertility and disorder. He punishes the hacks and scoundrels of his time with madness, moreover, in order to force their outer appearance into correspondence with what he conceives their inner state to be. Pope is as serious as Dante in his intention of manifesting and publishing the true characters of sinners, and indeed he seems to share that medieval hatred of madness we mentioned earlier, a righteous hatred of dangerous and unclean spirits, a hatred fueled by fear. But for us Pope also persistently chooses unprophetic madness as the external representation of the Dunces' inward nature because his audience understands madness only in that way, because a combination of historical changes has stripped madness of its classical ambiguity, its tragic or heroic possibilities, and has reduced it to the level of willful evil: no one could say of the Dunces that they are more sinned against than sinning.

In this chapter I want to draw the outlines of madness in *The Dunciad*, next to point out ways in which the social and intellectual history of the period confirms the representative character of the poem, and finally to suggest some tentative explanations. I should add that I shall be using the word *Augustan* to describe in the broadest sense the state and style of mind that dominates English culture roughly from the Glorious Revolution to the mid-eighteenth century. Its limitations in terms of accuracy are well understood, but in terms of suggestiveness it is a useful shorthand.

King Lear has given us a certain schematic approach for examining madness in *The Dunciad*, and as a beginning we may revisit the themes of poverty, blindness, and truth that we isolated earlier.

I

In *King Lear*, though specific interpretations differ, nearly every reader has in common, as we have said, the feeling that madness has improved or even redeemed Lear. Insanity in the great storm scenes of Act III has carried him forward toward a humane compassion for his fellow man, perfectly symbolized in his embracing of mad Tom; and in Act IV it has brought to him a certain worldly, lacerating wisdom, a satiric grasp of the truths of disorder forced upon him; it has brought him knowledge and also self-knowledge. Even within the context of the drama, where he is still a crazed old man, Lear takes on to some extent in our minds the robes of a prophet who finds reason in madness, *obscuris vera involvens.*[2] In this relationship, intense and certain, with higher knowledge, King Lear is the very type of the traditional madman or prophet, a man inspired, one who has been removed for a time from this world to look upon transcendent truths. He suffers, as Gellius said, "the disease of heroes."

We need only imagine ourselves applying that phrase to the actors of *The Dunciad* to see how far the Augustans have altered traditional views. For Pope these swarming madmen share all of the frenzy and obscurity of ancient prophets—but none of their prophecy. Dulness, he takes pains to inform us at the beginning, must be understood as "turning topsy-turvy the Understanding, and inducing an Anarchy or confused State of Mind." And lest we still suspect that there may possibly be reason in raving, he explains further: "*The native Anarchy of the mind* is that state which precedes the time of Reason's assuming the rule of the Passions." In taming the Passions, Pope admits, Dulness may sometimes have "the appearance of Reason," but only because she regulates or represses them; no Dunce is a Timon or a Lear

> Or that William Blake
> Who beat upon the wall
> Till Truth obeyed his call.[3]

Those still awake at the triumph of Dulness will

> See skulking *Truth* to her old Cavern fled,
> Mountains of Casuistry heap'd o'er her head!
> [*Dunciad*, IV.641—42]

This divorce of truth from madness need not be insisted upon unduly: it is one of the fundamental assumptions that organizes *The Dunciad*. Yet here as in all great literature such assumptions rarely exist simply as statements; we find them quite literally embodied in image, metaphor, or figure. Pope makes us certain of the Dunces' untruthfulness on the one hand by transforming their outward appearances into nauseating nastiness, and on the other hand by associating them with two conventional figures of untruth in his time, the religious enthusiast and the enthusiastic poet. One example of their degradation can be seen plainly in the games of the Dunces in Book II. Generations of readers have turned away in disgust from the antics of that book, just as they have turned from the spectacle of the Yahoos in *Gulliver's Travels*. In *The Dunciad*, the cause of their revulsion, most simply and obviously, is the obscenity of the Dunces' behavior; and the nature of that obscenity is excremental. Johnson some years later observed that "Pope and Swift had an unnatural delight in ideas physically impure, such as every other tongue utters with unwillingness, and of which every ear shrinks from the mention."[4] But, in truth, Pope's failing, at least, is less personal than Johnson imagined; and it is highly suggestive of the more general attitude toward mad creatures that we are exploring. For when Pope pits his lunatic Dunces against each other in heroic contests of urination or rolls them through the kennel, he is explicitly and literally *besmearing* them.

> Full in the middle way there stood a lake,
> Which Curl's Corinna chanc'd that morn to make:
> (Such was her wont, at early dawn to drop
> Her evening cates before his neighbour's shop,)
> Here fortun'd Curl to slide; loud shout the band,
> And Bernard! Bernard! rings thro' all the Strand.
> Obscene with filth the miscreant lies bewray'd,
> Fal'n in the plash his wickedness had laid.
> [*Dunciad*, II.69–76]

In three farcical, rather scurrilous pamphlets published by Pope in 1713, beginning with "The Narrative of Dr. Robert Norris," he draws a vivid picture of the bookseller Edmund Curl's domestic lunacy: "As the poor Man's Frenzy increas'd, he began to *void his Excrements in his Bed, read* Rochester's *bawdy Poems to his*

Wife, gave *Oldmixon* a *slap* on the *Chops,* and wou'd have kiss'd
Mr. *Pemberton's* A—— by violence."[5] As his victims thus wallow
in excrement, it is clear that the poet's satire here depends on the
efficacy of what psychiatrists call "fecalization"—the hurling of
"brown dishonours" at one's enemies. Accusations of disease,
particularly venereal disease, and perversion (he accuses more
than one Dunce of homosexuality) perform the same function for
Pope, but on a less heroic scale; it is no accident that a variation of
his phrase "Bedlam and the Mint" is "Bedlam and Soho" (both
notorious for prostitutes).[6]

The embrowning that Pope and other Augustans give satirical
madmen is frequently returned with interest. In their tour of
Bedlam, for example, Ned Ward and his guide stop before a cell
to listen to a madman who is eating and at the same time
mumbling extravagantly to himself. "At last he Counterfeits a
Sneeze, and shot such a Mouthful of Bread and Cheese amongst
us, that every Spectator had some share of his Kindness, which
made us Retreat; he calling after us *Masters, Masters;* some went
back to hear what he had to say, and he had provided them a
plentiful Bowl of Piss, which he cast very Successfully amongst
them, crying in a Laugh, *I never give Victuals, but I give Drink,
and you're Welcome Gentlemen.*"[7] (We should not ignore the
sarcasm of "Masters" and "Gentlemen" in Ned Ward's account.)
The Augustans by these means project their hostility, their own
fecalizing urges upon the image of madmen, insisting upon both
the degradation and the anger of unreason.

There is less anger than absurdity in the figure of the religious
enthusiast, which Pope along with most of his generation uses as a
synonym for madman. In temperament, if not in doctrine, Pope
stands with those who in New England were called "Old
Lights"—stubborn, sober opponents of the blindingly ecstatic
New Lights. Careful as he was, because of his Catholicism, about
religious pronouncements, Pope nevertheless must have felt
secure in gibing enthusiasm from time to time. Of George
Whitefield, the celebrated revivalist and "Field Preacher," Pope
writes in a *Dunciad* note that he "thought the only means of
advancing Christianity was by the New-birth of religious madness."[8] And in Boston the Reverend Charles Chauncy, likewise no

friend to Whitefield, doubtless spoke for Pope when he said that "the cause of this enthusiasm is a bad temperament of the blood and spirits; 'tis properly a disease, a sort of madness. . . . In nothing does the enthusiasm of these persons discover itself more, than in the disregard they express to the dictates of reason. They are above the forces of argument, beyond conviction from a calm and sober address to their understandings."⁹ (In an engraving entitled *Credulity, Superstition and Fanaticism: A Medley,* Hogarth sketches a wild mob scene in a Methodist church: in one corner an emotional thermometer climbs rapidly from prophecy to madness; and the text the preacher turns to is 2 Corinthians 11:23—"I speak as a fool." See plate 1.) Like Pope, Chauncy is asserting that the human personality is properly arranged—*safely* arranged—only when reason is in full charge of the affections. But the New Lights (we shall have cause to savor the image) on both sides of the Atlantic have rearranged the humanist priorities of the Renaissance; and to conservatives this new arrangement in its excess, like an overheated engine, seems always about to explode. Pope shrewdly notes of the ordinary Dunce: "he centers every thing in *himself.* The Progress of Dulness herein differing from that of Madness; one ends in *seeing all in God,* the other in *seeing all in Self.*"¹⁰

Another recurrent figure emblemizing madness's divorce from truth is, ironically enough, the poet himself—not Pope, of course, urbane and self-possessed, but the frenzied, god-possessed poet who comes to us out of early Greek literature, a character beyond reason like the enthusiast. Of such poets Pope speaks scornfully: "*Lethe* and the *Land of Dreams* allegorically represent the *Stupefaction* and *visionary Madness* of Poets, equally dull and extravagant."¹¹ And with unmistakable glee Pope torments his old enemy John Dennis (known to literary London as "tremendous Dennis") for his love of the sublime:

> She saw slow Phillips creep like Tate's poor page,
> And all the mighty Mad in Dennis rage.
>
> [I.105—6]

In a long note Pope goes on: "This is by no means to be understood literally, as if Mr. Dennis were really mad. . . . No—it is spoken of that *Excellent* and *Divine Madness,* so often mentioned by Plato; that poetical rage and enthusiasm, with which Mr. D. hath, in his time, been highly possessed; and of those *extraordinary hints and motions* whereof he himself so feelingly treats in his preface to the Remarks on *Prince Arthur.*" Pope's own opinion of the divine madness of poets rings clearly through his satiric purposes here; the author of *An Essay on Man* and the Horatian satires is not likely to classify himself with visionary or ecstatic madmen: his characteristic gesture is to "stoop to truth and moralize" his song. But it is ironic that he should refer to Dennis's book on the contemporary epic *Prince Arthur* for evidence: there like most neoclassical critics Dennis declares that genius, "this extraordinary thing in Poetry, which has hitherto been taken for something Supernatural and Divine, is nothing but a very common Passion, or a complication of common Passions."[12] True, he says, most men lack the fire to express themselves poetically, but the source of poetry is present in all of us. Sir William Temple, Swift's patron, says the same thing with more sober elegance: "I can easily admire poetry," he writes, "and yet without adoring it: I can allow it to arise from the greatest excellency of natural temper or the greatest race of native genius, without exceeding the reach of what is human, or giving it any approaches of divinity."[13] The doctrine of poetic inspiration has all but disappeared from Augustan criticism. Dennis's emphasis on the passions, the unreasonable and untruthful passions, is what draws Pope's fire. For that way disorder lies, and madness.

Besides enthusiasts and embrowned madmen, one other image particularly emphasizes the divorce of madness and truth. In the opening lines of Book III the king of the Dunces begins to dream.

> But in her Temple's last recess inclos'd,
> On Dulness' lap th' Anointed head repos'd.
> Him close she curtains round with Vapours blue,
> And soft besprinkles with Cimmerian dew.
> Then raptures high the seat of Sense o'erflow,
> Which only heads refin'd from Reason know.
> Hence, from the straw where Bedlam's Prophet nods,
> He hears loud Oracles, and talks with Gods. . . .

And now, on Fancy's easy wing convey'd,
The King descending, views th' Elysian Shade.
A slip-shod Sibyl led his steps along,
In lofty madness meditating song. . . .

[III.1–16]

Pope's scorn for dreams is plain enough and unsurprising, for wakefulness and sleeping are almost synonymous with sanity and madness in *The Dunciad*, a poem, after all, about the whole world going to sleep. Darkness, which we associate with sleep and dreaming and Dunces, threatens our well-regulated daylight selves ("Awake, my St. John!" begins the *Essay on Man*). The dreams that come to us in darkness, moreover, are in the Augustan psychology actual moments of madness. "It is true, we have sometimes instances of perception whilst we are asleep," Locke writes, "and retain the memory of those thoughts: but how extravagant and incoherent for the most part they are; how little conformable to the perfection and order of a rational being, those who are acquainted with dreams need not be told."[14] Medical opinion agreed without hesitation: Thomas Tryon, for example, in 1689 wrote of the "Affinity or Analogy between Dreams and Madness, so that the understanding of one will somewhat illustrate the other; for Madness seems to be a Watching or Waking Dream. . . ."[15] Throughout the Renaissance men could still hope to discover truth or guidance in their dreams, still look upon dreams as supernatural visitations. (Although Theseus scoffs at "The lunatic, the lover, and the poet" in *A Midsummer Night's Dream*, he is alone and unconvincing: to the dream-spirit Puck is given the play's last word.) But the Augustans, for whom a nascent science had stripped away so many alternatives, slammed shut the Gate of Ivory. Dreams were no longer an allegorical medium, a coherent narrative structure, a story told. The eighteenth century experienced dreams as chaotic, extravagant swarms of images. When the mind is "disordered by Dreams or Sickness," in the words of *The Spectator* (No. 421), "the Fancy is over-run with a Thousand hideous Monsters of its own framing." The analogy between dreams and madness, ironically enough, does in fact exist; but not until Freud would the irrationality of dreams that Locke insists upon be discredited and the allegorical interpretation re-established. In Pope's world, dreams, like madness, are imagination utterly uncontrolled, and the sleepless satirist paces their kingdom in an anxious dead patrol. The children of reason fear the darkness.

II

King Lear's madness, as the storm scenes of Act III have shown us, reduced him in his own mind to the state of "unaccommodated man," wrenching his sympathies away from his own plight and toward the "poor naked wretches" of his kingdom; and the shivering, demented figure of Tom o'Bedlam reinforced his new awareness of the state of human misery with an example of

> . . . the basest and most poorest shape
> That ever penury, in contempt of man,
> Brought near to beast.

This radical physic of exposing himself to what wretches feel brought forth in Lear profound compassion for the poor man—a Christian tenderness for the world's beggars, paupers, victims—and a satiric contempt for the hypocrisy of riches and pomp. By then poor himself, Lear responded to poverty by accommodating it within his tragic vision.

Though there is poverty as ample and as abject in *The Dunciad*, there is no comparable outpouring of compassion. Madness and poverty exist side by side in the fantastic world of the Dunces; but chained in helpless and inevitable partnership, madness and poverty represent for Pope complementary images of a human condition to be spurned utterly, a condition of spirit less tragic than demeaning.

That poverty abounds among Dunces is announced at the very beginning of *The Dunciad*. In the "Letter to the Publisher" that opens the volume, William Cleland, a front for Pope himself, indignantly rebuts the charge that Pope has unfairly mocked the poverty of his enemies, declaring that "Poverty itself becomes a just subject of satyr, when it is the consequence of vice, prodigality, or neglect of one's lawful calling." And the learned Martinus Scriblerus, another of Pope's fictitious commentators, also insists that the poet justly treats "the Causes creative of such Authors, namely *Dulness* and *Poverty;* the one born with them, the other contracted by the neglect of their proper talents, through self-conceit of greater abilities."[16] These denials register a certain sensitivity on Pope's part to what he was doing. The pride he attacks was a commonplace but very serious sin in Augustan eyes, the sin of stepping out of place and disturbing order.[17] ("As Folly is The Foundation of Pride," runs *Tatler* 127, "the natural Superstructure of it is Madness. If there was an Occasion for the Experiment, I would not question to make a proud Man a Lunatick in Three Weeks Time, provided I had it in my Power to ripen his Phrensy with proper Applications.") Fixed in their roles as Dunces, these Grub Street hacks and pedants must also be fixed—and firmly—in their insignificance by the image of their poverty. And it is no less suitable than subtle that the first English poet to grow wealthy from his art should return so often to this image for his ammunition.

The first book of *The Dunciad* sets the scene of action for us:

> Close to those walls where Folly holds her throne,
> And laughs to think Monroe would take her down,
> Where o'er the gates, by his fam'd father's hand
> Great Cibber's brazen, brainless brothers stand;
> One Cell there is, conceal'd from vulgar eye,
> The Cave of Poverty and Poetry.
>
> [I.29–34]

In a note to these lines Pope elaborates his description and offers a prospectus of the entire poem from just the point of view we are now taking.

> The cell of poor Poetry is here very properly represented as a little *unendowed Hall* in the neighbourhood of the Magnific *College* of Bedlam; and. as the surest Seminary to supply those learned walls with Professors. . . . The *Qualities* and *Productions* of the students of this private Academy are afterwards described in this first book; as are also their *Actions* throughout the second; by which it appears, how near allied Dulness is to Madness. This naturally prepares us for the subject of the third book, where we find them in union, and acting in conjunction to produce the Catastrophe

of the fourth; a mad poetical Sibyl leading our Hero through
the Regions of Vision, to animate him in the present un-
dertaking, by a view of the past triumphs of Barbarism over
Science.

The ironic reversal of Dryden's famous line—"Great Wits are
sure to Madness near ally'd"—should not go unnoticed. But more
important is the geography: Bedlam stands naturally next to the
cell of poverty; and although one spectacularly outshines (or
overshadows) the other, their relationship is almost symbiotic.
Pope's reference to "the Magnific *College* of Bedlam" is, of
course, a mocking one: expenditures for the hospital buildings in
1676 had seemed to many Englishmen ludicrously dispropor-
tioned. Ned Ward, whose *London Spy* I have already mentioned,
remarks to his guide that "I conceiv'd it to be my *Lord Mayor's
Palace*, for I could not imagine so stately a structure could be
design'd for any Quality inferior; he smil'd at my innocent
Conjecture, and inform'd me this was *Bedlam*, an Hospital for
Mad-Folks: In truth, said I, I think they were Society." Such
sarcasm calls into question the whole idea of taking any trouble
about the insane; it implies that the poverty of cells and caves is
their natural and just desert; indeed, Ned's guide, comparing
Bedlam to the great Monument of the Fire of London, sniffs that
"this, like the other, is but a *Monument* of the Cities *Shame* and
Dishonour, instead of its Glory."[18] The identification of the
Dunce Colley Cibber with his "brazen, brainless brothers" is a
fundamental one, but that identification is inseparable from the
accusation of being poor.

It is not an accusation Pope confines to *The Dunciad.* With
increasing frequency throughout the 1730s Pope's satires disclose,
whether by suggestive habits of phrasing or by open attack, an
assumption that dull wits are as sure allied to poverty as to
madness. The opening section of the *Epistle to Dr. Arbuthnot* is a
good example. The innocent poet besieged by literary madmen
groans:

> The Dog-star rages! nay 'tis past a doubt,
> All Bedlam, or Parnassus, is let out:
> Fire in each eye, and papers in each hand,
> They rave, recite, and madden round the land.

[3—6]

Calm in the midst of their furor, Pope serenely, silently, self-righteously sits:

> I never answer'd, I was not in debt:
> If want provok'd, or madness made them print,
> I wag'd no war with Bedlam or the Mint.
>
> [154—56]

The Mint was a sanctuary for debtors in Southwark; he liked the phrase "Bedlam or the Mint" enough to use it again in his *Imitations of Horace*—Book II, Satire I, 99—and a variation of it in Book II, Epistle I, 226: "Stretch'd to relieve the Idiot and the Poor." In *The Dunciad* at the conclusion of the games in Book II the mad poets all retire "to the neighb'ring Fleet," which Pope himself glosses as "A prison for insolvent Debtors on the bank of the Ditch." And in a longer note to another section of the games he explains, "Our indulgent Poet, whenever he has spoken of any dirty or low work, constantly puts us in mind of the *Poverty* of the offenders, as the only extenuation of such practices. Let any one but remark, when a Thief, a Pick-pocket, an Highwayman, or a Knight of the post are spoken of, how much our hate to those characters is lessened, if they add a *needy* Thief, a *poor* Pick-pocket, an *hungry* Highwayman, a *starving* Knight of the post, etc."[19] The point, however, is not merely to multiply instances of Pope's hostility toward starving Dunces: it is rather to underscore how far his "hate to those characters" differs from the more traditional attitude of a work like *King Lear*. There, where poverty and madness are also inseparable, we are called along with Lear to charity. Pope seems to call us only to contempt.

His attack on the Dunces' poverty, like his attack on madness, is metaphorical, of course, not literal (although Emrys Jones suggests that he finds the subject "interesting and stimulating"). In his own life and in poems like *Bathurst* Pope shows himself thoroughly sympathetic to honest poverty and at the same time thoroughly scornful of mindless avarice and tasteless riches: Sir Baalam is as much a Dunce as Colley Cibber. Just as the metaphor of madness shows the outer face of the Dunces' inner states, so likewise the metaphor of poverty reminds us of their moral insubstantiality and driving, single-minded greed. What makes men mad also impoverishes them.

Two special meanings of poverty seem attached to Pope's

descriptions: squalor, which suggests to him both disorder and disgust, and idleness. Book I of *The Dunciad* contains a striking picture of Bays's squalid chambers, littered with mangled books and papers:

> Round him much Embryo, much Abortion lay,
> Much future Ode, and abdicated Play. . . .
> Here lay poor Fletcher's half-eat scenes, and here
> The Frippery of crucify'd Moliere;
> There hapless Shakespear, yet of Tibbald sore,
> Wish'd he had blotted for himself before.
>
> [121–34]

Bays (Colley Cibber, poet laureate and chief victim of the satire) appears at the end of "a thin Third day," "swearing and supperless" because of the failure of his play. In a Scriblerian note Pope adds sarcastically, "It is amazing how the sense of this hath been mistaken by all the former commentators, who most idly suppose it to imply that the Hero of the poem wanted a supper. In truth a great absurdity! . . . The language of poesy brings all into action; and to represent a Critic encompassed with books, but without a supper, is a picture which lively expresseth how much the true Critic prefers the diet of the mind to that of the body." Cibber's unhappy state is not without its analogues in Pope's work. The nearest model for this Dunciad garret—perhaps its inspiration—is the description of John Dennis's apartment in "The Narrative of Dr. Robert Norris." Dennis he imagines as a raging maniac sitting furious on his bed while the doctor surveys the room. "By the Fire-side lay Three-farthings-worth of Small-coal in a *Spectator*, and behind the Door huge heaps of Papers of the same Title. . . . There was nothing neat in the whole Room, except some Books on his Shelves. . . . The whole Floor was cover'd with Manuscripts, as thick as a Pastry's Cook's Shop on a Christmas Eve. On his Table were some Ends of Verse and of Candles; a Gallipot of Ink with a yellow Pen in it, and a Pot of half-dead Ale cover'd with a *Longinus*."[20] Diverted though we may be by Pope's wit, we nonetheless recognize that he is discrediting Dennis by his familiar technique of making him both mad and poor, and that here as in *The Dunciad* such poverty is degrading because of its disorder and in part because it is so physically repellent. His description of Dennis's person makes the second point perfectly: "His flannel night-cap, which was exceedingly begrimed with sweat and dirt, hung upon his left ear; the flap of his breeches dangled between his legs, and the rolls of his stockings fell down to his ancles."[21] In another such description, taken from the *Epistle to Bathurst,* all humor is gone, and the melodrama of the Bedlam cell prevails:

> In the worst inn's worst room, with mat half-hung,
> The floors of plaister, and the walls of dung,
> On once a flock-bed, but repair'd with straw,
> With tape-ty'd curtains, never meant to draw,
> The George and Garter dangling from that bed
> Where tawdry yellow strove with dirty red,
> Great Villers lies—alas! how chang'd from him,
> That life of pleasure, and that soul of whim!
>
> [299—306]

Idleness has already been implied in these pictures of squalor, for though Pope takes care to explain that dulhness includes "Labour, Industry, and some degree of Activity and Boldness,"[22] this labor is not to be understood as in any sense productive; and in fact much of the inaction of *The Dunciad* belies Pope's claim. The games in Book II, for example, conclude with universal drowsiness, brought on by a public reading from the Dunces' works:

> Thus the soft gifts of Sleep conclude the day,
> And stretch'd on bulks, as usual, Poets lay.
>
> [II.419—20]

And in Book IV the goddess Dulness "sees loitering about her a number of Indolent Persons abandoning all business and duty, and dying with laziness." "Soft on her lap her Laureat son reclines" (IV.20), and all around her she

> . . . look'd and saw a lazy, lolling sort,
> Unseen at Church, at Senate, or at Court,
> Of ever-listless Loit'rers, that attend
> No Cause, no Trust, no Duty, and no Friend.
> Thee too, my Paridell she mark'd thee there,

> Stretch'd on the rack of a too easy chair,
> And heard thy everlasting yawn confess
> The Pains and Penalties of Idleness.
>
> [IV.337—44]

In a poem in which sleep is so important an image, we should not be surprised to find the charge of laziness leveled against so many Dunces. The goddess Dulness symbolizes, after all, the sleep of reason, from which, as Goya says, nightmares arise (Martin Price offers an illuminating comparison of Freud's conception of the unconscious and Pope's Dulness[23]). She also symbolizes the deadening of moral consciousness, the refusal to face up to the responsibility and the pain of being human. More than moral effort, however, is being shirked. In Pope's world idleness is one of the causes of poverty, and poverty is one of the punishments for idleness. Here Pope's yoking of poverty and madness points us toward an important social failing of the madman in Augustan eyes: he cannot or will not work.

The significance of the madman's idleness becomes clearer if we remind ourselves that the early eighteenth century marks yet another point in the unremitting, gravity-defying rise of the middle classes, a moment when the bourgeoisie took cultural as well as economic command of English life. Christopher Hill has called 1688 the turning point between two fundamentally different civilizations in England, the civilization of the Middle Ages and the Renaissance and the civilization of the coming Industrial Revolution and of Empire.[24] One civilization pits the satirist-humanists like Pope and Swift, defenders of hierarchical order and aristocracy, against the massive countermovement of the Dunces, whom they identify as fools and Whigs. The Tory satirists look nostalgically backwards to a life uncontaminated by easy money, political corruption, or social mobility. Making all allowances, for instance, for Pope's irony of tone and purpose, we still confront in lines like these a stubborn sincerity:

> Time was, a sober Englishman wou'd knock
> His servants up, and rise by five o'clock,
> Instruct his Family in ev'ry rule,
> And send his Wife to church, his Son to school.
> To worship like his Fathers, was his care;

To teach their frugal Virtues to his Heir;
To prove, that Luxury could never hold;
And place, on good Security, his Gold.
Now times are chang'd, and one Poetic Itch
Has seiz'd the Court and City, poor and rich.
[*First Epistle of the Second Book of Horace*, 161–70]

(Significantly he describes this "Poetic Itch" as a "raging fit" and calls its victims "these madmen.") Pope can hardly be understood as a spokesman for shopkeepers' virtues like Richardson and Defoe. Defoe, in fact, ally of Sir Robert Walpole and staunch Whig journalist, stands for everything Pope despises: economic scheming, paper money and credit, stockjobbing, and middle-class avarice and gentility. Yet yeoman frugality and industry lie near the center of the Tory vision of the past, alongside its more imposing classical ideals; and despite the lure of get-rich-quick projects, despite its Mandevillean acceptance of corruption, what we have learned to call the Protestant ethic lies also at the heart of the Whig assumptions shared by a remarkably broad spectrum of his society.[25]

Pope also reveals an anxiety about the continued stability of those values in a world of Dulness. For the idleness attached to the image of madness signifies at bottom an unspoken defiance of the established economic values in early eighteenth-century England—a defiance at once comical and disturbing. In chapter 2 of *Madness and Civilization* Michel Foucault analyzes the importance of work in eighteenth-century institutions of correction, both prisons and madhouses, concluding that the policy of these institutions was to *force* their inmates to work at some useful task in order to reintegrate them with the world of labor outside. Foucault's argument here (and sometimes elsewhere) tends to simplify the eighteenth-century response to madness into monolithic hostility, I think. Pope's complicated uses of the image of poverty, for example, mirrored in Swift's political writings on behalf of Ireland, serve to qualify and even subvert his picture of an Augustan war on madness. But if we can correct Foucault to some extent by remembering the metaphorical nature of much of the evidence, we can also connect the metaphor to social facts. What we see clearly from his researches is the tenacious belief of the Augustan mind that the

madman is basically hostile to the bourgeois order. Daniel Defoe
speaks for decent men everywhere when from the soapbox of his
weekly *Review* he denounces a nonsensical world.

> From mad statesmen, let us descend to mad Tradesmen,
> mad Creditors, and Companies, and all the Crowd of Shop-
> keeping Lunaticks, with which the World abounds—Some
> run in Debt to trust Lords, and are so mad, to think the
> other will be mad enough to pay them. Some are mad at the
> Diligence of Forreigners, and yet are idle themselves; some
> grow rich at Ale-houses, and some grow poor in their shops;
> some neglect their Business, loyter, and are drunk every
> day, and yet the World rowls into their Mouths; others
> pursue it with all manner of careful Industry and in vain rise
> early, wake late, and eat the Bread of Sorrow and scarcity.[26]

"Mad" is the only word—literally—that Defoe has for a topsy-
turvy world in which industry is not necessarily rewarded nor
idleness necessarily punished; in his definition of Dulness at the
beginning of the poem (quoted above), by no coincidence at all,
Pope also speaks of Anarchy and topsy-turvyness.

III

The possibilities of disorder become certainties in Book IV of
The Dunciad, written almost twenty years after the original
poem. Forebodings, of course, had gnawed at his poetry for many
years. Every student remembers lines from the *Essay on Man*
celebrating the immutable chain of being. "ORDER is Heav'n's
first law," Pope declares:

> Oh sons of earth! attempt ye still to rise,
> By mountains pil'd on mountains, to the skies?
> Heav'n still with laughter the vain toil surveys,
> And buries madmen in the heaps they raise.
> [IV.73–76]

And although he scoffs at "madmen" who would subvert divine
system, he nonetheless gives a nervously detailed picture of what
might happen if they succeed.

> And if each system in gradation roll,

Alike essential to th' amazing whole;
The least confusion but in one, not at all
That system only, but the whole must fall.
Let Earth unbalanc'd from her orbit fly,
Planets and Suns run lawless thro' the sky,
Let ruling Angels from their spheres be hurl'd,
Being on being wreck'd, and world on world,
Heav'n's whole foundations to their centre nod,
And Nature tremble to the throne of God:
All this dread ORDER break—for whom? for thee?
Vile worm!—oh Madness, Pride, Impiety!

[I.247—56]

A less cosmic example of "dread Chaos" occurs in *The Rape of the Lock* in Pope's description of "the gloomy Cave of Spleen." A few lines suffice to show how the unbalancing of the spheres may have its analogues in the human mind.

A constant Vapour o'er the palace flies;
Strange phantoms rising as the mists arise;
Dreadful, as hermit's dreams in haunted shades,
Or bright, as visions of expiring maids.
Now glaring fiends, and snakes on rolling spires,
Pale spectres, gaping tombs, and purple fires:
Now lakes of liquid gold, Elysian scenes,
And crystal domes, and Angels in machines.

[IV.39—46]

Martin Price calls this "one of the strongest pictures of disorder in the age: it gives us a measure of order, a sense of the strength of the forces that social decorum controls and of the savage distortion of feeling that it prevents."[27] We can even give those forces their modern names: they are the unconscious, the id. What Pope is describing in the Cave of Spleen is a turbulent succession of dreams and nightmares, the closest analogues the eighteenth century knew for madness. Internal order that protects the human personality from its own dark and brutal forces of unreason is society's first line of defense. In our discussion of Swift we shall look more closely into the individual's universal struggle for self-control; but Pope's expression of that struggle is nearly always public.

The fourth book of *The Dunciad* records the apocalyptic conclusion of the struggle for social self-control. Now the strange, fantastic anarchy of the Cave of Spleen and the literary and political anarchy of Walpole's England, as Pope sees it, are realized on a vast scale. "What is novel in the Fourth Book—and in parts of earlier books that resemble it most—is greatness of subject," writes Reuben Brower. "Pope sees the human drama, absurd and miserable as it is, against the 'huge scenic background of the stars,' and his feeling of the connexion between human folly and larger orders and disorders is religious in a quite primitive sense."[28] When the center no longer holds, Chaos is the rough beast that slouches toward London.

The metaphor of light dominates Book IV and carries us back to the third theme of madness in *King Lear*. In the story of Gloucester we saw how blindness, like madness, is traditionally associated with superhuman insight; and I suggested that the career of the image of sight should parallel that of madness. Yet in Pope's time blindness, like madness, could not persuasively be identified in any way with truth or insight.[29] In an age so dominated by Newton, blindness took on a new and negative meaning, for to be blind meant missing *the* essential principle of order; it meant being cut off symbolically from the greatest intellectual feat of the times, the most magnificent leap toward truth (like being an orphan in the age of Freud). Blindness meant both the chaotic, suffocating darkness of dreams, sleep, night, and, at the same time, error, the failure of reason. "God said, 'Let Newton be!' " as Pope's line ran, and all was light.

Both Newton and Milton in their roles as light-givers and defenders of order inspire Pope's invocation to the fourth book:

> Yet, yet a moment, one dim Ray of Light
> Indulge, dread Chaos, and Eternal Night!
> Of darkness visible so much be lent
> As half to shew, half veil the deep Intent.
>
> [IV.1–4]

The Miltonic allusions to light are almost self-evident ("darkness visible," etc.), but elements of Milton's Chaos and Night are surely present too. Few Augustan readers would have forgotten the picture of those two in *Paradise Lost:*

> . . . a dark
> Illimitable Ocean without bound,
> Without dimension, where length, breadth, and highth,
> And time and place are lost; where eldest *Night*
> And *Chaos*, Ancestors of Nature, hold
> Eternal Anarchy, amidst the noise
> Of endless wars, and by confusion stand.
>
> [II.891—97]

Just such "Eternal Anarchy" Pope now sees about to be restored, irresistible, inevitable, "inertly strong." Dulness returns, as he puts it, "To blot out Order, and extinguish Light." But his association of order and light at this juncture is, as we have said, Newtonian in a large sense. Pope further refines his allusions by commenting in a note that Dulness can thus be seen as an "*Eclipse of the Sun*," and rightly so, because the Eclipse "is occasioned by the *Moon's predominancy*, the very time when *Dulness* and *Madness* are in *Conjunction;* whose relation and influence on each other the poet hath shewn in many places."[30] Pope's sane readers, of course, choose order over chaos, light over darkness; but it is worth remarking for a moment that the human sense of what constitutes chaos and order can vary from culture to culture. The Renaissance, for example, ordinarily describes chaos by the image of things falling apart (as in Donne's *Anniversaries*) or of annihilation ("Nothing" in *King Lear*), whereas in the early eighteenth century chaos is often expressed by things merging into shapelessness. Renaissance-like inversions and disorders are present in *The Dunciad*, but few readers would deny that a vision of life deteriorating into shapeless, undiscriminated darkness is at the center (and the conclusion) of the poem. The fixed idea or obsession that Pope so often satirizes is another case in which everything is sucked into a single category, all distinctions lost.

The complex of images—light-sight-darkness-blindness—does not occur, of course, only here at the beginning of Book IV. It appears incidentally in the rest of the poem, but now with a density and intensity that unify the last part metaphorically. The other books seem at points to have such unifying imagery—noise in I, excrement in II—but not on the scale of light and darkness in IV. Even the most casual reading will accumulate a swarm of references to clouds, veils, eclipses, and so on; and very little care

is needed to appreciate how completely Pope fuses order, which
he calls "the Truth of Things," and light. All this is seen partially
in a passage from the previous book:

> But oh! with One, immortal one dispense,
> The source of Newton's Light, of Bacon's Sense!
> Content, each Emanation of his fires
> That beams on earth, each Virtue he inspires,
> Each Art he prompts, each Charm he can create,
> Whate'er he gives, are giv'n for you to hate.
> Persist, by all divine in Man unaw'd,
> But, 'Learn, ye DUNCES! not to scorn your GOD.'
>
> Thus he, for then a ray of Reason stole
> Half thro' the solid darkness of his soul. . . .
>
> [III.217—26]

Intelligence and light are clearly one; but the image of the sun as
"the Source of Light itself" (note to III.213) leads naturally to
astronomical considerations. In words ironically suggestive of the
conclusion of *The Dunciad* Pope goes on to picture what will
follow when Newtonian light is "polluted" and order shattered
by a "sable Sorc'rer," when "one wide conflagration swallows
all":

> Thence a new world to Nature's laws unknown,
> Breaks out refulgent, with a heav'n its own:
> Another Cynthia her new journey runs,
> And other planets circle other suns.
> The forests dance, the rivers upward rise,
> Whales sport in woods, and dolphins in the skies;
> And last, to give the whole creation grace,
> Lo! one vast Egg produces human race.
>
> [III.241—48]

Book IV elaborates in nearly every line these values and fears. A
description of the crowds of Dunces buzzing around Dulness
expands into a long parody of planetary order, a miniature solar
system whirling, it might be said, around a dark star. And conceits
of eyesight turn up everywhere, usually signifying moral or

rational myopia. "The critic Eye, that microscope of Wit," sees only part of any given whole and thus quite misperceives the harmony of system.

> O! would the Sons of Men once think their Eyes
> And Reason giv'n them but to study *Flies!*
> See Nature in some partial narrow shape,
> And let the Author of the Whole escape.
>
> [IV.453–56]

The famous conclusion to *The Dunciad* compresses these images of human light and darkness into unforgettable language. And the scene that Pope so powerfully shows—akin to that in Archibald MacLeish's "You, Andrew Marvell"—is that of lights going out one by one, everywhere: a vision, so to speak, of universal blinding. *King Lear* also closes on an apocalyptic note—"Is this the promis'd end?" Kent asks—but there are actors left on the stage to continue after that curtain falls. Pope's vision is starker. With excruciating irony he makes the elements of truth enact a brief, irreversible paradigm of madness:

> *Physic* of *Metaphysic* begs defence,
> And *Metaphysic* calls for aid on *Sense!*
> See *Mystery* to *Mathematics* fly!
> In vain! they gaze, turn giddy, rave, and die.
>
> [IV.645–48]

The images of mountains and caves reappear:

> See skulking *Truth* to her old Cavern fled,
> Mountains of Casuistry heap'd o'er her head!
>
> [IV.641–42]

"*Night* Primaeval" and "*Chaos* old" stand forth again; blinding becomes literal and physical as Argus's eyes are put out by Hermes' wand, until at last

> Nor *public* Flame, nor *private*, dares to shine;
> Nor *human* Spark is left, nor Glimpse *divine!*
> Lo! thy dread Empire, CHAOS! is restor'd;

Light dies before thy uncreating word:
Thy hand, great Anarch! lets the curtain fall;
And Universal Darkness buries All.

[IV.651–56]

And the restoration of Dulness is also, because they are inextricably joined in poverty, error, and blindness, the restoration of madness. The Christian allusions of the poem—the metaphorical light of right reason and the large inverted Christian structure of Book IV, complete to apocalypse and second coming—all serve to underscore our feeling for the Satanic character of the Dunces here. They swarm forward like troops of the damned, linked in their sinfulness to the ancient traditions of demonic madness. "So much has error the odds of Truth," wrote one of Pope's favorite poets, Samuel Butler, "that the Kingdom of Darkness is more frequently taken by violence than that of Heaven."[31]

IV

When we turn from *The Dunciad* to the society it speaks for (or against), we find the representative character of its vision of madness confirmed in a number of ways. Michel Foucault has argued in *Madness and Civilization* that the seventeenth and eighteenth centuries began the modern invention of madness as a secular disease, the division of madness from truth, and the division of madmen from their former place in society.[32] In earlier times madness had been constantly, physically present in human life, a phenomenon encountered daily in cities and towns, and one to be worshiped or feared according to its source of inspiration. The madman who walked so prominently through European culture drew such attention largely because of the supernatural causes of his affliction, the belief that madness was a visible sign of sacred or demonic possession. Even *King Lear*, a creation of the late Renaissance, presses upon us the sense that madness has *struck down* the king, has come downwards upon him from a higher force. When Lear stands in the midst of the storm and shakes his fists at the sky, we feel the instinctual rightness of the direction. Although he brings his madness upon himself, he brings it *down* upon himself. Moreover, the storm that heralds his madness is one more example of the tie men often feel, as Foucault says, citing Ophelia and the Lorelei, between madness and water. Water purifies, absolves, blesses, washes away; and the absolving fury of Lear's mad storm is an important reason that we judge his madness, in the end, to have been of sacred rather than demonic character. Some higher power has blessed him. The water that the Dunces make and sink in will not easily be confused with Lear's great tempest.

What seems to have broken down in the Augustan period was the relationship men had experienced for centuries with higher powers like these. In the age of Newton and Locke men no longer shook their fists with much conviction at the gods, no longer spoke directly with witches or devils or angels, not even indirectly through dreams and visions. The eighteenth century is the great century of demystification, taking away the sacramental element from all common vital acts of experience; it naturally marks the disappearance of "holy" madness. The forces that move men, that cause madness, became depersonalized, secular, and inaccessible. Awareness of such forces remained, of course; but for many years to follow the evil and beneficent gods would go by the unsatisfactory names of reason and imagination, whom we cannot confront and speak with and who bring neither absolution nor damnation; not yet. Paradoxically, however, the question of madness preoccupied Augustan thought as almost never before. In nearly every significant intellectual formulation in the eighteenth century, I think, madness appears in the matrices, a concept buried in the center of other concepts or surrounding them and exerting pressure as an inescapable boundary. It is only slight exaggeration to say that Augustan life verged on obsession with the negative meanings of irrationality; by no coincidence, obsession itself is the most familiar Augustan definition of madness. So one-sided a relationship, from which responsive nonhuman forces have been banished, generates a frustrating intensity. The Dunces embody folly not on behalf of someone else, but inexplicably on their own behalf, in the teeth of reason; it is the chief source of Pope's frustration and anger with them. We can turn now to see the same frustration and anger expressed in analogous developments from the social and intellectual history of the period.

All of the important associations that Pope and the Augustans attach to madness are comprised within the single image of Bethlehem Hospital, whose ordinary name is Bedlam; indeed, conceivably an adequate history of madness throughout the eighteenth century could be drawn from the vicissitudes of that famous hospital's reputation.[33] From the point of view of *The Dunciad*, however, the image of Bedlam seems both to complement and to complete Pope's pictures of squalor and poverty, those recurring expressions of disapproval tempered with disgust we saw in the opening book of the poem. For Pope and his contemporaries Bedlam and "Bedlam's straw" represent the last step in the human declension, a nadir of poverty, filth, and "darken'd walls" that invites and at the same time embodies a moral judgment against its inhabitants, just as the "worst inn's worst room" makes concrete the moral bankruptcy of Villers in the *Epistle to Bathurst*. Doubtless the best-known rendering of the miseries of the place is the concluding plate of Hogarth's series of engravings *The Rake's Progress*, an illustrated eighteenth-century morality play (see plate 2). Tom Rakewell, who has squandered his fortune in vice, now raves within the confines of Bedlam. His head is shaved according to the custom with violent inmates in the eighteenth century; and he lies shackled and forcibly held down by two attendants, surrounded by a sordid assembly of fellow madmen, while two silly young women of fashion, tourists or perhaps whores, stand to one side of the room observing. Behind Tom we see into the gloomy, squalid cells where other madmen lie on their beds of straw and where one of them is urinating; nearby is a ranting religious enthusiast. Only the girl whom long ago Tom seduced shows pity for him here, but her tears are not meant to call forth our own; they are to add to the moralistic warning, stern and final, that the artist has given us.

The squalor of Bedlam, of course, existed in fact as well as in Augustan imagination. Although Ned Ward calls it a "magnific College," we know from many sources just how disheartening it was, even in comparison with the conditions in previous times. During the medieval period, in fact, patients had to some degree been treated kindly, though by the early seventeenth century squalor and exploitation had begun to set in. Patients were occasionally used for medical experimentation, testing the effects of massive emetics or bloodletting or experimental torture. One popular curative theory required that they be plunged repeatedly into baths of ice water. (Foucault points out the themes of purification and rebirth behind such medical baptism.[34]) Most were housed in crowded, unheated wards, segregated by sex and not allowed to move about. Violent inmates were chained to the walls or beds, and the most outrageous were elaborately rigged with chains, weights, handcuffs, iron collars, and straps. An American sailor in Bedlam, James Norris, was found to have lived for more than nine years confined to his bed and carrying an iron weight of about twenty-eight pounds; his head was attached to a supporting column by a chain only twelve inches long.[35] Even in the early nineteenth century the squalor was astonishing. One reformer stumbled upon secret rooms in a northern asylum: "about eight feet square, in a very horrid and filthy situation, the straw almost saturated with urine and . . . the walls . . . daubed with excrement." He found one cell "twelve feet by seven feet ten inches . . . [in which] there were thirteen women. . . . I became very sick, and could not remain longer."[36] Often these patients were left naked or given a single blanket for warmth in the winter; nearly always they were starved and beaten by the untrained and indifferent staff.

Bedlam was thrown open to visitors every Sunday afternoon, and for a few pennies' admission Londoners could promenade past cells arranged like a circus sideshow (see plate 3); whores and pickpockets frequently put the sideshow to their own specialized uses. In Paris the madmen confined in Bicêtre were also exhibited on Sundays, as Mirabeau writes in familiar phrases, "like curious animals, to the first simpleton willing to pay a coin."[37] Toward the end of the century inmates were permitted to exhibit each other and finally to perform their own dramas, an innovation we associate today with the Marquis de Sade. Bethlehem closed its doors to visitors for a period during the Commonwealth of Oliver Cromwell, but they were soon opened again, and by the early eighteenth century the hospital sometimes cleared more than 400 pounds annually from its sightseers' fees; the practice continued at least until 1815. A number of these visitors have left vivid if not sympathetic descriptions. A Frenchman, Pierre Grosley, wrote,

"One entire ward of Bedlam contains a row of large cells, in each of which was a poor unfortunate wretch, chained down in bed. Whilst I was going round, one of the madmen, having disengaged himself from his chains, lept stark naked upon the back of the person that accompanied me, who was the keeper of the ward. The keeper seized him by the arms and carried him back to the cell, without giving him time to change his attitude."[38] Thomas Legg in *Low-Life; or, One Half the World Knows Not How the Other Half Lives* (1752), one of those innumerable surveys-cum-guidebooks of London vice, remembers "The Nurses of *Bethlehem* Hospital, carrying the appointed Messes in wooden Bowls, to the Poor People under their Care, and putting by the best Part of it for their ancient Relations, and most intimate Friends, who are to come and visit them in the Afternoon." And he remarks casually: "The unhappy Lunaticks in St. *Luke's* and *Bethlehem* Hospitals in *Moorfields*, and the Mad-houses in *Clerkenwell* and *Bethnal-Green*, are employ'd in breaking their Wooden Bowls, drawing Figures with Chalk on their Partitions, rattling their Chains, and making a terrible Out-cry, occasioned by the Heat of the Weather having too great an Effect over their rambling Brains."[39] Not until the late eighteenth century, after reform has begun, do we hear the word *asylum* used to describe a lunatic hospital; its connotations of retreat and shelter hardly conform to the realities of Bedlam—Bedlam, as Dryden put it, "slovenly and sad."

Thomas Legg's mention of the private madhouses in Clerkenwell and Bethnal Green points us toward another important change in the treatment of madmen. A very few private madhouses existed in London in the seventeenth century, and they seem to have been managed by clergymen; by the early eighteenth century, however, private madhouses were to be found everywhere, and their number in all likelihood ran into the dozens.[40] These establishments were operated by unskilled managers, sometimes clergy, more often mere keepers; some had arrangements more or less scrupulous with physicians (Dr. Monro, the head of Bethlehem whom Pope mentions several times, prescribed for patients in these houses without ever seeing them), but many more did not. Private madhouses received men and women who could not or would not be received in Bethlehem (or later St. Luke's), but they were also frequently used simply as repositories for sane persons who had proved troublesome to their friends or relatives. Alexander Cruden, author of the *Biblical Concordance* and a well-known London eccentric, is a case in point. He was nicknamed "The Corrector" by himself and his friends, partly because of his occupation as proofreader for printers, partly because it was his habit to correct the profane habits (like swearing on the Sabbath) of his townsmen according to his own inner spiritual light. After suddenly correcting one profane offender with a handy shovel, Cruden was seized by his neighbors and carried off secretly to a private madhouse, where he was at once clapped in a "Strait-Wastecoat" and held prisoner in isolation. While a captive he was treated with demeaning and dangerous barbarity and at first kept incommunicado. His patrons paid a guinea a week for his confinement, though rates were cheaper in other houses. The keeper and his wife, Cruden observes, "seem to have such an insatiable thirst after Money, that if the most judicious and prudent persons upon earth were sent thither with a good weekly allowance, they must be their Prisoners either with *Handcuffs, Chains,* or *Strait-Wastecoats.*"[41] "The way to be mad," he wrote later, "was to be sent to a Madhouse." Some weeks after his abduction a thoughtful visitor, betraying a conventional logic, remarked to Cruden "that if he had not seen him in this place, he should not have suspected him of the least Disorder." Although he was chained constantly to his bedpost at night and weakened by purgatives, Cruden managed to escape after several months, and he wrote a series of pamphlets describing his experience and calling for reform. A few other writers also attacked the conduct of these private madhouses and proposed government regulation—Daniel Defoe in both his *Review* and his *True-Born Englishman* made spirited attacks on the problem and recounted several tales of scandalous abuse. And at mid-century Tobias Smollett's novel *Sir Launcelot Greaves,* itself a parody of *Don Quixote,* concludes with both hero and heroine innocently trapped in a private madhouse, in this case run by a Mr. Shackle, who terrifies his charges into silence with the mere whisper of the ominous word "waistcoat." Sir Launcelot, like Defoe, protests this outrageous imprisonment and with a telling aim for English pride compares unregulated madhouses to the Inquisition or Bastille: in liberty-proud England, he says, "the most innocent person upon earth is liable to be immured for life under the pretext of lunacy, sequestered from his wife, children, and friends, robbed of his fortune, deprived even of necessaries, and subjected to the most brutal treatment from a low-bred barbarian."[42] Goaded by such critics, Parliament opened an investigation into private madhouses in 1763, and regulation of them was finally established in 1774.

Sir Launcelot's loss of fortune takes us back to Pope's frequent association of madness and poverty in *The Dunciad*. Robbery of one kind or another, usually enlivened by motives of illicit sexuality, appears to have been at the bottom of a great many abductions to private madhouses. Wives put away their husbands in this manner, goes one anonymous complaint in 1740, "that they may enjoy their Gallants, and live without the Observation and Interruption of their Husbands; and Husbands put their Wives in them, that they may enjoy their Whores, without Disturbance from their Wives; Children put their Parents in them, that they may enjoy their Estates before their time; Relations put their Kindred in them for wicked Purposes, Guardians to cheat their Pupils, Managers those with whom they are entrusted either by Law or Choice."[43] After a lunatic hospital had been opened in Dublin under the sponsorship of Jonathan Swift, a friend wrote to him: "I own to you, I was for some time averse to our having a public Bedlam, apprehending we should be overloaded with numbers under the name of mad. Nay, I was apprehensive our case would soon be like that in England; wives and husbands trying who could first get the other to Bedlam. Many, who were next heirs to estates would try their skills to render the possessor disordered, and get them confined, and soon run them into real madness."[44] In our own time political dissidents have been silenced in mental institutions in the Soviet Union, but the English Augustans used the same technique to pursue other ends. They seem always prepared to strip their victims of both sanity and property at once, and it is the lucky heir who, like Hogarth's Rake, manages to rob himself.

The vast majority of such incidents, moreover, concern young women, especially young women with money at their disposal who refuse to cooperate with their families, generally on the

matter of marriage. Defoe describes the plight of one such girl:
"It may suffice to tell you for the present, they kept her bound
Hand and Foot in her Bed, such a one as it was, and ty'd to the
Bed Post for several Days, reduc'd to strange Extremity, beat and
pinch'd her by cruel and barbarous wretches called Nurses, and
forc'd nauseous Draughts down her Throat, *which they call'd
Physick,* and which she, being apprehensive they design'd her
Destruction, and might poyson her, *refus'd;* but they forc'd her
Mouth open with Iron Instruments, and pour'd into her, what
they thought fit, wounding her very much with their Violences
and Inhumanities." Even the most casual reader will respond to
the insinuations in such an account, the erotic overtones of
Beauty and the Beast that make it sound like an eighteenth-
century *Story of O.* These tormented women are plausible
forerunners of the heroines of Gothic novels later in the century:
"During her confinement," Defoe wrote of another case, "the
Villain of the Mad-House frequently attempted her chastity; and
the more she repuls'd him, the worse he treated her: till at last he
drove her mad in good earnest. Her distressed Brother, who is
fond of her to the Last Degree, now confines her in part of his
own House, treating her with great Tenderness; but has the
Mortification to be assured by the ablest Physicians, that his poor
Sister is irrecoverably distracted."[45] But many of the famous
novels of incarceration in the century, like *Pamela, Clarissa,* and
Diderot's *La Religieuse,* share both the titillations of Defoe's story
and the conception of marriage as a serious financial transaction,
designed mainly for profit. (The English historian Christopher
Hill has written interestingly on the early eighteenth-century use
of marriage as a means of family aggrandizement.[46]) But the
situation can be seen in another way, a way relevant to our
discussion of madness and money. The girls put away in this
manner are put away because they have refused to be good
bourgeois daughters; they have refused, as every reader of
Clarissa knows, to contribute to the family fortune in the only
way they possibly can, by marrying well. And when such a girl
refuses to do her monetary duty she is locked in a madhouse. It is
the association that should be emphasized here: hostility to
ordinary middle-class values is associated instantly, automat-
ically, with insanity; and insanity with confinement. Madness is a

failing of the aristocracy or the poor; the middle class cannot accept it.

In other, similar cases the madhouses were openly used for the punishment of perverse wives. The celebrated Dr. Battie (who was notorious for his own rather rambling brain and from whom I think we get our word *batty*) testified before the Parliamentary committee in 1763 that he had often met with sane persons in private madhouses. "He related the Case of a Woman perfectly in her Senses brought as a Lunatic by her husband to a House under the Doctor's Direction, whose Husband upon Doctor Battie insisting he should take home his Wife, and expressing his Surprise at his Conduct, justified himself by frankly saying, he understood the House to be a Sort of Bridewell, or Place of Correction."[47] (That the subjects of this correction seem almost invariably to be women is a fact of no little interest, and we will return to it in the next chapter.)

Although the inmates of Bedlam and of the private madhouses of London lived in wretchedness, there was a far worse side to their situation: even within their squalor they were not free. Imprisonment, as the archetypal poverty of Bedlam suggests, is another of the meanings of poverty for the Augustan mind—not simply the specter of debtor's prison that looms so often in eighteenth-century literature, but the terrible cell of madness toward which any Dunce may be traveling. The widespread practice of confining madmen, Michel Foucault argues, began in Europe in the mid-seventeenth century, roughly the beginning of what we have been calling the Augustan Age; as a convenient date he chooses 1656, the year of the founding of the Hôpital Général in Paris, though it should be noted that the first laws requiring the incarceration of indigent lunatics in England appeared only at the beginning of the eighteenth century.[48] In earlier periods madmen normally lived among relatives or upon the charity of the community, and the devils thought to cause madness were exorcised openly, driven out in public ceremony (Foucault does tell how some German coastal villages at the end of the Middle Ages would bribe passing ships to transport and unload elsewhere the local mad, thus creating an actual ship of fools). The imprisoning of the insane stands in startling contrast to the freedom of movement of Don Quixote and King Lear, and even Tom o' Bedlam—freedom from convention, in fact, was one of the traditional privileges of the insane—and confinement helps to mark a new era, a new tone of life. For confinement implies a desire on the part of ordinary men to avoid (except on Sundays!) the very sight—the shocking and scandalous sight—of madness; it reshapes the social landscape and experience of the community, and it makes the madness thus hidden somehow shameful. In no possible way divinely inspired, the insane now belong properly only within the walls of a quasi-medical prison alongside other criminals, degraded and exiled and also punished; madness is indistinguishable from crime.

The degradation of confinement was not limited to the degradation of poverty. Caged, chained, beaten—the madman of the Augustan Age was brutalized in fact: regarded as an animal, he was treated exactly like one. The madman's supposed powers to endure the coldest weather without clothing or shelter were proof of his inhumanity; and some unscrupulous keepers had actually set their charges to pulling a plow or hauling wagons. The cells of Bedlam were in reality the cells of a human zoo. The animality of madness cannot be too much emphasized. Medical theory in Augustan England considered most kinds of mental illness incurable (and inexplicable)—hysteria seemed the only exception—and the raging insanity of *homo furiosus* fell utterly beyond the pale of science. More than at other periods men of the early eighteenth century stressed the differences between men and animals; the animality that the madman displayed—and which was forced upon him—removed him from the category *human* and dumped him within a wild beast's cage.

Another scene from Ned Ward's *London Spy*, a trip through the Tower Zoo, incorporates most instructively the animal and the excremental themes. "In another Apartment, or *Ward*," he relates, "for the conveniency of drawing a Penny more out of the Pocket of a Spectator, are plac'd the following Animals: First a *Leopard*, who is grown as cunning as a cross Bedlamite that loves not to be look'd at; for as a *Madman* will be apt to salute you with a Bowl of Chamber-Lie, so will the *Leopard*, if you come near him, stare in your Face, and Piss upon you."[49] Here the identification between the lunatic and the worst kind of animalism is automatic and complete, even to the price of

PLATE 1. *William Hogarth's* Credulity, Superstition and Fanaticism: A Medley *(1762). A satire against enthusiasm. The thermometer leading to madness replaces the conventional hourglass. The witch on the broomstick represents the Trinity. At bottom left is Mary Toft, who gained great notoriety by claiming to give birth to rabbits—one a day.*

PLATE 2. *William Hogarth's last engraving in the series* Rake's Progress *(1735). The Rake and the madman in the cell to the left of him were modeled on "Cibber's brazen, brainless brothers," the two statues over the entrance to Bedlam. The coin on the wall signifying the madness of all Britain was added in 1763.*

A VISIT TO BEDLAM

PLATE 3. *Richard Newton's* A Visit to Bedlam *(1794). It depicts a scene like that described in* The London Spy, *by Ned Ward, much earlier in the century. For a few pennies' admission sightseers were permitted to gawk at the inmates.*

PLATE 4. The Mad Artist in Chains, *an eighteenth-century etching by an anonymous artist. An attack on Hogarth, showing him like his own Rake in a Bedlam cell. "The Line of Beauty" and "the precise Line" refer to Hogarth's book* The Analysis of Beauty *(1753) and are used to satirize his "fixation."*

admission to see them in their cages; identical, too, is their antisocial response to the curiosity of uncaged men. In fact, of course, the Augustans are speaking from first-hand observation; schizophrenics do dabble in their own excrement or fling it angrily at their attendants. Yet what interests us at this point is not the clinical accuracy of Pope or Ned Ward: it is what such carryings-on mean to them. The sequel to the Tower Zoo episode, a stay in the Poultry Countner Prison, combines spectacularly all of the accustomed associations. The most dramatic adventure is an epic battle between prisoners, whose weapons are supplied from a great central "stink-tub." At a particularly nasty moment in the fight (which would not be out of place in *The Dunciad*) Ned Ward comments: "This put the Court, as well as the other Spectators, into an excessive Laughter, to see the poor Lawyer Spit, Splutter, Spew, and run about Swearing and Cursing, Raving, and Crying, like a Bedlamite that had broke his Chains." And in another part of the prison "Some lay round the Fire, almost cover'd with Ashes, like *Potatoes* Roasting, with their Noses in Conjunction with one anothers A——s, like *Hogs* upon a Dunghill: These, I suppose, were tender Mortals bred up at the *Forge*, and as great Enemies to Cold Weather, as the Mad Fellow that walks about the Town Naked."[50] Madmen, convicts, animals—all reduced to one level, "their Noses in Conjunction with one anothers A——s, like *Hogs* upon a Dunghill." Utterly separate from normal men, mocked away or locked away.

V

At the very beginnings of the Augustan Age Thomas Hobbes had pronounced magisterially that "madness is nothing else, but too much appearing passion," and a particularly outrageous form of it, he says, is "Private Spirit" or religious "Enthusiasm." Of persons possessed by it he notes sourly that "if there were nothing else that bewrayed their madness; yet that very arrogating such inspiration to themselves is argument enough."[51] The widespread attack of the late seventeenth century against the claims of enthusiasm (an attack in which Pope happily joined) was due partly to the rise of natural science and its new standards of truth, partly to sheer weariness after four decades of political and religious turmoil, and partly to the ridiculous figures the revivalists cut. With the inspired rantings of their meetings in mind, Hobbes calls it one aspect of enthusiastic madness "when men speak such words, as put together, have in them no signification at all; but are fallen upon by some through misunderstanding of the words they have received, and repeat by rote; by others from intention to deceive by obscurity."[52] Nowhere does Shaftesbury's conception of ridicule as the test of truth meet more success than in the case of field preachers (of no small importance here is the fact that, broadly speaking, enthusiasm is a lower-class phenomenon, not usually espoused by the sophisticated, affluent, or educated). Underlying all of these reasons, however, is the firm experience of seventeenth-century England that dissenters are disrupters: not only does subjective inspiration fail to produce objective truth, it also brings down upon a society far-reaching disorder, disorder that may seem after a time even to the most sympathetic citizen apocalyptic.

Both complicating and strengthening the charge of madness against enthusiasts is their persistent identification with enthusiastic poets. For the late seventeenth century, weary of the private ecstasies of religious enthusiasts, grew similarly impatient with their counterparts in literature—imagination and false inspiration are treated as much the same thing—and critical theory of the period is nearly unanimous in its insistence on a controlled, not to say hobbled, poetic imagination. John Evelyn's *Diary*, for example, in an entry made at the beginning of the age, contains a laconic but suggestive observation: "I stepped into Bedlam, where I saw several miserable creatures in chains; one of them was mad with making verses."[53] In the unspoken associations Evelyn communicates we are far from Aristotle's account of his friend Marascos, who was a bad poet sane but much improved when mad. Even Abraham Cowley speaks from a new position of wariness when he remarks of his odes: "If a man should undertake to translate Pindar word for word, it would be thought that one madman had translated another." This skepticism about the divine madness of poets was distinctly an Augustan phenomenon. Distrust of rhetoric had for a generation been converging from several directions: from a general feeling that passionate, highly charged political language had driven the nation toward its devastating civil wars; from the impressive

insistence of the natural scientists, newly organized into a Royal
Society, that language concentrate on clarity and logic rather
than "untruthful" imaginative rhetoric; and again, especially
from the obnoxiousness of the enthusiasts, who scorned logic and
clarity and valued instead a kind of transcendent incompre-
hensibility—who spoke, in other words, "in tongues." Dryden,
for example, attacks the fanatic in poetry who "has a light within
him, and writes by an inspiration; which (like that of the heathen
prophets) a man must have no sense of his own when he receives;
and no doubt he would be thought inspired, and would be
reverenced extremely in the country where Santons are
worshipped."[54] The Tatler (No. 11) reports on the progress of the
author of The Modern Prophets, "a most unanswerable satire
against the late spirit of enthusiasm. . . . My friend designs to go
on with another work against winter, which he intends to call,
The Modern Poets, a people no less mistaken in their opinions of
being inspired than the other." Indeed, pretentious poets are
thrown into the same jumble of degrading associations as the
other madmen we have examined. Ned Ward captures the spirit
of the hunt, if little else:

> But what a Pox is't I am doing?
> Or where the Devil am I going?
> Now Pegasus I've once bestriden,
> Methinks I Gallop like a D——n;
> And pleas'd I'm in the Vein, Egad,
> Blunder out Verse like any Mad.

> This Ignis Fatuus in my Brains
> That kindles up these Rambling Strains,
> Makes my Head Light as any Feather,
> And leads me wand'ring God knows whither.[55]

In Peri Bathos, with redoubled entendre, Pope calls such poetry
"a morbid Secretion from the Brain," whose expulsion brings
relief and a deadened tranquility.[56] Elsewhere poetry is like sleep
or nightmares or like the mobs that so often symbolize insanity to
the Augustans:

> Our King return'd, and banisht Peace restor'd,
> The Muse ran Mad to see her exil'd Lord;

On the crack't Stage the Bedlam Heroes roar'd,
And scarce cou'd speak one reasonable word.[57]

Unguarded poetry can be dangerous: frenzied satire "like a sword in the hands of a madman . . . runs a Tilt at all manner of Persons without any sort of distinction or reason."[58] Imagination, poetry, or wit run mad all formed part of a dangerous challenge to the hard-won order of the Restoration; and any one kind of disorder, if unchecked, seems to have signaled a storm of it. Augustan culture valued the style of scientific simplicity; and Lockean psychology, as we shall see in a moment, further encouraged a distrust of private styles and insights as inherently untrue and potentially disordering. Defoe speaks for everyone except Methodists and madmen when he says: "If any man were to ask me what I should suppose to be a perfect style . . . I would answer, that in which a man speaking to five hundred people, of all common various capacities, idiots or lunatics excepted, should be understood by them all, and in the same sense in which the speaker intended to be understood."[59]

The ideal poet for the Augustans, thus, had become not only a man among other men but also a moral figure, a truthful and responsible public voice. In *The Dunciad* Pope stings equally cruelly the visionary poet and "the *Muse's Hypocrite,* . . . one who thinks the only end of poetry is to amuse, and the only business of the poet to be witty; and consequently who cultivates only such trifling talents in himself, and encourages only such in others."[60] Madness and knavery, amplification and diminution, are the images Pope chooses for such deliberately untruthful poets, while the responsible poet, as delineated in *Arbuthnot* and elsewhere, counsels and safeguards like a literary ombudsman:

> Truth guards the Poet, sanctifies the line,
> And makes Immortal, Verse as mean as mine.
> [*Epilogue to the Satires,* II.246–47]

VI

In a long note to the passage introducing Book III of *The Dunciad* (describing Cibber's dream of Dulness), Pope's friend and editor Warburton recapitulates the themes we have been touching upon. Of the Sibyl who leads Cibber he says:

This allegory is extremely just, no conformation of the mind so much subjecting it to real *Madness*, as that which produces real *Dulness*. Hence we find the religious (as well as the poetical) Enthusiasts of all ages were ever, in their natural state, most heavy and lumpish; but on the least application of *heat*, they run like lead, which of all metals falls quickest into fusion. Whereas *fire* in a Genius is truly Promethean, it hurts not its constituent parts, but only fits it (as it does well-tempered steel) for the necessary impression of art. But the common people have been taught (I do not know on what foundation) to regard Lunacy as a mark of *Wit*, just as the Turks and our modern Methodists do of Holiness. But if the cause of Madness assigned by a great Philosopher be true, it will unavoidably fall upon the dunces. He supposes it to be the *dwelling over long on one object or idea:* Now as this attention is occasioned either by Grief or Study, it will be fixed by Dulness; which hath not quickness enough to comprehend what it seeks, nor force and vigor enough to divert the imagination from the object it laments.

The "great Philosopher" whom he quotes is John Locke, and his deference to the most renowned intellect of the time, after Newton, illuminates further the Augustan strictures on madness. ("The authority of this great man is doubtless as great as that of any man can be," Burke was later to write.[61])

In the passage Warburton has in mind, in the *Essay Concerning Human Understanding,* Locke is distinguishing between "naturals" (idiots) and madmen: idiots, he says, "are deprived of reason; whereas madmen . . . seem to suffer by the other extreme. For they do not appear to me to have lost the faculty of reasoning, but having joined together some ideas very wrongly, they mistake them for truths; and they err as men do that argue from wrong principles."[62] Thus madmen are simply *mistaken,* not inspired (though the Dunces, of course, are willfully mistaken). "The ultimate language of madness," Foucault asserts, "is that of reason."[63] Madmen attach themselves to wrong principles by dwelling too long on some passion or other until it becomes a fixed idea, like Don Quixote's knight-errantry; and thereupon what Johnson calls the "tyranny of imagination" is established. What is important to notice, however, is how easily the mind can be mistaken. Locke's description of the human mind, to rehearse briefly a complex matter, contained two major innovations: first he denied the presence of innate ideas like justice or duty in our minds and declared instead that we receive all our ideas through our five senses; and second he argued that our complex or abstract ideas arise from the combination or association of these initial sensory ideas. Now, an atmosphere of gloom (never sufficiently noted) hangs over Locke's analysis. For if the mind is a blank tablet, a *tabula rasa*, on which the senses write their information, the mind is also a *camera obscura:*

> For, methinks, the understanding is not so much unlike a closet wholly shut from light, with only some little opening left, to let in external visible resemblances, or ideas of things without: would the pictures coming into such a dark room but stay there, and lie so orderly as to be found upon occasion, it would very much resemble the understanding of a man, in reference to all objects of sight, and the ideas of them.[64]

The somber feeling of *limitation* that such a description conveys is confirmed when we consider, as Locke does over and over, that the senses themselves are not always reliable receptors of information; indeed, they can be actively deceitful (as in visual perspective, for example) and in any case they are only "some little opening," the outward, insuperable circumferences of our knowledge. The principle of the association of ideas is even more problematic, and Locke himself expresses misgivings about its liability to error. Illogical free association was a sign of weakness of mind to the eighteenth century; carried far enough, a proof of madness. That great Lockean novel *Tristram Shandy* goes to the barricades, if not beyond.

One implication of the Lockean model is that all minds, since they receive the same sensory information in the same way, will perceive the same reality and come to the same conclusions about it. Hence the "public" character of so much Augustan literature, the interest in the greater genres like epic rather than in the private meditative lyric. And hence too the "insanity" of private, unverifiable experiences like those of the enthusiasts. Of course, every man has certain quirks or hobbyhorses that tyrannize him at

some time in some way, take him from the public to the private
realm; and Locke duly takes that into account: "I shall be
pardoned for calling it [idiosyncratic opinion] by so harsh a name
as madness, when it is considered, that opposition to reason
deserves that name, and is really madness; and there is scarce a
man so free from it, but that if he should always, on all occasions,
argue or do as in some cases he constantly does, would not be
thought fitter for Bedlam than civil conversation."[65] Like Locke,
who strikes a tone of urbane tolerance here, Pope understands
(and even enjoys) ordinary human foibles. But in another light
their attitude toward human nature is marked by suspicion and
tension. Possibilities latent in every man, private and
unreasonable, spring grotesquely to life in the Dunces. Johnson
expresses that nervousness more directly when he advises Boswell
(and himself) to avoid singularity of behavior. Singularity, insofar
as it runs counter to public opinion, runs counter to truth and into
the jaws of madness.

Locke's model of the human mind, in other words, for all the
complexity of his *Essay*, was too simple. Reason and certainty are
too easily lost (he compares a fit of momentary madness to being
lost in the streets of a strange city),[66] and there is no place for
redemptive intuition, for inspiration. Apart from divine
revelation—now as extinct as witchcraft—men cannot discover or
even guess at anything more than their senses permit. "Were our
senses altered, and made much quicker and acuter, the
appearance and outward scheme of things would have quite
another face to us."[67] But as it is, fantastical or chimerical ideas
are merely combinations of simple sensory ideas, combinations
that do not conform to routine probability. Madmen *cannot* see
some other reality, unperceived by normal men, because to the
poor, limited human understanding no other reality is accessible:
another sense or set of senses would be needed. Madness *must* be
wrong reasoning, for no other possibility exists. But those who
rejected Lockean psychology in the years thereafter were few and
unsuccessful (one thinks particularly of Christopher Smart and
Blake). "Men of the early eighteenth century," Perry Miller
observes, "were not so much the beneficiaries of Locke as they
were his prisoners."[68] The majority accepted what he himself
would have called the half-light of his vision.

VII

Why did this change come about? Why did the English evaluation of madness change so dramatically from one of complex possibilities to one of intense hostility? Why did Augustan society begin to lock madmen in cages, to transform them into wretched, ludicrous animals? It may well be that no single answer will account for so startling a shift in sensibility. It may well be that human forms and institutions, like radioactive elements, have only a half-life of energy and that inevitably their energy falls away. The cultural forms (especially the literary forms) that contain and shape ideas in the Renaissance, in other words, may simply have worn out over the course of several centuries. The outlines of Renaissance humanism persisted into a new era, but faded and weakened, while the energies that they once contained pushed through and outwards in search of new forms. That is the kind of explanation (or non-explanation) that C. S. Lewis offers for a similar shift in sensibility, when he considers the sudden appearance of courtly love in fourteenth-century France: who can say precisely why the winds of the mind take one direction rather than another?[69] And yet in the case of madness some suggestions, far more tentative than precise, may nonetheless be offered. One reason may lie in the experience of two generations with the confusion that private values always bring to public order. The religious enthusiast, for example, so closely bound up with the political conflicts of the earlier seventeenth century, even without a political role would have come to seem dangerous somehow to humanistic values. In his madness he had, after all, dispensed with the older priority of reason and trusted instead to private voices and visions, unverifiable by other men; and as with every madman his privacy suggested subversion. Another reason for the change from classical to Augustan ideas about madness appears to lie, as we have seen, in the implications of John Locke's epistemology, which reinforced—as it may have been intended to do—the growing English preference for what was publicly, generally knowable.

Yet behind these reasons we may discern another. The identification of insanity with animality and excrement conveys perfectly the degradation that madness meant to the early

eighteenth century. The comradeship of madmen and convicts
sharpens our sense that to the Augustan mind madness also meant
punishment: the madman was punished for being what he was.
But this perception of madness seems determined by something
more than simple disgust; so systematic and so general an
overreaction comes, not from a natural distaste for what is ugly or
unfamiliar, but from fear. The intensity of the Augustan revulsion
was too great not to suggest to us as its cause a deep-seated,
barely controlled terror.

Fear of the insane, of course, is common to many cultures. In
earlier times men recoiled from the gods or witches who inflicted
madness: their presence, even if it denoted supernatural
protection, was frightening. But in the Augustan Age fear of the
insane springs from the inescapable conclusion that it is *ourselves*
who cause madness, that human beings possess an unpredictable
self-altering, self-destructive potential. (Present in both cases
seems to be that primitive terror of irrationality we mentioned
earlier, the irrationality that destroys all order.) The alternative
external explanations of human madness that had served earlier
cultures held their ground poorly in the face of an advancing,
skeptical science and a weary, often defensive religious
establishment. Homer or Shakespeare might account for the
insanity of a hero by pointing toward external interventions, like
Athena's in the opening of *The Iliad* or the devils and gods so
often named in *King Lear;* but for the Augustans external
explanations of the human personality no longer worked, and an
internal mythology was not available and would not be until
Freud. Medicine offered only unconvincing theories. ("What is
Dr. *Monro?*" Cruden asks. "A mad-doctor: and pray what great
matter in that? what can mad-doctors do? prescribe *purging*
physic, letting of *blood,* a *vomit, cold bath,* and a *regular diet?*
how many incurables are there? when the brain is in great
disorder, a cure is past the power of man."[70]) The Homeric gods
were no longer believable, as the lifelessness of classical
mythology in eighteenth-century poetry ineloquently testifies.
Witchcraft was officially pronounced defunct in 1736: where else
could men locate the forces of unreason except within
themselves?

And yet if the Devil can no longer be exorcised, at least the

madman can be. The Augustans send him away; they twist almost
beyond recognition his human qualities. They project upon
madmen those characteristics within themselves that seem mad
or mad-creating. They fear what they cannot understand. And so,
frightened of the inexplicable disordering forces of madness, the
Augustans simply deny their presence within normal men; by
transforming madmen into animals, they only insist thereby that
physical appearances correspond to inner realities: if demonic
explanations do not exist, it will be easy to invent them.

It would be wrong to say—if we may anticipate for a
moment—that the Romantic period would recognize and accept
those basic forces of unreason as part of our natures; only Blake
among the Romantics honestly does so. But the others, like
Wordsworth and Coleridge, admit them in indirect ways,
disguised as dreams, reveries, visions, exalted madmen or poets.
In their personifications of nature and of abstractions middle and
late eighteenth-century poets take tentative steps toward
restoring that relationship with nonhuman forces which the
Augustans had by and large severed. Not really until our own
time is the animalistic side of our nature fully recognized, indeed
insisted upon, in writers like D. H. Lawrence and Norman
Mailer. In them the qualities that cause madness are accepted as
valuable parts of ourselves; but the path to such self-knowledge
(or self-exposure) takes most of the nineteenth century to travel
and passes through a dark Romantic forest where those qualities
are not repressed, but neither are they openly expressed:

> L'homme y passe à travers des forêts de symboles
> Qui l'observent avec des regards familiers.
>
> [Baudelaire, "Correspondances"]

Rather, they appear in the characteristic Romantic mode of
symbols.

The most obvious meaning of the image of madness in the
Augustan Age, then, is a traditional one profoundly darkened:
folly—willful, inexplicable, life-denying folly. The fools of *The
Dunciad* lack the robustness or the wit or even the holiness of
earlier fools like Lear's or Rabelais's; nor are they mouthpieces for
dark or satiric truths. Pope's fools are insects, mad droning

creatures present in such numbers that their very numbers menace. Pope and his contemporaries do not say it is a mad world so much as they say it is a world full of madmen; and there is a difference. For a mad world makes no sense, but in a world swarming with madmen we can still hear the voice of sanity; it is a world contested between the sane and the mad, but stubbornly, righteously, despite the danger, sanity maintains itself. We may catch this same quality of anxiety about the power of folly sometimes in Horace; we miss it for the most part in earlier English literature; and nowhere else do we find the converging circumstances that give so much force to fear and so much energy to counterattack. And yet when we consider the Augustan denunciation of folly, we should also consider its correspondingly high standard of sanity. The Augustans are fully aware of the difficulty of not being Dunces; alongside their insistence on the rational, the civilized, the ordered is their recognition—not tragic because not abandoned or defeated—that to be rational, decent, and sane is uncertain business at best and requires effort forever and costs pain forever. The kind of behavior that Pope and Swift call madness tends to be behavior that denies, in Johnson's phrase, "the pain of being a man." Denies it in the way ecstatic visionaries do, by ignoring what is corrosive and irreversibly destructive in life. Or denies it in the way that Grub Street hacks do, by abdicating the standards of art and intellect that men can reach only with endless labor, but that they are obliged by their best natures to strive for. The Romantics speak—perhaps too easily—of the promise of being a man, instead of the pain. To the Augustans promise is precarious; the humanity so carefully sustained is always threatening to fly apart into its components. Like the passage from *The Dunciad* with which we began, this too is an Augustan note from Pope: "My lord *Bolingbroke* and Mr. *Bethel* have not forgotten to visit me: the rest (except Mrs. *Blount* once) were contented to send messages. I never pass'd so melancholy a time, and now Mr. *Congreve*'s death touches me nearly. It is twenty years that I have known him. Every year carries away something dear with it, till we outlive all tenderness, and become wretched Individuals again as we begun." Here are the terms of what Johnson calls "the great law of mutual benevolence." The public context, the mutuality of sane men and women, was never clearer. "Wretched Individuals again" is not what we shall hear from Blake or Wordsworth. In Pope's world to be properly human is to resist slipping backwards toward where we began, not to collapse into private knowledge, darkness, animalism, folly, madness.

In explanation of such a world it may be that those social and intellectual changes that indirectly we have been following constitute easily, as the lawyers say, sufficient reason. One difficulty for the historian—it is also significant evidence—lies in the available perspective. In the Augustan Age we can only hear writers speaking out, anxiously and pessimistically, against the meanings of madness; by the end of the century we hear the authentic voice of the madman speaking for himself.

CHAPTER THREE

Swift

Much of what Pope expresses about the Augustan image of madness Jonathan Swift, the friend and literary ally to whom *The Dunciad* is dedicated, expresses too, and it would be an easy task to trace in his writings those same characteristic attitudes and postures. But Swift demands special attention, not only for the variations a gifted writer inevitably brings to familiar themes, but also for the conspicuous role he plays in the history of English literature: the unrelenting satirist who expired, as Johnson wrote, "a driv'ler and a show" like one of his own imagined madmen; "a hater of his kind," Stephen Dedalus calls him, who "ran . . . to the wood of madness, his mane foaming in the moon, his eyeballs stars"; the great English misanthrope who sleeps, his epitaph tells us, "where savage indignation can no longer lacerate his heart."[1]

Scholarship has dispelled the fiction that Swift went mad at the end of his life, and modern medicine has explained away his giddiness and his occasional senile incoherence as the effects of Ménière's disease, a severe disturbance of the inner ear.[2] But despite these authorities, the idea that he was mad remains stubbornly attached to the figure Swift takes in our imaginations. It makes obscure sense; it satisfies us that a writer whose best works all end (or begin and end) with madness should at last sacrifice himself upon that common altar, a violent and outrageous lunatic. We spoke earlier of the Swiftian tones and preoccupations in the climactic phase of King Lear's madness, when he encounters Gloucester in the fields near Dover; and indeed in all literature there may be no one whom Swift so much resembles to our minds as Lear in the fourth act of his tragedy, Lear before he is reclaimed by charity. Whoever reads Swift's letters and studies his life can scarcely believe in his madness, but whoever reads *A Tale of a Tub* or Book IV of *Gulliver's Travels* must surely hesitate, unable quite to comprehend the vehemence with which Swift damned the madness that surrounded him. "There's hell, there's darkness," Lear says,

> There is the sulphurous pit—burning, scalding,
> Stench, consumption; fie, fie, fie! pah, pah!
> Give me an ounce of civet, good apothecary,
> To sweeten my imagination.

I

The evidence suggests that Swift's imagination could have used sweetening almost from the beginning. In his early Pindaric odes (1690–93), poetically inept and virtually unreadable today, the only "serious" poetry he ever attempted, we see put baldly some of the themes that we meet over and over again in Swift's vision of madness.

Of these pieces the most interesting for our purposes is the unfinished "Ode to Dr. William Sancroft," a poem almost equally divided between panegyric and passionate denunciation. What Swift is praising, of course, is the symbol of fixed truth that Sancroft, the archbishop of Canterbury martyred by James II, has become. "Truth is eternal," he begins, and Sancroft now basks in its "immortal ray" beside "the Son of Heav'n."[3]

> Thou daily seest Him face to face,
> Nor does thy essence fix'd depend on giddy circumstance
>   Of time and place,
> Two foolish guides in ev'ry sublunary dance:
> How shall we find Thee then in dark disputes?
> How shall we search Thee in a battle gain'd,
>   Or a weak argument by force maintain'd?
> In dagger-contests, and th' artillery of words,
> (For swords are madmen's tongues, and tongues are madmen's
>   swords)

Contriv'd to tire all patience out,
And not to satisfy the doubt.

[6—16]

What Swift is denouncing in labored contrast is the mutable and
uncertain state of the "sublunary dance," the "giddy
circumstance" that tires and confuses, and satisfies no doubts;
and in describing this confusion he turns to an image of madmen
at war, endlessly battling with words and swords. We may put
aside his elaboration of these images for a moment to consider the
significance of this particular Augustan version of chaos—for the
effect Swift creates here is surely one of chaos and, apart from
scale and skill, much in it reminds us of the peroration to *The
Dunciad*. Reflexively, students of eighteenth-century literature,
citing the *Encyclopédie* or the great chain of being, affirm that
age's love of order and its horror of the uncontrolled; but in Swift
we see a rare chance to reduce that truism from rhetoric to
experience, from astronomy to personality. In *Jonathan Swift and
the Age of Compromise* Professor Kathleen Williams has
speculated on Swift's lifelong fear of madness and has suggested
how deeply Swift needed to believe in an "ordering mind," the
human power to interpret and direct that strange "sublunary
dance" of flux and circumstance; and she points out how
paradoxically uncertain and even inadequate reason had come to
seem to many members of what we now call its age—it had
burrowed disruptively into old ground, and it threatened to
change utterly man's intellectual landscape, superseding or
destroying the older world of fantasy and myth.[4] For Swift, by
nature a conservative man (like Johnson and for much the same
reasons), the complicated and large-scale seismic changes going
on about him resolved quickly into the kind of contest dramatized
in the first stanza of "Sancroft"; for someone like Pope the war
against chaos seems to have come later in life—it has little place
in his early poems—and never with the personal intensity Swift
gives it. The ode to Sancroft (like Johnson s poem "The Vanity of
Human Wishes") is filled with words like "giddy" and "wild"
and with images of crowds, herds, swarms, and incoherent motion
until its attacks on error come very close to being attacks on
human life itself:

But zeal is weak and ignorant, tho' wond'rous proud,
Though very turbulent and very loud;
The crazy composition shews,
Like that fantastic medley in the idol's toes,
Made up of iron mixt with clay,
This, crumbles into dust,
That, moulders into rust,
Or melts by the first show'r away.
Nothing is fix'd that mortals see or know,
Unless, perhaps, some stars above be so. . . .

[135—44]

Elsewhere we find less ponderous statements on human disorder—the opening of *Some Thoughts on Free-Thinking*, for example:

Discoursing one day with a prelate of the kingdom of
Ireland, who is a person of excellent wit and learning, he
offered a notion applicable to the subject, we were then
upon, which I took to be altogether new and right. He said,
that the difference betwixt a mad-man and one in his wits,
in what related to speech, consisted in this: That the former
spoke out whatever came into his mind, and just in the
confused manner as his imagination presented the ideas.
The latter only expressed such thoughts, as his judgment
directed him to chuse, leaving the rest to die away in his
memory. And if the wisest man would at any time utter his
thoughts, in the crude indigested manner, as they come into
his head, he would be looked upon as raving mad. And
indeed, when we consider our thoughts, as they are the
seeds of words and actions, we cannot but agree, that they
ought to be kept under the strictest regulation. And that in
the great multiplicity of ideas, which ones mind is apt to
form, there is nothing more difficult than to select those,
which are most proper for the conduct of life.[5]

Here almost casually Swift sets forth a view of the human mind
remarkable for distrust, suspicion, pessimism. At best, he is
saying, even among the wisest, the mind resembles nothing so
much as a cauldron of ideas bubbling randomly to consciousness.
He offers no trust in the mind's own organization: in its natural

state every man's mind is a madman's, and only by the "strictest regulation" do we harness the chaotic forces built into our very constitution. At such a moment Swift is closest to the Johnson of *Rasselas*, miserably sensitive to the human potential for self-confusion, conceiving the mind only in terms of a battleground where ill-matched powers struggle to subdue each other; for them the fear of the mind is the fear of madness.

The first stanza of the ode to Sancroft ends in battle, but many of Swift's later works point up more directly the *psychological* character of the continuing battle. He concludes, for example, a list of conversational offenses (like contradiction) "with the Disease called the Wandering of the Thoughts, that they are never present in Mind at what passeth in Discourse; for whoever labours under any of these Possessions, is as unfit for Conversation as a Mad-man in Bedlam."[6] And his grim imitation of Petronius's poem "On Dreams" darkens and enlarges the mind's seething world of nightmares. (We may think of the role of dreams and sleep in *The Dunciad*.) But by far the best-known instance is the long series of horse-and-rider images in *A Tale of a Tub*, extraordinary symbols of ordinary mental commotion as Swift sees it. "The mind of Man," he says, "when he gives the Spur and Bridle to his Thoughts, doth never stop, but naturally sallies out into both extreams of High and Low, of Good and Evil. . . ."[7] And he goes on in "A Digression concerning . . . Madness . . ." to demonstrate what happens "when a Man's Fancy gets *astride* on his Reason, when Imagination is at Cuffs with the Senses, and common Understanding, as well as common Sense, is Kickt out of Doors,"[8] his mad narrator at last confessing that "even, I my self, the Author of these momentous Truths, am a Person, whose Imaginations are hard-mouth'd, and exceedingly disposed to run away with his *Reason*, which I have observed from long Experience, to be a very light Rider, and easily shook off. . . ."[9] The image, of course, is an ancient one—we see it in Plato, for example; in those lines of the *Aeneid* beginning "*At, Phoebi nondum patiens, immanis in antro / bacchatur vates*"[10]; and in medieval and Renaissance iconography too. And it is fascinating to see how in our time exactly the same image serves another student of the human mind. "The ego's relation to the id," wrote Sigmund Freud in 1932, "might be compared with that of a rider to his horse. The horse supplies the locomotive energy, while the rider has the privilege of deciding on the goal and of guiding the powerful animal's movement. But only too often there arises between the ego and the id the not precisely ideal situation of the rider being obliged to guide the horse along the path by which it itself wants to go."[11] But while the basic pattern of the metaphor, the explosive and repressive faculties of the mind in conflict, is timeless, the energy and frequency of these clashes among the Augustans startle us.

Swift exploits such tension more completely than most of his contemporaries. In his pictures of mobs, for example, a favorite Augustan emblem of irrationality, Pope is always breaking away from censure into cleverness:

> Now thousand tongues are heard in one loud din:
> The Monkey-mimics rush discordant in;
> 'Twas chatt'ring, grinning, mouthing, jabb'ring all,
> And Noise and Norton, Brangling and Breval,
> Dennis and Dissonance, and captious Art,
> And Snip-snap short, and Interruption smart.
>
> [*Dunciad*, II.235–40]

But Swift keeps a certain grim focus on what appalls him, as here in his proposal for a new insane asylum in Dublin: "What a mixed multitude of ballad-writers, ode-makers, translators, farce-compounders, opera-mongers, biographers, pamphleteers, and journalists, would appear crowding to the hospital; not unlike the brutes resorting to the ark before the deluge."[12] And in what he praises, as the tribute to Sancroft has already shown us, he chooses to emphasize firmness, consistency, loyal and virtuous endurance. The poems written to Stella on her birthday, especially those of 1723/24 and 1726/27, return often, even in jest, to her stoical patience, her steadiness. Like Sancroft or like Swift himself in his self-portraits,[13] the Stella figure exemplifies fixed virtue, principled and even manly, in perfect opposition to the turbulence and "giddy turns" of ordinary life—or of ordinary women. (And it is hardly surprising that Swift, who suffered periodic bouts of giddiness throughout his life, should be so emotionally certain of the terrors of mental and moral giddiness.)

The conditions of sublunary disorder, as the second stanza of the ode to Sancroft makes plain, are also the conditions of human blindness, another of Swift's recurrent themes.

> For this inferior world is but Heaven's dusky shade,
> By dark reverted rays from its reflection made;
>   Whence the weak shapes wild and imperfect pass,
> Like sun-beams shot at too far distance from a glass;
>   Which all the mimic forms express,
> Tho' in strange uncouth postures, and uncomely dress;
>   So when Cartesian artists try
>   To solve appearance of sight
>   In its reception to the eye,
> And catch the living landscape thro' a scanty light,
>   The figures all inverted shew
>   And colours of a faded hue,
>   Here a pale shape with upward footstep treads,
>   And men seem walking on their heads;
>   There whole herds suspended lie
>   Ready to tumble down into the sky;
>   Such are the ways ill-guided mortals go
>   To judge of things above by things below.
> Disjointing shapes as in the fairy-land of dreams,
>   Or images that sink in streams;
>   No wonder, then, we talk amiss
>   Of truth, and what, or where it is. . . .

[21–42]

So unreliable is our vision that it removes us even further from the "Bright effluence of th' immortal ray," separating us from settled and eternal truth and condemning us to the "fairy-land of dreams." Inevitably, as Professor Williams points out, the consequence of our blindness is deception, usually self-deception. "In 'Day of Judgment,' " she notes, "it is not humanity's wickedness but its blindness of which Jove complains":

> Jove, nodding, shook the Heav'ns, and said,
> "Offending Race of Human Kind,
> By Nature, Reason, Learning, blind, . . .
>
> The World's mad Business now is o'er,
> And I resent these Pranks no more."[14]

And Swift echoes Jove's complaint time and time again, using blindness invariably to mean error, just as madness does. "Mistaken Ideots!" he cries in the ode to Sancroft, "see how giddily they run, / Led blindly on by avarice and pride."[15] Of the "Blind and thoughtless Croud" he remarks less poignantly elsewhere,

> Happy Nation were we blind,
> Or, had only eyes behind.

And indecently he riddles of "The Posteriors"

> Because I am by Nature *blind*,
> I wisely chuse to walk *behind;*
> However to avoid Disgrace,
> I let no creature see my *Face*.[16]

In particular two sorts of visionaries—the word itself is an Augustan sneer—gall Swift with their blindness: the enthusiast and the poet. "Vision is the Art of seeing Things invisible," he observes tartly in his journal,[17] and for the dean of St. Patrick's the season never closes on dissenters. But Swift also measures out an acid and strangely disconcerting scorn for the thing he was never to be, the serious, "poetic" poet. In the last of his youthful odes, a celebration of Sir William Temple's recovery from illness, he abruptly turns on that "Malignant goddess" the Muse:

> Ah, should I tell a secret yet unknown,
> That thou ne'er hadst a being of thy own,
> But a wild form dependent on the brain,
> Scatt'ring loose features o'er the optic vein;
> Troubling the chrystal fountain of the sight,
> Which darts on poets eyes a trembling light;
> Kindled while reason sleeps, but quickly flies,
> Like antic shapes in dreams, from waking eyes:
> In sum, a glitt'ring voice, a painted name,
> A walking vapor, like thy sister fame,
> But if thou be'st what thy mad vot'ries prate,
> A female pow'r, loose-govern'd thoughts create;
> Why near the dregs of youth perversely wilt thou stay,
> So highly courted by the brisk and gay?[18]

Not unexpectedly this poem marks Swift's farewell to elevated
poetry, but the metaphorical associations strung together
here—deceitful poetic vision, the sleep of reason, antic dreams,
madness, corrupt and corrupting women—reappear in all his
later writing; the farewell is in reality a preview:

> Madness like this no fancy ever seiz'd,
> Still to be cheated, never to be pleas'd;
> Since one false beam of joy in sickly minds
> Is all the poor content delusion finds.—
> There thy enchantment broke, and from this hour
> I here renounce thy visionary pow'r;
> And since thy essence on my breath depends,
> Thus with a puff the whole delusion ends.
>
> [147–54]

Swift's disgust with the Muse clearly grows from distrust of her,
his conviction that poetry, like vision, deceives the reason and
manipulates the passions. "Thus the *deluding Muse* oft blinds me
to her Ways," he wrote to the Athenian Society; by her "blind
and eager Curiosity" she has been "forc't to grope her uncouth
way / After a *mighty Light* that leads her wandring Eye."[19]
Deceitful, enchanting, inconstant—Swift comes very close to
calling his Muse a bawd. "Tis with a foul design the muse you
send, / Like a cast mistress to your wicked friend," he proclaims
to Congreve;[20] and two suggestive lines in the ode to Sancroft
denouncing the errors of crowds weave together these themes of
blindness and womanhood:

> Th' daz'ling glory dimms their prostituted sight,
> No deflower'd eye can face the naked light.
>
> [221–22]

In the context of madness and blindness Swift's misogynistic
pose takes on unusual significance; for just as in the previous
chapter we saw images of animality and excrement used to dis-
credit (at the very least) the madman's experience, so here in
Swift we find images of femaleness used in the same way:
madness is womanish.

The Muse, quickly demoted in his satiric verse to Everywoman, deludes and blasts whoever comes near her, and through pox and blindness she points toward madness. The denunciation of woman and insanity, though he invests it with unusual energy, is by no means uniquely Swiftian—we have only to think of King Lear again or of the Christian antifeminist tradition scornfully recorded by the Wife of Bath—yet more than a convention, it seems part of the very air, the syphilis-plagued air, of the Augustan Age. Like Swift's Muse, Pope has his goddess Dulness. And the disease of hysteria was by definition and etymology a woman's disease (blindness was often a symptom of hysteria). "I never dare to speak of Vapours," says Mandeville, "the very name is become a Joke, and the general notion the Men have of them, is, that they are a malicious mood, and contriv'd Sullenness of Willful, Extravagant and Imperious Women, when they are denied, or thwarted in their unreasonable desires; nay, even Physicians, because they cannot Cure them, are forc'd to ridicule them in their own Defence, and a Woman, that is really troubled with Vapours, is pitied by none but their unhappy fellow Sufferers, that labour under the same Affliction."[21] This affliction he ascribes complacently to women's inherent weaknesses: "One Hours intense Thinking wastes the Spirits more in a Woman, than six in a Man."[22] Dr. Arbuthnot describes the illness of John Bull's mother in terms by now familiar to us: "She, that was the cleanliest creature in the world, never shrunk now, if you set a close-stool under her nose. . . . At last the distemper grew more violent, and threw her downright into raving fits; in which she shrieked out so loud, that she disturbed the whole neighborhood. . . . *Dr. Garth.* 'This case seems to me to be plainly hysterical; the old woman is whimsical; it is a common thing for your old women to be so; I'll pawn my life, blisters, with the steel diet, will recover her.' "[23] It is this last aspect, the excremental, that we find so often in Swift's images of women, sometimes as a metaphor for madness, sometimes in fact as a cause of it. The idealized woman turns out to be human, and the shocked lover, as in "Cassinus and Peter" or "Strephon and Chloe," frequently collapses in madness:

> Nor wonder how I lost my Wits;
> Oh! *Caelia, Caelia, Caelia* shits.[24]

Swift's excremental disgust with women may translate into more
general sexual disgust—a point irresistible for most biographers—as in the remarkably ugly poem "A Beautiful Young
Nymph Going to Bed"; but typically his antifeminist stance
reflects a cultural motif:

> But see, the Female Club disbands,
> Each twenty visits on her Hands.
> Now all alone poor Madam sits,
> In Vapours and Hysterick Fits....
> A dreadful interval of Spleen!
> How shall we pass the Time between?[25]

Nothing could contrast more completely with Swift's poetic,
idealized view of himself—urbane, controlled, deliberately Roman, "A perfect Stranger to the Spleen."[26]

II

Swift never tries to render the *experience* of madness like Kafka
and certain other modern writers; on the contrary, it is usually our
awareness, insistent and ironic, of the distance between Swift's
personae and the truth that forms the whole point of his satire.
But in *A Tale of a Tub* satiric distance sometimes vanishes,
plunging the reader into a terrifying confusion of purpose and
tone. For the most part, however, the *Tale* only embodies
dramatically the themes of madness we have been discussing.
Here the religious enthusiasts, the second of the two kinds of
visionaries we mentioned, whirl and jerk like shooting gallery
targets before Swift's wit, mindless creatures, entirely mad.
Of the three brothers with whom the *Tale* occasionally
concerns itself, two of them, Peter and Jack, unquestionably run
crazy. Peter, standing for the Church of Rome in the allegory,
falls first: "alas, he had kept his Brain so long, and so violently
upon the Rack, that at last it *shook* it self, and began to *turn
round* for a little Ease. In short, what with Pride, Projects, and
Knavery, poor *Peter* was grown distracted, and conceived the
strangest Imaginations in the World."[27] But Swift evenhandedly
leaves Catholicism to one side and turns next to the English

Calvinists: "what, alas, was left for the forlorn *Jack* to do, but after a Million of Scurrilities against his Brother, to run mad with Spleen, and Spight, and Contradiction. . . . *Jack* went immediately to *New Lodgings,* and in a few Days it was for certain reported, that he had run out of his Wits. In a short time after, he appeared abroad, and confirmed the Report, by falling into the oddest Whimsies that ever a sick Brain conceived" (p. 141).

In satires like these against enthusiasm Swift expands the scope of earlier English satire and rearranges its emphases, adding to the usual criticisms of Puritanism the charge of madness and stressing its destructive, chaotic effects. Until Samuel Butler, seventeenth-century satires rarely stressed insanity among the major Puritan failings; they concentrated instead on accusations of hypocrisy, ignorance, and sexual looseness. But in the eighteenth century no complaint is more common: we find it in Shaftesbury, for example, in Smollett, in Hogarth, in Graves's *Spiritual Quixote,* and in *The Dunciad.* In 1739, according to Denis Leigh, John Wesley first preached to a London crowd, "in full view of Bethlehem Hospital. To the wits and caricaturists Wesley was often linked with Bethlem and even serious writers attributed many cases of lunacy to the influence of his preaching. He was forbidden to enter Bethlem, as an extract in his diary for 22 February 1750 shows: 'I went to see a young woman in Bedlam; but I had not talked to her long before one gave me to know that none of the preachers were to come here. So we are forbidden to go to Newgate for fear of making them wicked, and to Bedlam for fear of making them mad.' "[28] Even David Hume joins the chorus, describing the summit of enthusiasm as the point when "every whimsey is consecrated: human reason, and even morality, are rejected as fallacious guides; and the fantastic madman delivers himself over, blindly and without reserve, to the supposed illapses of the Spirit."[29] And yet at the level of personality it may not be inappropriate to speculate that for Swift himself these "illapses" of the spirit are part of the risk a religious man necessarily runs. Because it draws so deeply from the mind's reservoirs of emotion, religion itself is a potentially dangerous activity. We can guess at a comparable anxiety in Pope, whose strictures against the enthusiastic poet always contain at the edges an awareness of the dangers *any* poet, Horatian or enthusiastic, faces.

> Whether the darken'd room to muse invite,
> Or whiten'd wall provoke the skew'r to write:
> In durance, exile, Bedlam, or the Mint,
> Like Lee or Budgell, I will rhyme and print.[30]

Swift's own religious sensibility shares perhaps even more of that peripheral unease. Just as Pope more or less consciously attacks something disruptive in the very nature of poetry, so Swift, with a clearer sense of his private temptations, attacks something to him insane in the very nature of religion. (See, for example, his censure of emotional sermons in A *Letter to a Young Gentleman, Lately Entered into Holy Orders*.) Dunces or religious fanatics represent appropriate personal manifestations of an enemy already within the walls.

Swift's distrust of the enthusiastic mind makes itself plainly felt in the history of the learned Aeolists, a race of priests puffed up by the wind (or spirit) figuratively and physically, who take their beginnings from the distempered Jack. In the midst of the comedy, however, as so many critics have seen, Swift is making the serious point that "the corruption of the Senses is the Generation of the Spirit" and—Professor Norman O. Brown asserts it emphatically—he is anticipating the heart of the Freudian theory of sublimation.[31] One long passage in the *Tale* explains the Aeolian mechanism that produces what we call "Madness or Phrenzy":

> For the *upper Region* of Man, is furnished like the *middle Region* of the Air; The Materials are formed from Causes of the widest Difference, yet produce at last the same Substance and Effect. Mists arise from the Earth, Steams from Dunghils, Exhalations from the Sea, and Smoak from Fire; yet all Clouds are the same in Composition, as well as Consequences: and the Fumes issuing from a Jakes, will furnish as comely and useful a Vapor, as Incense from an Altar. Thus far, I suppose will easily be granted me; and then it will follow, that as the Face of Nature never produces Rain, but when it is overcast and disturbed, so Human

> Understanding, seated in the Brain, must be troubled and
> overspread by Vapours, ascending from the lower Faculties,
> to water the Invention, and render it fruitful.
>
> [p. 163]

Just as in the remarks of the Irish prelate on a madman, the
human personality here is unregulated, unorganized, subject to
no authority but chance; and the climate of the mind (like the
world of Dunces) seems so *busy*, always restless and troubled, full
of rising mists and falling rain. Swift's language, incidentally,
almost spells out the chief difference between his and Pope's use
of excremental imagery: to Pope fecalization is no more than a
drastic weapon between enemies, an extreme form of
denigration; to Swift the role of excrement is fundamental to the
working of human nature, a repulsive symbol of the power of our
nonintellectual selves. Yet as a concept, psychological weather
seems charming beside another elaborate description of the mind,
in the *Discourse Concerning the Mechanical Operation of the
Spirit, &c.*

> It is the Opinion of Choice *Virtuosi*, that the Brain is only a
> Crowd of little Animals, but with Teeth and Claws
> extremely sharp, and therefore, cling together in the
> Contexture we behold, like the Picture of *Hobbes's
> Leviathan*, or like Bees in perpendicular swarm upon a Tree,
> or like a Carrion corrupted into Vermin, still preserving the
> Shape and Figure of the Mother Animal.
>
> [p. 277]

Whimsy is utterly absent from such an image, and nightmare
dangerously close. Elsewhere Swift more cheerfully ponders the
physics of "the Notions of all Mankind," comparing them to
atoms jostling and bouncing in the void, like so much Brownian
motion of the mind (pp. 166—67).

In all these conceits from the *Tale*, including of course the
horse-and-rider images, Swift is depicting for us the chaotic
potentialities of our own nature, the necessity for counterpressure
against our "lower Faculties": "if the *Moderns* mean by
Madness, only a Disturbance or Transposition of the Brain, by
Force of certain *Vapours* issuing up from the lower Faculties;

Then has this *Madness* been the Parent of all those mighty Revolutions, that have happened in *Empire*, in *Philosophy*, and in *Religion*" (pp. 170–71). And he is warning us that at the social and political level our individual disorder becomes translated into intolerably disruptive movements, and the security of order, so precariously enjoyed in England, is destroyed. Indeed, Jack at last introduces a "new Deity, who hath since met with a vast Number of Worshippers; by some called *Babel*, by others, *Chaos*" (p. 194). The consequences of madness are chaos and all those mighty revolutions, and madness is what we call them.

The *causes* of madness, however, are beyond our control. Swift's devastating contempt for enthusiasts like Jack has paradoxically carried him to a point where logically responsibility ceases. If the madness of the Aeolists or of any man is brought about entirely and simply by physical mechanism, beyond our control or our knowledge, madness no longer remains for Swift an image of willful folly, as it was for Pope. Hence, just as the narrator is about to show why vapors sometimes cause Bedlam-madness and sometimes "Greatness" (by which he means the insane conquests of Alexander the Great or Jack of Leyden), Swift humorously but rather helplessly inserts a large gap in the text, with the marginal note *Hic multa desiderantur*. Yet helpless is hardly the word we should choose to describe Swift's tone in these passages. At certain moments, A. E. Dyson has observed, Swift's irony is "turned against states of mind or existence, which cannot be changed at all. The irony intended to 'wonderfully mend the world' transmutes itself into a savage exploration of the world's essential unmendability. . . . When this happens, Swift seems to generate his fiercest intensity. The restless energy behind the style becomes a masochistic probing of wounds. The experience of reading him is peculiarly disturbing at such moments; and it is then that his tone of savage indignation deepens into that *disgust* which Mr. T. S. Eliot has called his distinctive characteristic."[32] At such moments, too, Swift abandons the satiric premise that reform is possible; he "irrationally implies," as Gardner D. Stout, Jr., says, "that mankind is *guilty* of defects intrinsic to the human condition," of possessing body as well as spirit.[33] When the narrator permits us only the choice "of being a Fool among Knaves" (p. 174), the resonance of Renaissance "fool" has disappeared; Lear and his Fool have exited.

In his images of religious madness, Swift also plays a good deal, as we might expect, with the enthusiast's "inward light" and at several points in the *Tale* supplements his ironic praise of madness with panegyrics on blindness. "How fade and insipid," he asks, "do all Objects accost us that are not convey'd in the Vehicle of *Delusion?* How shrunk is every Thing, as it appears in the Glass of Nature? So, that if it were not for the Assistance of Artificial *Mediums,* false Lights, refracted Angles, Varnish, and Tinsel; there would be a mighty Level in the Felicity and Enjoyments of Mortal Men" (p. 172). In the *Discourse* he repeats his joke about vision and seeing things invisible (p. 287). And he has Jack sermonize at length, after falling in a kennel, on the virtues of blindness:

> Now, had my Eyes been open, it is very likely, the Business might have been a great deal worse; For, how many a confounded Slip is daily got by Man, with all his Foresight about him? Besides, the Eyes of the Understanding see best, when those of the Senses are out of the way; and therefore, blind Men are observed to tread their Steps with much more Caution, and Conduct, and Judgment, than those who rely with too much Confidence, upon the Virtue of the visual Nerve, which every little Accident shakes out of Order, and a Drop, or a Film, can wholly disconcert; like a Lanthorn among a Pack of roaring Bullies, when they scower the Streets; exposing its Owner, and it self, to outward Kicks and Buffets, which both might have escaped, if the Vanity of Appearing would have suffered them to walk in the Dark.
>
> [p. 193; italics omitted]

We feel in this how much meaning Swift gives to darkness, apprehending in it, not the mere absence of reason, but the terrifying presence of evil; Pope achieves such an effect, too, in the closing lines of *The Dunciad,* but as always Swift works on a smaller, more personal scale. Irrationality is adumbrated for him in some creature of the darkness: we are meant to taste our fear as we draw back from "Shadows, / Phantoms, bodiless and vain, / Empty Visions of the Brain" or from the satanic powers that fly "At Midnight, through the dark'ned Air."[34] The repulsive darkness of "A Privy" literally assaults us, and at night we discover the corruptions of "The Progress of 'Beauty" or "A Beautiful Young Nymph Going to Bed." *In noctis spatium miserorum vulnera durant,* Petronius observes.[35]

Similarly, Swift's pose of antifeminism manifests itself in the Aeolist section of the *Tale,* but once again he does more than simply mock the enthusiast's notorious weakness for lady saints ("She was of that blend of licentiousness and enthusiasm we see so often," Boswell says of a complete stranger). Like the excremental functions, sexuality becomes another cause as well as effect of madness, another example of men's lower faculties directing their higher. Vapors rise from unnameable parts, giving both "carnal Extasie" and inspiration to women, provoking men to greater and greater deeds of disorder. In this acute sensitivity to the physical springs, however polluted, of conduct, Swift is expressing a perception later much more widespread in the eighteenth century. Leslie Fiedler cites the author of *Rameau's Nephew* as another writer fascinated by the underground of the mind; and he notes that Diderot's pornographic novel *Les Bijoux indiscrets* also deals with a second self (the genitals) with a life of its own.[36] It may be more than idle speculation to wonder how much the eighteenth century's pronounced feeling for human duality contributed to the rise of of pornography and sentimental eroticism toward the middle of the century. Surely the sense of a vast, other, personal world, forbidden but free, tantalizing and chaotic, tempted more than one explorer. "Fair Liberty" was all Swift's cry, but by the time the Marquis de Sade embarked upon his drama, liberty—political as well as psychological—had entered another province. The dark world of the human personality, at once so alluring and so frightening to Swift, though not flooded with light by the end of the century, did grow less frightening. And as we shall see, new conceptions of liberty and slavery and also of childhood all contributed to this change. The id, the subconscious, the horse, the darkness seemed less unpredictable, less hostile toward men's better natures; all truly of the devil's party, the men of Blake's generation appeared not altogether unwilling to look closely at the part of themselves that Swift and the Augustans had cruelly mocked. Indeed, there were to be some who dug in their spurs.

III

Northrop Frye tells the story of the poet and dramatist Nathaniel Lee, a contemporary of Dryden, who "remarked when confined to a madhouse: 'They said I was mad; and I said they were mad, and, damn them, they outvoted me.' "[37] Inevitably, what most readers remember best from *A Tale of a Tub* is its Augustan version of the medieval ship of fools, the remarkable conclusion to the digression on madness in which Swift declares Bedlam to be merely the ordinary world in miniature. "IS any Student tearing his Straw in piece-meal," he asks, "Swearing and Blaspheming, biting his Grate, foaming at the Mouth, and emptying his Pispot in the Spectator's Faces? Let the Right Worshipful, the *Commissioners of Inspection*, give him a Regiment of Dragoons, and send him into *Flanders* among the *Rest*. Is another eternally talking, sputtering, gaping, bawling, in a Sound without Period or Article? What wonderful Talents are here mislaid!" (p. 176). And so he continues through lawyers, merchants, courtiers, tailors—until every kind of sane and upright citizen has his twin among the Bedlamites; Swift holds our faces up to the bars and forces us to see the madness that stirs in each of us, in our human cages.

It is a very old idea, of course, that mankind is mad perhaps as a result of Adam's fall, and Swift would not have lacked instances of it. Horace, whom we know he was reading at the time he wrote the *Tale*,[38] composed one of his most famous satires on the theme; and we have already seen it in Defoe and Pope. The seventeenth-century poet Thomas Traherne likewise felt that

> Mankind is sick, the World distemper'd lies,
> Opprest with Sins and Miseries.
> Their Sins are Woes; a long corrupted Train
> Of Poyson, drawn from *Adam's* vein,
> Stains all his Seed, and all his Kin
> Are one Disease of Life within.
> They all torment themselves!
> The World's one *Bedlam*, or a greater Cave
> Of Mad-men, that do alwaies rave.[39]

But when we think of Defoe together with Pope—especially Pope of *The Dunciad*—and with Swift and so many other of their contemporaries, we may be forgiven an impression that the Augustan Age made rather more of calling the world mad than an amusing leitmotif. In general the mad world theme seems somehow connected to the tragic fear of universal irrationality that I mentioned earlier. And it is also a response to the madman's power of metamorphosis—the madman is himself transformed into a beast or a fool, and a similar transformation of others is part of his threat. The satirist who calls the world mad defuses such dangers; his comic distance and his own (presumed) sanity control that terror. But when Swift drags us forward to "behold a surley, gloomy, nasty, slovenly Mortal, raking in his own Dung, and dabling in his Urine" (p. 178), we suffer a shocked recoiling that is not Horatian.

Like Pope, Swift is here employing the image of madness to attack supposedly sane men and women; but largely because of the intensity of his own disgust, Swift fails to leave the reader a space apart from the satire, a sane retreat from which to see the irony. Pope consistently distinguishes himself from his satiric victims and maintains his tone of innocent and outraged sanity:

> A knave's a knave, to me, in ev'ry state:
> Alike my scorn, if he succeed or fail,
> Sporus at court, or Japhet in a jail. . . .
> [*Arbuthnot*, 361–63]

But at the beginning of this passage in *A Tale of a Tub* Swift's narrator has already confessed to membership in Bedlam society (p.176), and the confession is repeated at the end of it. Critics frequently argue that this mad narrator is merely a persona, not to be confused with Swift himself. Yet Gardner D. Stout, Jr., has recently rejected this argument, pointing out that Swift's practice in the *Tale* is to parody the various objects of his satire, as one might in conversation, and that at last he parodies and attacks himself: "The satirist, as Swift sees him, has much in common with the other Bedlamites of the crazy world of all human aspiration. Perpetually collecting the ordure of human nature—including his own—he has disturbing affinities with that 'surley, gloomy, nasty' Greshamite . . . in his hellish vision of

Bedlam: the 'best Part of his Diet, is the Reversion of his own
Ordure, which exspiring into Steams, whirls perpetually about,
and at last reinfunds.' "⁴⁰ Why is Swift's satiric persona insane,
while Pope's is not? The answer, I think, lies partly in the
mechanical explanation of the causes of madness Swift has
already given: his satire cannot reform a glandular imbalance, his
lashes cannot soften "so callous and insensible a Member as the
World's Posteriors" (*Tale*, p. 48). But surely another part of the
answer lies in that disgust with human nature itself that
sometimes takes command of his irony. For at certain moments
Swift speaks with detachment of what the satirist has in common
with his victims: "*Satyrical Poets* . . . tho' indeed their business is
to rake into *Kennels*, and gather up the *Filth* . . . yet I have
observed they too have themselves very foul *Cloaths*, and like
dirty *Persons* leave more *Filth* and *Nastiness*, than they sweep
away."⁴¹ But in such moments as the digression on madness he
breaks down the walls of Bedlam in a kind of desperate unease,
leaving himself as well as his readers no escape from the
conclusion that every man's mind is a madman's. It is finally this
note of personal complicity that distinguishes Swift's vision of
madness from Pope's and makes of madness not merely a
metaphor for folly but a mirror for our own sad, vicious,
inescapable irrationality.

One further speculation may be in order here, concerning the
kinds of targets Swift and Pope chose to attack. Modern sociology
has discovered much about the nature and treatment of deviants
in various societies, and some aspects of its theory would seem to
bear directly upon the practices of Augustan satire. There seem,
for example, to be two important types of deviants in a society:
those who violate social norms deliberately, to challenge or
offend; and those, as Kai T. Erikson says, who "clumsily violate a
norm in their very eagerness to abide by it."⁴² Alexander Cruden,
the mad Corrector, or Pope's Dunces belong clearly to this second
category; their foolishness results from an excessive or even
aggressive conformity, not from a spirit of independence. It is in
this group, moreover, that we find the origins of the oft-noted
paradoxical resemblance between deviant and conformist,
particularly between criminal and policeman. We have only to
recall the outlines of the popular detective story to remind

PLATE 5. *Wash drawing by Thomas Rowlandson (1756–1827) of a doctor and a lunatic. It satirizes the "mad-doctors" as much as it does the madmen. As was customary, the lunatic is chained and naked under his blanket.*

PLATE 6. St. Luke's Hospital *(1809), a colored aquatint and etching by Thomas Rowlandson and Augustus Pugin. Founded in 1750 under the direction of Dr. William Battie, St. Luke's was intended as a reform measure, an alternative to the cruelty and squalor of Bedlam.*

PLATE 7. Madness, *an eighteenth-century mezzotint by an anonymous artist. Exemplifying the new sensibility toward madness, this exopthalmic madwoman, half-naked and confined in a dungeon, is presented as an object of interest and power in herself, not of satire.*

PLATE 8. Crazey Kate *(1815), a colored aquatint by G. M. Brighty after George Shepheard. The seaside setting of this portrait of another Romantic madwoman is typical, as is her tragic expression.*

ourselves how often the private eye and the crook appear interchangeable: they both share, after all, the same styles of life and the same ideas about what is valuable. Other varieties of deviants bear disturbing resemblance to the conformists that a society appoints to control them—Erikson cites the witchcraft hysteria of eighteenth-century New England, when witches were thought to take on the guise of pious persons, to do the Devil's work in the Lord's clothes, as Cotton Mather saw it. Given this similarity, Erikson comments, "It is not surprising that deviant behavior should seem to appear in a community at exactly those points where it is most feared. Men who fear witches soon find themselves surrounded by them; men who become jealous of private property soon encounter eager thieves."[43] And men who fear madness may soon create a world of madmen. "For the thing which I greatly feared is come upon me, and that which I was afraid of is come unto me" (Job 3:25—26). Satirists are also policemen, self-appointed guardians of social values. Do Pope and Swift, like Cotton Mather, create madmen in their own image? We have already noted how conscious both are of the potential for insanity buried in writing or religion, how roughly they denounce enthusiastic poets and preachers. The sociological principle of the identity of opposites suggests that, like all great writers, they speak from painful psychic intuitions, far more intense in Swift's case, of what human beings may become. What they feared, in a cultural and perhaps in a personal sense, they therefore created through the metaphor of madness in order to excoriate or exorcise or to unite the community of the sane against a common enemy. There is an element of *psychomachia* about *The Dunciad*, as Emrys Jones has noted; and Swift more than most writers would understand the ominous quality of Virginia Woolf's recurrent image of creativity, a fin breaking sharply through water. It is a final irony—Locke had insisted upon it earlier—that their madmen are so often parodies of sane men, as in *A Tale of a Tub* or *A Modest Proposal.*

In the perspective of Swift's whole career, it must be added, the mutual identification of satirist and victim, sane and mad, is still here only tentative; the *Tale* does not stamp men as irrevocably mad. Swift speaks with a young man's confidence, and we sense everywhere beneath his irony the unshaken assumption of the

Pindaric odes that truth is fixed and certain and that standards exist to which all of us would willingly repair. To be sure, man's capabilities for perceiving and holding fast to truth are limited—the digression on madness marks those men as mad, like conquerors and demagogues, who trust too much in their own powers—but learning and religion rightly understood do steady us; Swift can say with assurance what he believes, what is mad and what is sane. The ordinary premise of his satire, after all, is that reform is possible, the reader to be trusted. ("I could never let people run mad without telling and warning them sufficiently," he writes to Arbuthnot.)[44] Whatever the rhetorical reality of the conclusion by the narrator of the *Tale* that "a Man truly wise, creams off Nature, leaving the Sower and the Dregs, for Philosophy and Reason to lap up" (p. 174), Swift surely intended us to know that he is mad and to condemn his madness.

Much later in his life, in one of his last important poems, "A Character, Panegyric, and Description of the Legion Club" (1736), the image of Bedlam is hopeless, the trust and certainty withdrawn.[45] Intended as an attack upon the Irish House of Commons, the "Legion Club" like the digression on madness taps some deeper current of Swift's energy; it reaches far beyond political invective to become in certain ways Swift's Dunciad, in intensity if not in scope. Yet no standards are implicit, no attempt made to draw the reader in and tease him back to truth; abuse, not satire, shapes the poem. Swift flogs for the sake of flogging. It is a dismal confirmation of all that we have been saying about the Augustan response to madness to find Swift turning thus, in a moment of extravagant anger, almost naturally to a metaphor of universal Bedlam. All of the associations that the Augustans habitually attach to madness—poverty, idleness, bestiality, disorder, excrement—stand out here like so many wounds upon Swift's enemies; and the condition of madness transcends one place to become ironically (but not comically) the human condition.

The title of the poem comes from a passage in the Gospel according to Mark, an encounter between Jesus and a demoniac madman; Jesus asks the name of the man's unclean spirit, "And he saith unto him, My name is Legion; for we are many." The narrator of the poem at first indulges in angry fantasies of

destroying these creatures by the help of the Devil (21–34), then
peeps (a recurring activity in Swift's poems) into their cells.

> Let them, when they once get in
> Sell the Nation for a Pin;
> While they sit a picking Straws
> Let them rave of making Laws;
> While they never hold their Tongue,
> Let them dabble in their Dung. . . .
>
> We may, while they strain their Throats,
> Wipe our Arses with their Votes.
>
> [47–62]

He descends into their Stygian world (reminiscent at points of
Pope's Cave of Spleen) with Clio his guide:

> When she saw three hundred Brutes,
> All involved in wild Disputes;
> Roaring till their Lungs were spent,
> Privilege of Parliament,
> Now a new Misfortune feels,
> Dreading to be laid by th' Heels.
> Never durst a Muse before
> Enter that infernal Door;
> *Clio* stifled with the Smell,
> Into Spleen and Vapours fell;
> By the *Stygian* Streams that flew,
> From the dire infectious Crew.
> Not the Stench of Lake *Avernus*,
> Could have more offended her Nose. . . .
>
> [113–26]

Clio retreats, and the poet stays to explore the scene alone.

> When I saw the Keeper frown,
> Tipping him with Half a Crown;
> Now, said I, we are alone,
> Name your Heroes one, by one.
>
> [133–36]

And he calls on another eighteenth-century artist of the insane:

> How I want thee, humorous *Hogart?*
> Thou I hear, a pleasant Rogue art;
> Were but you and I acquainted,
> Every Monster should be painted. . . .
>
> [219–22]

Despite its singsong and its waggish rhymes, the "Legion Club" is a cheerless vision of society as madhouse; it falls short of calling the whole world mad, but its trajectory lies unmistakably in that direction. In his catalog of the brutish inmates and their sins Swift adds nothing new to the Augustan portrait of madness, but he also leaves nothing out.

It strains our credulity, therefore, almost too much to consider that, only a few years after the "Legion Club" and *The Dunciad*, the motif of the world gone mad was transformed into a matter of genuine pride for eighteenth-century England. After all, Augustan England frequently regarded itself through what Louis Landa calls a "gloom-thickened atmosphere."[46] The apparently immoral and opportunistic politics of the time were paralleled, to many eyes, by the more general decline of English cultural vigor. Italian opera, French foppery, a licentious theater, ineffectual religious and educational institutions, the ravages of gin-drinking among the lower classes, and a shrinking population—all seemed so many signs of a great fall. And this is of course the atmosphere of the great satires: Gulliver remarks that it gave him

> melancholy Reflections to observe how much the Race of human Kind was degenerate among us, within these Hundred Years past. How the Pox under all its Consequences and Denominations had altered every Lineament of an *English* Countenance; shortened the Size of Bodies, unbraced the Nerves, relaxed the Sinews and Muscles, introduced a sallow Complexion, and rendered the Flesh loose and *rancid.*
>
> I DESCENDED so low as to desire that some *English* Yeomen of the old Stamp, might be summoned to appear; once so famous for the Simplicity of their Manners, Dyet and Dress; for Justice in their Dealings; for their true Spirit of Liberty; for their Valour and Love of their Country.[47]

But at other literary levels books like Bishop Berkeley's *Essay*

towards Preventing the Ruin of Great Britain and John Brown's
Estimate of the Manners and Principles of the Times reflect this
sense of decline; and in America a whole literature sprang up, for
a multitude of reasons, contrasting contemporary Britain with its
former virtue. To call such a world mad not only suited a mood, it
also seemed true. But in the middle of the eighteenth century, as
we shall see in the next chapter, this atmosphere lifted: England's
madness shaded delicately into melancholy, and that melancholy
came to be admired, even cultivated as a sign of an undeniably
high civilization.

IV

Paradoxically, Swift's distrust of our restless mind extends also
to the rider upon the horse, to reason itself. The religious fanatic,
as Irvin Ehrenpreis points out, is for Swift the paradigm of human
folly;[48] but balance matters most, and in all the variety of madness
spread out before us in Swift's work the next most common type is
unquestionably the man gone crazy with too much reason.

The eighteenth century called such men "projectors"—someone with a fixed idea (like Lear). In the madcap
author of *A Tale of a Tub* we have already encountered one
projector, but his relationship to reason is too uncertain and his
personality too rarely in focus for him to be typical. Without
doubt Swift's archetypal projector is the blood-chilling personage
who puts forth *A Modest Proposal,* that notorious scheme for
marketing Irish infants as food and skins. What shocks us in
Swift's satire, of course, is the gulf between the modest, well-
intentioned author and all normal human feelings, indeed all
sense of reality. His fixed idea, encrusted with elaborate
reasonableness, drives a wedge between him and the truth and
makes him appear to us as horribly, disfiguredly insane. The
enthusiast detaches emotions from reason, but the projector, as
we see in these sentences, detaches his reason from his emotions
and even turns it against them:

> the remaining Hundred thousand, may, at a Year old, be
> offered in Sale to the *Persons of Quality* and *Fortune,*
> through the Kingdom; always advising the Mother to let
> them suck plentifully in the last Month, so as to render them

plump, and fat for a good Table. A Child will make two
Dishes at an Entertainment for Friends; and when the
Family dines alone, the fore or hind Quarter will make a
reasonable Dish; and seasoned with a little Pepper or Salt,
will be very good Boiled on the fourth Day, especially in
Winter.⁴⁹

In such a passage and in phrases like "a Child, *just dropt from its
Dam*" the mad projector, ironically enough, animalizes ordinary
human beings. He does not place them in Bedlam-like cages or
cover them with dung, but in the same way that the Augustans
deny the humanity of the insane, *he* denies the humanity of sane
men and perceives them instead entirely as animals; only a mad
world could listen to him with equanimity. The point is not, however, that Swift here suddenly recognizes the failure of the
Augustan response to madness—his satiric tactics are determined,
after all, by his satiric strategy—rather it is to see how for Swift
even reason, when it aspires to more than common sense, pulls
the seesaw of the mind off balance and makes a man mad.

Academies are assemblies of particularly ludicrous and
energetic projectors, less sinister than the Modest Proposer
perhaps, but no less insane; they might be called the intellectual
equivalent of mobs for Swift. The greatest academy of the age,
the Royal Society, founded in 1662 at the Restoration, was
already luminous as a center of scientific research, and its
membership included such titans as Newton and Sir Robert
Boyle. But to many Augustans, the Royal Society also symbolized
the absurdities and excesses inherent in projecting, and out of its
annals the stock figure of the mad scientist was already beginning
to grow. In Swift's hands this august institution becomes the
Grand Academy of Lagado, the insane highpoint of Gulliver's
third voyage. Here, where fixed ideas of scientific progress have
driven everyone mad, a parental Warden keeps kindly watch over
yet another scene of Bedlam. Gulliver tours the cells of the
projectors and inspects, not altogether uncritically, such projects
as removing sunlight from cucumbers, transforming ice into
gunpowder, and the breeding of naked sheep. And here too the
familiar signs of Augustan madness reappear. Almost predictably
we encounter the project of a man "born blind, who had several
Apprentices in his own Condition: Their Employment was to mix

Colours for Painters, which their Master taught them to
distinguish by feeling and smelling. It was indeed my Misfortune
to find them at that Time not very perfect in their Lessons; and
the Professor himself happened to be generally mistaken: This
Artist is much encouraged and esteemed by the whole
Fraternity." And yet more typically in chapter 5 Gulliver recounts
this visit:

> I WENT into another Chamber, but was ready to hasten
> back, being almost overcome with a horrible Stink. My
> Conductor pressed me forward, conjuring me in a Whisper
> to give no Offence, which would be highly resented; and
> therefore I durst not so much as stop my Nose. The Projector
> of this Cell was the most ancient Student of the Academy.
> His Face and Beard were of a pale Yellow; his Hands and
> Clothes dawbed over with Filth. When I was presented to
> him, he gave me a very close Embrace, (a Compliment I
> could well have excused.) His Employment from his first
> coming into the Academy, was an Operation to reduce
> human Excrement to its original Food, by separating the
> several Parts, removing the Tincture which it receives from
> the Gall, making the Odour exhale, and scumming off the
> Saliva. He had a weekly Allowance from the Society, of a
> Vessel filled with human Ordure, about the Bigness of a
> *Bristol* Barrel.

Here again we feel the pointless energy of the climate of the mind
in *A Tale of a Tub,* its insensible motion. But from our point of
view the Grand Academy belongs to a larger prospect, one that
includes Ned Ward and *The Dunciad* and the "Legion Club" as
well as the Bedlam of the digression on madness.

It is Gulliver himself who represents the last great embodiment
of the madness of too much reason. The fourth book of his *Travels*
records the story of a man who, like the Modest Proposer and the
academicians of Lagado, loses his humanity because he worships
reason. And ironically Gulliver's *passion* for *reason* becomes his
fixed idea; the truth of what he is deserts him, leaving him a
madman who declares himself a horse, a fit professor for any
Bedlam. Surely, too, it is the ultimate complication of the horse-
and-rider image when Swift endows the Houyhnhnms with

reason and makes their ordinary riders, Gulliver and the Yahoos, stand for unbridled passion.

> When I happened to behold the Reflection of my own Form in a Lake or Fountain, I turned away my Face in Horror and detestation of my self; and could better endure the Sight of a common *Yahoo,* than of my own Person. By conversing with the Houyhnhnms, and looking upon them with Delight, I fell to imitate their Gait and Gesture, which is now grown into a Habit; and my Friends often tell me in a blunt Way, that I *trot like a Horse;* which, however, I take for a great Compliment: Neither shall I disown, that in speaking I am apt to fall into the Voice and manner of the *Houyhnhnms,* and hear my self ridiculed on that Account without the least Mortification.
>
> [chapter 10]

Gulliver's alienation equals that of any maid who thinks herself a bottle or any tramp who thinks himself a king. And while Gulliver is mad like the academicians with his fixed idea, the models who have inspired him seem also to our minds a little suspect. The Houyhnhnms are not projectors—their reason gives them "a general Disposition to all Virtues"—but their reasonableness borders on fanaticism: in their chilling impersonal way they remind us of the Modest Proposer, and even Gulliver complains of their rigor.

Gulliver, while he whinnies and eats straw, seems a ludicrous but amusing madman, a classic of self-delusion yet not a repulsive figure. His companions in passion, on the other hand, the Yahoos, are Swift's greatest Bedlamites, the fullest Augustan expression we have of the degradation of madness. Behind the image of the Yahoos lies surely that widespread obsession of the age with the negative meanings of irrationality, for they embody completely almost every quality that the Augustans in general and Swift in particular ascribe to madmen. The Yahoos *are* repulsive—some readers, like Thackeray, never recover from the obscenity of them—and from Gulliver's first encounter Swift makes us see them as monsters of outward deformity and inward depravity. Excrement pervades their lives: they dabble in it like the inmates of Bedlam, they fling it at each other like Ned Ward's cellmates, and they even use it as medicine ("a Mixture of *their own Dung and Urine*") for their numerous diseases, somewhat like the projectors in Laputa. Preoccupation with excrement, however, is only one aspect of their "strange Disposition to Nastiness and Dirt." Like all Augustan madmen they resemble animals—they are monkeys, jackdaws, weasels, and foxes in the space of two pages—and they are compared ironically throughout with higher beasts, horses of course, and hounds; only the pig is assigned a lower ranking. (Yahoos are in fact unnatural creations, the Houyhnhnms speculate, "produced by the Heat of the Sun upon corrupted Mud and Slime, or from the Ooze and Froth of the Sea.") Swift even manages to interject antifeminist sentiments in his accounts of the salacious behavior of the female Yahoos, who admit males when pregnant and leap amorously upon poor Gulliver. The Yahoos in all their ferocious appetite are the creatures of unreason, abiding elements of human nature, prevented from their uncreating work of anarchy only by the presence of their strong masters, the keepers of reason. Our disgust with them is the measure of the tension within ourselves. Our disgust is also a reminder of what we saw in opposite balance in *King Lear:* the satiric meaning of madness casts a sinister, tragic shadow.

There is one further way in which *Gulliver's Travels* may comment on the meaning of madness in the early eighteenth century. Ernst Cassirer in his great study of *The Philosophy of the Enlightenment* traces the age's physiological speculations on the phenomenon of human blindness from Bishop Berkeley to Diderot and after. But questions of physiology and philosophy converge, and the very truth of our perceptions, their reliability and objectivity, at first in terms of eyesight alone, comes into open doubt; and that doubt introduces the much larger problem of the relative value of intellectual, political, and religious truths, depending upon their places in history and in different cultures.

> Swift treated the subject with great satirical power and intellectual acumen in his *Gulliver's Travels,* and from here its influence spread to French literature, where it is especially felt in Voltaire's *Micromegas.* . . . Relativity extends into the sphere of the highest, the so-called purely

intellectual ideas. The concept and word 'God' cannot mean the same thing for the blind as for those who can see. Is there then a logic, a metaphysics, or an ethics which can emancipate itself from the bondage of our sense organs? Or are not all our statements about the physical world as well as the intellectual merely about ourselves and the peculiarity of our organization? Would not our being have to undergo a fundamental change if we were endowed with a new sense or deprived of one of the senses we already have?[50]

We have only to substitute "madness" for "blindness" to understand the direction in which the eighteenth century was traveling. If the blind man may comprehend existence or any part of it in a different and yet "true" way, may not a madman? Locke, as we have seen, was already moving toward such a question. By the time he wrote *Gulliver's Travels* personal crisis had shaken Swift's confidence in his youthful standards, weakened his trust in the traditions and institutions that upheld them; his view of life had become darker, less positive about man's ability to know the truth; at the end he leaves us in the air deliberately. The relativism of the book betrays this insecurity, and our response to its satire, like the impulse of its creator, is ambiguous. It would not be the least irony of Swift's career if indeed his own masterpiece helped teach the European mind that truth was no fixed star, and if through Gulliver the dark secrets of the madman's mind came to be regarded as belonging to a different life, but perhaps not a worse.

CHAPTER FOUR

Johnson

J ohnson was "a great enemy," Sir John Hawkins observes, "to
the present fashionable way of supposing worthless and
infamous persons mad."[1] Like Pope, like Swift, Samuel Johnson
belongs temperamentally and intellectually to the Augustan
generation; indeed he represents the culmination of that
Augustan vision of madness we have been tracing. But even as
Johnson was looking backwards, the sands shifted under his feet:
in the decades of the 1740s and '50s the current began to go
against his hostility, and new attitudes began to make themselves
felt and visible. For as the Augustan satiric intensity failed,
suggestively madness entered fashion's circle, and the eighteenth
century came to regard it with interest as an excuse of even a
commendation for formerly "worthless and infamous persons."
In these years pity and sometimes fascination replaced disgust
and fear; a new sensibility spoke; and the Bedlam cell, if not
swept clean, at least won exposure to air and light. Johnson
himself, despite his Augustan lineage, betrays something of this
new attitude, tempering even his hottest attack with a
contradictory expression of his understanding and fellow feeling.
As Mrs. Thrale says of him, "All he did was gentle, if all he said
was rough."[2]

We can glance quickly at the dramatic (but by no means
steady) change that came over the old Augustan order in the
three following descriptions of Bedlam, arranged in chronological

order, before we turn logically from them to their great conclusion in Johnson's portrait of the mad astronomer in *Rasselas* (1759).

I

At the beginning of the 1740s Samuel Richardson had already described a visit to Bethlehem Hospital in a conspicuously un-Augustan way. In Letter CLIII of his *Familiar Letters*,[3] popular examples of the letter-writing art, Richardson imagines a sensible young lady recounting her experience to an aunt in the country.

A more affecting scene my eyes never beheld; and surely, madam, any one inclined to be proud of human nature, and to value themselves above others, cannot go to a place that will more effectually convince them of their folly: For there we see man destitute of every mark of reason and wisdom, and levelled to the brute creation, if not beneath it; and all the remains of good sense or education serve only to make the unhappy person appear more deplorable! . . .

I was much at a loss to account for the behaviour of the generality of people, who were looking at these melancholy objects. Instead of the concern I think unavoidable at such a sight, a sort of mirth appeared on their countenances; and the distemper'd fancies of the miserable patients most unaccountably provoked mirth and loud laughter in the un-thinking auditors; and the many hideous roarings, and wild motions of others, seemed equally entertaining to them. Nay, so shamefully inhuman were some, among whom (I am sorry to say it!) were several of my own sex, as to endeavor to provoke the patients into rage to make them sport.

. . . the heart must be abandoned indeed, that could be viscious amidst so many examples of misery, and of such misery as, being wholly involuntary, may overtake the most secure.

In part all this is only too familiar: madmen are "destitute of every mark of reason and wisdom, and levelled to the brute creation, if not beneath it." Madness is brutal, "miserable," "deplorable." Yet when we remember how Pope or Swift or Ned Ward saw Bedlam, Richardson's letter becomes remarkable to us for the undeniable mood of charity he introduces. Significantly he omits those details most prominent in earlier accounts, the excrement, the filth, and the explicit animality. And he emphasizes the affecting nature of the scene, its misery and the concern its visitors ought to feel. Madness here is "wholly involuntary," not the result of choice or folly as it is in Pope and Swift, and it can overtake any of us, even "the most secure." The inmates have become "patients," and the satire is shading into a sermon.

We should notice, however, that Richardson's sermon involves only a few unexceptional phrases. His letter communicates not a lesson about madmen but a mood, a mood sensible and sentimental and also titillating in its way. For although we see nothing really of the horrors of madness here, we are teased by the references to "hideous roarings" and "wild motions." And the young lady dwells with shock on the rumor she has heard that Bedlam is a resort for "lewd persons," an insensitivity impossible for her to comprehend. But this is Richardson's familiar mixture of piety and sensationalism, and its presence need not distract us from the genuine humanity of his perception.

A more indignant, less affective treatment of the same subject appears midway between Johnson and Richardson in *The World*, 7 June 1753. An anonymous correspondent reflects on his recent trip to Bedlam in the Richardsonian vein.

> To those who have feeling minds, there is nothing so affecting as sights like these; nor can a better lesson be taught us in any part of the globe than in this school of misery. Here we may see the mighty reasoners of the earth, below even the insects that crawl upon it; and from so humbling a sight we may learn to moderate our pride, and to keep those passions within bounds, which if too much indulged would drive reason from her seat, and level us with the wretches of this unhappy mansion.

Like Richardson's young lady he complains of the riotous behavior of the visitors, and goaded by anger he declares the experience has revived an old opinion of his, "that the maddest people in this kingdom are not *in* but *out* of Bedlam." We have heard Swift and the other Augustans talk in this vein before; but they contented themselves with an equation between Bedlam and the outer world; at mid-century we begin to hear more of degrees of madness, and they are madder who laugh at madness. Seized by the satiric fit, *The World*'s informant goes one more logical step and proposes that there be two hospitals for the insane. In a

> hospital for incurables, I would have all such persons conveyed that are mad through folly, ignorance, or conceit; there to be shut up for life, not only to be prevented from doing mischief, but from exposing in their own persons, the weaknesses and miseries of mankind. These incurables, on no pretence whatsoever, to be visited or ridiculed; as it would be altogether as inhuman to insult the unhappy wretches who never were possessed of their senses, as it is to make jest of those who have unfortunately left them.

The other hospital has a different charge:

> all young noblemen and others within the bills of mortality, having common sense, who shall be found offending against the rules of decency [as in cavorting at Bedlam] . . . shall immediately be conducted to a hospital for demoniacs, there to be exorcised, physicked, and disciplined into a proper use of their senses, and . . . full liberty to be granted to all persons whatsoever to visit, laugh at, and make sport of these demoniacs, without let or molestation from any of the keepers, according to the present custom of Bedlam.

We hardly need pause over the contradictions of this quarrelsome humanitarian. His compassion for Bedlam's inmates is blunted by self-righteousness, yet he stands squarely nonetheless with the new sensibility; he refuses to mock insanity, and if he is too willing to "mock mockers after that," he means only to silence them. The conception of madness as punishment, Bedlam as an elaborate stocks, is fully Augustan, of course, as is the wish to lock away from human sight the truly insane, to deny their existence. But we can see the anger shifting toward other targets; a certain confidence is needed to turn one's back to madness; to take aim at its enemies is almost to defend it.

One final example deserves to be mentioned, though it appeared a bit past the mid-century decades we are considering.

Henry MacKenzie's famous (and to modern readers, incredible) sentimental novel *The Man of Feeling* (1771) includes a short visit to Bedlam by that ceaselessly vibrating organ of sensibility, the hero Harley. Harley naturally objects to the whole idea of such an exhibition: "Harley objected to it, 'because,' said he, 'I think it an inhuman practice to expose the greatest misery with which our nature is afflicted, to every idle visitant who can afford a trifling perquisite to the keeper; especially as it is a distress which the humane must see with the painful reflection, that it is not in their power to alleviate it.' "[4] His tender feelings, however, and his compassionate idea of insanity as "the greatest misery with which our nature is afflicted" do not prevent his visit in chapter 20. Once there he looks upon a sight that we may by now be hardened to.

> Their conductor led them first to the dismal mansions of those who are in the most horrid state of incurable madness. The clanking of chains, the wildness of their cries, and the imprecations which some of them uttered, formed a scene inexpressibly shocking. Harley and his companions, especially the female part of them, begged their guide to return: he seemed surprised at their uneasiness, and was with difficulty prevailed on to leave that part of the house without showing them some others; who, as he expressed it in the phrase of those that keep wild beasts for a shew, were much better worth seeing than any they had passed, being ten times more fierce and unmanageable.

Like Richardson, MacKenzie supplies only enough physical details to sketch in the outline of this "scene inexpressibly shocking," for his real interest too is in the emotions roused by it in Harley and in us. We are to share Harley's distress (not disgust) at the wretchedness of madness, and we are to turn away with him from the unfeeling keeper, himself more a beast than any of his charges. We have only to recall Swift's cozy understanding with the keeper of the Legion Club to feel the difference:

> When I saw the Keeper frown,
> Tipping him with Half a Crown;
> Now, said I, we are alone,
> Name your Heroes one, by one.

True to the principle of titillation, MacKenzie does not lead a trembling Harley from this dungeon, as we might expect; the tour continues among less dangerous inmates, and Harley falls behind to talk with several of them. These madmen are more or less stock characters, driven mad by some ruling passion, in one case a former mathematician scribbling numbers on his walls, in another a ruined merchant charting imaginary profits. Among the females, however, "stood one, whose appearance had something of superior dignity. Her face, though pale and wasted, was less squalid than those of the others, and showed a dejection of that decent kind, which moves our pity unmixed with horror: upon her, therefore, the eyes of all were immediately turned." This lady has been driven to Bedlam (like all its victims, Boswell thinks) by a disappointed love. She sees Harley, who has paid her story "the tribute of some tears," and cries out that he seems the very image of her drowned lover—" 'Twas when the seas were roaring—I love you for resembling my Billy. . . .' " Further tribute irresistibly follows. The pathos of the scene perhaps exacts a very different tribute from us: in the episode with mad Maria at the conclusion of *Tristram Shandy*, doubtless the model for MacKenzie, Laurence Sterne undercuts such sentimentalism, though it is his own, with a joke. But even tears of laughter should not blind us to the reversal of emotions the mid-eighteenth century is displaying here toward the sight of madness. Items of the familiar comedy certainly persist, but the climax taps our sympathy, not our hatred. We are drawn into the madwoman's world, made a part of her story. The lunatic steps forward to show us an appearance that has "something of superior dignity," and explicitly we are permitted "pity unmixed with horror." (Both Sterne and MacKenzie also correct to some extent the Augustan misogyny by making their pathetic victims women. Far from being objects of Popean and Swiftian scorn, women now appear as creatures of extraordinary delicacy, sensitivity, genius; these mad ladies, whom we saw earlier in the factual narratives of the private madhouses, are first drafts of the virtuous heroines of Mrs. Radcliffe's Gothic novels.) Pope's or Ned Ward's laughter was raucous, cruel, unmixed with pity, informed ultimately by fear as well as horror. MacKenzie's and Richardson's tears spring from sympathy, compassion, and even from self-recognition.

II

Visitors like these to Bedlam by no means mark the re-establishment of classical attitudes toward madness, but they do signify change in the Augustan imagination, chinks in the Augustan armor. And the elements of sympathy and identification they tentatively set forward now realize their fullest expression in the writings and also in the person of the moral arbiter of the age. We know that Johnson, as Boswell says, sometimes "visited the mansions of Bedlam," and he defended the practice once, referring to apartments near the hospital, by declaring that "it is right that we should be kept in mind of madness, which is occasioned by too much indulgence of imagination. I think a very moral use may be made of these new buildings: I would have those who have heated imaginations live there, and take warning."[5] Johnson has left no account of his own visits, but in the story of the mad astronomer in *Rasselas* we discover such an encounter, and also such a warning.

When Prince Rasselas declares toward the close of the book that his choice of life is concluded and that he will henceforth spend all his days in the solitude of his study, his mentor Imlac cautions him to consider, before he decides, the actual experience of "those who are grown old in the company of themselves." As an example Imlac describes his friend the astronomer, a man renowned for learning, who has by degrees gone mad after so many years of loneliness and has at last been deceived by his imagination into believing that he alone has been given the powers of the "regulation of the weather, and the distribution of the seasons" over the whole earth.

> "About ten years ago, said he, my daily observations of the changes of the sky led me to consider, whether, if I had the power of the seasons, I could confer greater plenty upon the inhabitants of the earth. This contemplation fastened on my mind, and I sat days and nights in imaginary dominion, pouring upon this country and that the showers of fertility, and seconding every fall of rain with a due proportion of sunshine. I had yet only the will to do good, and did not imagine that I should ever have the power.
> "One day as I was looking on the fields withering with heat, I felt in my mind a sudden wish that I could send rain

on the southern mountains, and raise the Nile to an inundation. In the hurry of my imagination I commanded rain to fall, and, by comparing the time of my command, with that of the inundations, I found that the clouds had listened to my lips. . . . I reasoned long against my own conviction, and laboured against truth with the utmost obstinacy. I sometimes suspected myself of madness, and should not have dared to impart this secret but to a man like you, capable of distinguishing the wonderful from the impossible, and the incredible from the false."

[chapter 42]

With this declaration the astronomer then asks Imlac to succeed to his power. "The prince heard this narration with very serious regard, but the princess smiled, and Pekuah convulsed herself with laughter. 'Ladies, said Imlac, to mock the heaviest of human afflictions is neither charitable nor wise. Few can attain this man's knowledge, and few practise his virtues; but all may suffer his calamity. Of the uncertainties of our present state, the most dreadful and alarming is the uncertain continuance of reason.' "

In Imlac's words we see at once how completely Johnson belongs to the Augustan tradition and at the same time how far he has advanced it. For madness, which Johnson calls significantly the loss of reason, is an unmitigated evil, "the heaviest of human afflictions," a "calamity," "dreadful" and "alarming." Yet Johnson does conspicuously what no earlier Augustan ever did: he stops our laughing at it. His language with its insistent moral-medical imagery, his solemn tone, his simple declaration, and above all his intense identification, at once private and general, with the madman rebuke the habitual eighteenth-century response to madness and draw us toward another: we are to pity and be fearful.

When we remember the other representations of madness we have seen, Johnson's version in *Rasselas* amazes us by its gentleness: the astronomer is mild, harmless, full of goodwill; his madness begins in a benevolent wish. He does not disgust us and is not meant to; no roaring, dung-dabbling maniac out of Ned Ward or *The Dunciad*, placed in the way for our amusement or our terror—literally and figuratively he is freed from Bedlam and all its horrific associations. We are not to laugh at him, we are not to fear him, and as we have already seen, all this marks a profound change in tone and sensibility. Madness is not for Johnson the indispensable metaphor of folly, error, or malice that it was for Pope and his contemporaries. Neither the emblem of a dunce nor the just punishment of a villain, it has become a human (but not a superhuman) affliction.

If in Johnson's hands madness is no longer the metaphor around which satire may be constructed, then it may be traveling back along the literary spectrum toward tragedy: though Johnson will not laugh at madness, he will cry for it. "Of the uncertainties of our present state, the most dreadful and alarming is the uncertain continuance of reason": the Augustan voice is unchecked, and it is telling us what the Greeks and moderns never do, that the greatest tragedy we can suffer is to lose our reason. The astronomer has in common with most Augustan madmen both illusion and error; unlike Lear he offers no secret, satiric truth, no reason in madness; he speaks only nonsense. Johnson does not fear the madman, but he fears his madness, and what the astronomer demonstrates, Imlac declares: "All may suffer his calamity." The "mad world," hyperbole for earlier Augustans, has become dreadful possibility for Johnson, and fecalization therefore gives way to sympathy and to identification.

To gauge the extent of the change that Johnson is here marking we have only to recall the outlines of Swift's digression on madness in *A Tale of a Tub*, published fifty-five years earlier. What Johnson has added to that classic Augustan presentation of madness—and what he has left out—is substantial. We have just mentioned his sympathy, the point that subsumes all others, and its corollary, identification: never in all the complicated shiftings of perspective in *A Tale of a Tub* are we intended to identify ourselves fully with the mad narrator; his insanity is too spectacularly outrageous to accept as our own; and even when he calls the world mad and invites it into a Bedlam cell, we understand him to be talking about the foolish, irrational world, not our well-behaved world, normal and reasonable.

Johnson has added to the Augustan account considerable psychological precision. Where Swift spoke in a general way of the contest between reason and imagination for the control of the

mind, Johnson speaks deliberately of the operation of those two
faculties and gives us concrete notions of what he means. After he
has rebuked Pekuah and the princess for their laughter, Imlac
goes on to discuss "The Dangerous Prevalence of Imagination":

> "Disorders of the intellect, answered Imlac, happen much
> more often than superficial observers will easily believe.
> Perhaps, if we speak with rigorous exactness, no human
> mind is in its right state. There is no man whose imagination
> does not sometimes predominate over his reason, who can
> regulate his attention wholly by his will, and whose ideas
> will come and go at his command. No man will be found in
> whose mind airy notions do not sometimes tyrannise, and
> force him to hope or fear beyond the limits of sober
> probability. All power of fancy over reason is a degree of
> insanity; but while this power is such as we can controul and
> repress, it is not visible to others, nor considered as any
> depravation of the mental faculties: it is not pronounced
> madness but when it becomes ungovernable, and
> apparently influences speech or action."
>
> [chapter 44]

Much in this is undeniably Swiftian: the sense of struggle, the
sense that forces of disorder at all times threaten, the sense, in
short, that every man's mind is potentially a madman's. But Swift
leaves us with the impression that imagination is largely the
sublimation of destructive forces (usually sexual) or the egoism of
enthusiasm. Johnson tells us that imagination operates primarily
in two ways: by hope or fear. The *Rambler* papers, as we shall see,
document the bizarre, ingenious ways in which we set ourselves
to hope for some blessing or gain or to fear some disaster, and
then as Imlac says, "By degrees the reign of fancy is confirmed;
she grows first imperious, and in time despotick. Then fictions
begin to operate as realities, false opinions fasten upon the mind,
and life passes in dreams of rapture or of anguish." For Johnson
the hopes and fears of the imagination exist not in the present but
in "boundless futurity," or in the irretrievable past; and the
garrisons of fiction thus posted menace and displace our present
realities. "The truth is," says Imlac meditating upon the
pyramids, "that no mind is much employed upon the present:
recollection and anticipation fill up almost all our moments." (See

also *Rambler* 41 and BLJ, II, 360−61.) For Swift too, reality lies at the mercy of time and imagination, but what more he means by imagination than a force—one that "is at Cuffs with the Senses, and common Understanding"—a force in control of enthusiasts and villains, we cannot say.

> 'Tis manifest, what mighty Advantages Fiction has over Truth; and the Reason is just at our Elbow; because Imagination can build nobler Scenes, and produce more wonderful Revolutions than Fortune or Nature will be at Expence to furnish. Nor is Mankind so much to blame in his Choice, thus determining him, if we consider that the Debate meerly lies between *Things past*, and *Things conceived*; and so the Question is only this; Whether Things that have Place in the *Imagination*, may not as properly be said to *Exist*, as those that are seated in the *Memory*; which may be justly held in the Affirmative. . . .
>
> [*Tale*, p. 172]

His tone, ironic, scornful, the very reverse of Johnson's serious sincerity, is too pugnacious; it works to reduce our awareness of the threat imagination poses: something so patently against all "common Understanding" does not touch us. Johnson, on the other hand, free of Swift's satiric purposes, presses forward insistently against us, setting down in detail not only the mechanics of our wily imagination, but also the conditions that encourage it.

He warns us against solitude like the astronomer's, for example, because solitude is temptation. Undistracted by society or work, the mind swivels back to its favorite fancies like the needle of a compass. Solitude, Johnson says out of his own painful experience, "is dangerous to reason, without being favourable to virtue. . . . Remember . . . that the solitary mortal is certainly luxurious, probably superstitious, and possibly mad: the mind stagnates for want of employment, grows morbid, and is extinguished like a candle in the foul air."[6] Hence Johnson urges us to channel our imaginative energies or else to "controul and repress" them: when you feel your madness returning, Imlac tells the astronomer, "fly to business or to Pekuah." Imlac's prescription underscores that powerful public sense of life we encounter so often in eighteenth-century literature, just as Johnson's aversion to solitude reminds us of the more general aversion of the age to private experience. Johnson dismisses one acquaintance as "unclubable," and the astronomer is cured of his madness eventually by his introduction to the society of Rasselas and his party: "If I am accidentally left alone for a few hours," he tells Imlac, recalling familiar patterns of light and darkness,

> "my inveterate persuasion rushes upon my soul, and my thoughts are chained down by some irresistible violence, but they are soon disentangled by the prince's conversation, and instantaneously released at the entrance of Pekuah. I am like a man habitually afraid of spectres, who is set at ease by a lamp, and wonders at the dread which harrassed him in the dark, yet, if his lamp be extinguished, feels again the terrours which he knows that when it is light he shall feel no more."
>
> [chapter 46]

Another condition favorable to madness, a condition worse than solitude, is imagination "complicated with the dread of guilt," and Imlac fears the attachment of imagination in any way to questions of religious or moral duty: "fancy and conscience then act interchangeably upon us, and so often shift their places, that the illusions of one are not distinguished from the dictates of the other" (cf. *Rambler* 126). Imagination thus merges with sin in Johnson's mind. He prays in his diary that God may "look down with mercy upon me depraved with vain imaginations, and entangled in long habits of Sin." And he weaves together guilt, imagination, and idleness:

> My indolence, since my last reception of the Sacrament, has sunk into grosser sluggishness, and my dissipation spread into wilder negligence. My thoughts have been clouded with sensuality, and, except that from the beginning of this year I have in some measure forborn excess of Strong Drink my appetites have predominated over my reason. A kind of strange oblivion has overspread me, so that I know not what has become of the last year, and perceive that incidents and intelligence pass over me without leaving any impression.

> This is not the life to which Heaven is promised. I purpose
> to approach the altar again tomorrow.[7]

But Johnson's distrust of the imagination is traditional as well as personal. Arieh Sachs points out that for centuries Western men have thought of the primary meaning of imagination as evil, literally diabolical. To the medieval mind imagination was irreligious, an attribute of the Devil; imagination was the force by which he drove his human victims to sin and madness. "The devil himself," in fact, "was regarded as proverbially out of his wits."[8] The protruding donkeylike ears on a court fool's headgear may have been vestigial reminders of the Devil's horns. The roots of Johnson's associations extend far backwards in time as well as down deep into his own personality.

We have a clear idea of what the earlier Augustans mean by reason. For Swift it is usually common sense, but it can be something more, the divine faculty, that is, which distinguishes men from brutes, "right reason": *animal rationis capax*. The perversion of reason that Swift attacks in madness is a perversion of man's heavenly likeness, and there can be no denying that the shadow of blasphemy hovers over his Bedlam. But for Johnson, though it would include the great classical and humanistic elements, reason is often simply regulation. Indeed, it is sometimes merely arithmetical: we know from Boswell and from Mrs. Thrale how he occasionally resorted to elaborate exercises in computation to combat his own imagination. Arithmetic, chemistry, translation—these to Johnson are reasonable, and they are real. "I cannot prove it by an external evidence," the astronomer tells Imlac, "and I know too well the laws of demonstration to think that my conviction ought to influence another, who cannot be conscious of its force. I, therefore, shall not attempt to gain credit by disputation. *It is sufficient that I feel this power*" (italics mine). Swift sardonically pays tribute to illusion in the *Tale*, but Johnson never could. Religious questions aside (and Bertrand Bronson has pointed out how violently Johnson struggled with his religious doubts[9]), what cannot be proved cannot be. In answer to Berkeley's phenomenalism, as everyone knows, Johnson kicked a nearby stone, crying out to Boswell, "I refute it thus."[10] Yet Swift and Johnson do share the

Augustan conception that reason leads us to truth, though the path is difficult and long; madness presents no such avenue.

It is instructive to notice for a moment what Johnson leaves out of Swift's attack on madness. Obviously he leaves out Swift's palpable disgust: no excrement, no sexuality makes him recoil. His madman is benevolent and though deeply learned, not witty; but Swift's madmen manifest a certain diabolic cunning, and the exigencies of satire make them say at some point what we must acknowledge as true and penetrating. (In this subversive sense, and only in this sense, can the Augustan allow reason in madness.) We may note in passing, too, how different Johnson's condemnation of idleness is from Pope's and Swift's. He attacks idleness not because it leads to poverty—no one is more charitable toward poverty than Johnson—but because of the personal debilitations it entails. His diary echoes over and over his efforts and failures to overcome idleness, to rise before noon, to read the Scriptures diligently, to go to church. "Almighty God," he prays on Easter Eve, 1757, ". . . Enable me to shake off Sloth, and to redeem the time mispent in idleness and Sin." Like a desperate, more human Ben Franklin he makes long lists of resolutions, until "I have resolved, I hope not presumptuously, till I am afraid to resolve again" (Easter 1761). And begins again:

> To avoid Idleness.
> To regulate my sleep as to length and choice of hours.
> To set down every day what shall be done the day following.
> To keep a Journal.

"His soul was not different from that of another person," Mrs. Thrale says, "but . . . greater."

Finally, Johnson does not place madness in its social or political context as Swift does. The persona of the *Tale* devotes much of his energy to driving the reader toward conclusions like this: "Then has this *Madness* been the Parent of all those mighty Revolutions, that have happened in *Empire*, in *Philosophy*, and in *Religion*" (p. 171). Swift like Pope calls madness whatever threatens the standards and stability of truth, and his concern is frequently public: the reform of evils. But Johnson never deals with public institutional madness. It is the secret, inner madness in each of us, in ourselves, that he turns to. "That the self may destroy the self by the very energies that define its being, that the self may be preserved by the negation of its own energies—this, whether or not we agree, makes a paradox, makes an irony, that catches our imagination."[11] Lionel Trilling's words suit Johnson better than Swift. Swift sets up madness like some grotesque, flapping scarecrow to drive us from forbidden ground. Johnson speaks habitually of it as chains and shackles.

III

In one sense, then, Johnson is quite limited in what he means by madness, in another sense extraordinarily expansive. In her remarkable essay "Johnson's 'Vile Melancholy'" Professor Katherine Balderston argues that "a study of all Johnson's pronouncements on and descriptions of melancholy and madness shows conclusively that his conception of madness involved only one type—the type that I believe he discovered incipiently in himself—that which arose from obsessive indulgence in culpable fantasy, which aroused melancholy despair in the victim, and finally impaired or destroyed his sense of reality."[12] Few students will quarrel with Professor Balderston's observation: this is the madness that we encounter again and again in the pages of the *Rambler*, in the other periodicals, and in *Rasselas*, the madness of the "hunger of imagination." Johnson uses the term madness consistently in this limited sense (his restraint suggests to us the spending of the Augustan fury). But the expansiveness of the term comes from the application he makes of it, his sleepless awareness that every human activity in which imagination has a part poses a threat to human sanity. "Perhaps, if we speak with rigorous exactness," says Imlac, "no human mind is in its right state."

The sweep of the danger is nowhere better seen than in the pages of Johnson's first great achievement, the *Rambler*, whose two-hundred-odd numbers he composed during the years 1750—52, even while work on the Dictionary went steadily on. In *Rasselas* we saw carefully explained the working mechanics of our treacherous imagination; in the *Rambler* we take a survey of examples. Bleak and solemn, they show us the myriad ways in which imagination encroaches upon reason in human conduct, the myriad ways, to put it in Swiftian terms, that the horse runs away with the rider. Vain hopes and vain amusements fill its pages: the petulance of Suspirus, the insolence of Prospero, the futility of Seged, rash attachments, the ravages of interest and envy. The *Rambler*'s catalog of misery is another dictionary really, unalphabetical but inclusive, an unabridged account of the possibilities for unhappiness in this world. Yet what all these sufferings have in common is that they are self-inflicted. Johnson lectures, not to warn us against fortune's turn, but to warn us against ourselves. Quite as insistently as Swift he pictures the human mind in a Manichean state of battle, in constant tension between reason and imagination; and whenever reason is stampeded, no matter how trivial the occasion, he is fearful. Swift despises the forces that generate these frightening, random pressures in the mind; Johnson fears only imagination, or as Professor Balderston puts it, "culpable fantasy." Swift waits anxiously for an explosion, a subterranean eruption; Johnson sees skirmishes at every moment, rarely bunching into one great battle, but wearing away defenses slowly, subtly, until our minds are captured by obsession. The characters in the *Rambler* appear to us not as willful lunatics but as victims caught in a long, caged trap, lured and lulled there by their imaginations, aware only at the end of the bars that hold them in.

Johnson uses another metaphor to describe them. Frequently a *Rambler* paper takes for its subject some "intellectual malady" like procrastination or idleness or envy and ponders a remedy. Number 112 seems typical: Johnson quotes the ancient physician Celsus on the best ways of maintaining bodily health, then applies the same regimen to "intellectual health." His analogical way of proceeding suggests how sensitive he is, surely in part because of his own lifelong poor health, to the relationship between body and mind. One of the funniest and most famous *Ramblers*, on the benefits of a garret, makes the serious point that "the faculties of the mind are invigorated or weakened by the state of the body, and that the body is in a great measure regulated by the various compressions of the ambient element."[13] (It is odd to find Johnson elsewhere stubbornly disputing the eighteenth-century commonplace that national character depends on climate and that the wind and weather cause melancholy [*Idler* 11]; but in *Rambler* 117 what he seems to be objecting to is the "reproachful" surrender of reason and responsibility to these elements, not the idea that they do affect us.) The medical imagery that occurs so frequently in the *Rambler* helps further to mark Johnson off from the earlier Augustans, for no matter how relentlessly he tracks down and blasts human folly, he understands it to be illness—and what is more remarkable, he understands it to be human. No man of sympathy, least of all Johnson, blames other men for their sicknesses.

It is characteristic of Johnson that he should have spoken in this way, and at the same time it is characteristic of his age that the medical analogy should have gained more general acceptance. The earlier eighteenth century, ignorant of the medical nature of madness and uninterested in it, rejected madness as a *human* experience and sought to transform it into something malevolent, bestial. In Johnson's lifetime madness was increasingly coming to be regarded as a disease—we will return to this question in the next chapter—though little real progress in its treatment was effected. But Johnson's own massive personal compassion rather than his medical knowledge (which was considerable) interrupts and prevents the kind of contempt for folly that we have seen in Pope and Swift; he is, as W. J. Bate tells us, a satirist *manqué*,[14] and where Swift in his rage might call the world mad to mock it, Johnson sees not a mad world, but a melancholy one. Far more than Swift's, Johnson's satire in the little fables and narratives of the *Rambler* is built upon the hope (if not the conviction) that reform is possible and devoutly to be wished for.

Despite his sympathy, Johnson does not willingly tolerate intellectual maladies. The *Rambler* may not satirize in the Swiftian mode, but he does censure. In an age of medical self-help Johnson's moral writings diagnose and prescribe for mental ailments, just as hundreds of pamphlets and books do for the physical. And he is a determined foe of those ominous symptoms affectation and singularity. "I, for my part, amused myself a while with her fopperies," a character says in *Rambler* 115, "but novelty soon gave way to detestation, for nothing out of the common order of nature can long be borne." This may seem paradoxical coming from a man whose love of novelty drove him to seek it out everywhere in order to fill the hours of the day. ("The vacuity of life," observes Mrs. Thrale, "had at some early period of his life struck so forcibly on the mind of Mr. Johnson, that it became by repeated impression his favourite hypothesis, and the general tenor of his reasonings commonly ended there, wherever they might begin."[15]) But what Johnson faults is not novelty itself, in literature or science or in life, but *fixed* originality in behavior, that is, eccentricity. "Singularity," he remarks, "is, I think, in its own nature universally and invariably displeasing: in what ever respect a man differs from others, he must be considered by them as either worse or better." He praises Newton significantly: "he stood alone, merely because he had left the rest of mankind behind him, not because he had deviated from the beaten tract."[16]

This aversion is based partly upon the conviction—widespread among Johnson's contemporaries—that obsession is the basic shape of madness, partly, as Balderston has said, upon Johnson's own personal experience. When imagination overpowers reason, the result is usually what the age calls the tyranny of a "ruling passion." A typical representation of insanity depicts—perhaps more frequently in the mid-eighteenth century than before—some kind of fanaticism carried to the point of delusion. So necessary an element is it for Johnson that he cannot allow the poet Collins, despite his confinement in an asylum, really to be insane: he suffers instead, Johnson says, from vitiation of the intellects.[17] Johnson condemns obsessions wholesale, even in their mildest guises as the habits and self-indulgences we all innocently practice, because they spoil our lives, because they crumble our rational strengths and surprise us too late by how far they have advanced. *Rambler* 95, the story of Pertinax the skeptic, is an example. Pertinax begins in a familiar vein:

> SIR, There are many diseases both of the body and mind, which it is far easier to prevent than to cure, and therefore I hope you will think me employed in an office not useless either to learning or virtue, if I describe the symptoms of an intellectual malady, which, though at first it seizes only the passions, will, if not speedily remedied, infect the reason, and, from blasting the blossoms of knowledge, proceed in time to canker the root.

He relates that he grew up in "the house of discord," where he learned early to dispute with ease on any side of any question, according to convenience or expediency; the habit grew during his years at the university, and his entrance into one of the Inns of Court provided the last stimulus; out of vanity and habit he paraded his sophisms before every possible issue, with no regard at all for truth or principle.

> I had perplexed truth with falsehood till my ideas were confused, my judgment embarrassed, and my intellects distorted. The habit of considering every proposition as alike uncertain, left me no test by which any tenet could be tried; every opinion presented both sides with equal evidence, and my fallacies began to operate upon my own mind in more important enquiries. It was at last the sport of my vanity to weaken the obligations of moral duty, and efface the distinctions of good and evil, till I had deadened the sense of conviction, and abandoned my heart to the fluctuations of uncertainty, without anchor and without compass, without satisfaction of curiosity, or peace of conscience, without principles of reason, or motives of action.

Finally he resigns his profession, represses his habits by sheer will, and after many months emerges cured. "I am at length recovered from my argumental delirium," he concludes, "and find myself in the state of one awakened from the confusion and tumult of a feverish dream. I rejoice in the new possession of evidence and reality, and step on from truth to truth with confidence and quiet." Pertinax is not a madman, but by Johnsonian lights he stands in danger of becoming one; certainly, Imlac would say, he is not in his right mind. Two things in particular make plain his danger: his obsessive, one-dimensional frame of mind and his loss of the basic sense of reality—the language emphasizes how from "truth" and "reality" he has wandered into "delirium" and "a feverish dream." In his strictures against dreams and dreaming, in fact, Johnson aligns himself firmly with Pope and Swift and all the Augustan forces of antidarkness. For him sanity is almost literally sleepless, and dreams, even daydreams, invite a kind of carnival of vice: "Other vices or follies are restrained by fear, reformed by admonition, or rejected by the conviction which the comparison of our conduct with that of others, may in time produce. But this invisible riot of the mind, this secret prodigality of being, is secure from detection, and fearless of reproach. The dreamer retires to his apartments, shuts out the cares and interruptions of mankind, and abandons himself to his own fancy . . ." (*Rambler* 89). Thus, although Pertinax's habit is a quasi-logical one, it has in fact "heated [his] imagination with needless controversies"; his intellects are distorted (not vitiated) by his ruling passion. The moral consequences, moreover, of losing our hold on reality, unstressed in the astronomer's case, are formidable here, for we weaken first our sense of duty and lose finally all "distinctions of good and evil." "Such, therefore," Johnson writes in *Rambler* 8, "is the importance of keeping reason a constant guard over imagination, that we have otherwise no security for our own virtue. . . ." His language organizes the human personality much as Locke and Jefferson arrange the political state: by a system of checks and balances guarding its full "security."

IV

One other reason, as I have suggested, accounts in part for Johnson's aversion to singularity and to indulgence of the imagination. He himself was among the most singular of men: his puffing and muttering, his convulsive starts and jerks, even his ugliness and involuntary grimaces astonished everyone who met him. Boswell describes Hogarth's first meeting with Johnson, at the home of the novelist Samuel Richardson:

> While he was talking, he perceived a person standing at a window in the room, shaking his head, and rolling himself about in a strange ridiculous manner. He concluded that he was an ideot, whom his relations had put under the care of Mr. Richardson. . . . To his great surprise, however, this figure stalked forwards to where he and Mr. Richardson were sitting, and all at once took up the argument. . . . In short, he displayed such a power of eloquence, that Hogarth looked at him with astonishment, and actually imagined that this ideot had been at the moment inspired.
>
> [BLJ, I, 146-47]

Any number of other witnesses confirm the peculiarities of Johnson's manner and appearance—Horace Walpole thought him really mad—indeed, his oddities are inseparable from the figure of "Doctor Johnson" of tradition, the Great Cham of literature.

But his disfiguring mannerisms were only the signals of some deeper personal distress. As Katherine Balderston says, the madness that Johnson so vigorously condemned was the madness that he believed he had found in himself; and her essay supplies strong evidence that Johnson, if he did not go actually insane for a time, poised very close to the brink. In all probability at one point in his life he believed he had gone mad. Certainly the fear of madness—so intimate, so insistent in Johnson and so unlike the coarseness of the Augustan fear—recurs again and again in what he said and wrote. "Johnson's fear of death," W. J. Bate observes, "is closely paralleled by his even greater horror of insanity as the 'heaviest of human afflictions.' Each explains and extends the other. For in either case the fear is of the loss of the strong rational grip on reality toward which Johnson's most strenuous efforts were always bent, at times with the desperation of a drowning man."[18] Like Lincoln, whom he resembles in so many ways, Johnson made no attempt to conceal his chronic depressions and melancholy. " 'I inherited, (said he,) a vile melancholy from my father, which has made me mad all my life, at least not sober,' " he tells Boswell. ("Dr. Lawrence told him one day, that if he would come and beat him once a week he would bear it; but to hear his complaints was more than *man* could support," wrote Mrs. Thrale.[19]) In his diary for Easter 1777, a period of great unhappiness for him, he reflects movingly: "When I survey my past life, I discover nothing but a barren waste of time with some disorders of body, and disturbances of the mind very near to madness; which I hope that he that made me, will suffer to extenuate many faults, and excuse many deficiencies."

The friend in whom he came to confide his darkest suspicions, we now know, was Mrs. Thrale. She observes acutely, but with some annoyance, that "his over-anxious care to retain without blemish the perfect sanity of his mind, contributed much to disturb it. He had studied medicine diligently in all its branches; but had given particular attention to the diseases of the imagination, which he watched in himself with a solicitude destructive of his own peace, and intolerable to those he trusted."[20] How intolerable he became to those around him she relates in a terrible scene:

> Mr. Thrale's attentions and my own now became so acceptable to him, that he often lamented to us the horrible condition of his mind, which he said was nearly distracted; and though he charged *us* to make him odd solemn promises of secrecy on so strange a subject, yet when we waited on him one morning, and heard him, in the most pathetic terms, beg the prayers of Dr. Delap, who had left him as we came in, I felt excessively affected with grief, and well remember my husband involuntarily lifted up one hand to shut his mouth, from provocation at hearing a man so wildly proclaim what he could at last persuade no one to believe; and what, if true, would have been so very unfit to reveal.[21]

How intolerable he sometimes became to himself we can see in his relationship with Mrs. Thrale in the years 1768—84, when she apparently acted secretly as Johnson's keeper, by his own wishes padlocking and confining him to his room like an inmate in a madhouse. As he told Boswell in 1777,

> 'A madman loves to be with people whom he fears; not as a dog fears the lash; but of whom he stands in awe.' I was struck with the justice of this observation. . . .
> He added, 'Madmen are all sensual in the lower stages of the distemper. They are eager for gratifications to sooth their minds and divert their attention from the misery which they suffer: but when they grow very ill, pleasure is too weak for them, and they seek for pain. Employment, Sir, and hardships, prevent melancholy. I suppose in all our army in America there was not one man who went mad.'
> [BLJ, III, 176]

This is, Balderston says, like "all Johnson's comments on 'madness,' clearly a commentary on his own case,"[22] and she finds it evidence that Johnson's mental disturbances took the form of masochistic fantasies involving Mrs. Thrale. *De pedicis et manicis insana cogitatio*, he notes in his diary in 1771.

For Johnson, then, the imagination holds two dangers. The first, which all Augustans see, is the danger of obsession: the risk that the mind will fasten itself exclusively to a single passion, to a single hope or fear. Then follows the familiar madness that Locke and others describe, the man who imagines himself a king or a glass bottle or a horse. The other danger for Johnson lies clearly in *what* the mind imagines. The darkened sexuality present in his relationship with Mrs. Thrale is inescapable, but it often appears to be present as well in his moral thought, especially in the guilt and fear he associates with fantasy. Can we say that he fears sexuality because it, like death, means loss of self-control, that obliteration of rational consciousness Bate mentions? It is certain in any case that sensuality, solitude, and imagination are inextricably entangled in Johnson's associations, and framed by his twin fears of insanity and death. In this entanglement, we can add, he resembles no one so much as his friend Samuel Richardson. For in Richardson's novels sexual life is understood by the reader as complete loss of control, as rape or seduction, as a threat to the heroine's selfhood, to the integrity of her personality: sexuality comes to Clarissa Harlowe in a swoon, for example, and its consequence is her death; and it is their fantasies of sexual indulgence that make villains of Lovelace and Mr. B. "*Why, why, did my Mother bring me up to bear no control?*" Lovelace cries out in rage; and envisions himself driven by lust to a madhouse: "—The sport of enemies! the laughter of fools! and the hanging-sleev'd, go-carted property of hired slaves; who were perhaps to find their account in manacling, and (abhored thought!) in personally abusing me by blows and stripes!" Richardson, in other words, whom Johnson praised for exposing the innermost workings of the human mind, sees sexuality in much the same way that Johnson sees the imagination, and both of them issue endless calls for repression and control. It seems no accident that the Oriental tale, the genre to which *Rasselas* belongs, was sometimes in eighteenth-century England a pornographic medium.[23]

These bits and pieces of evidence, at once tantalizing and shocking, fill out another dimension for us. No reader can fail to catch the anxious undertone running through Johnson's conventional pronouncements on madness, the sympathetic identification that undercuts his castigation. Augustan and rational Johnson may be, yet once we are attuned to it we hear this other note of anguish everywhere. Swift struck us by his resemblance to Lear in the great mad scene of Act IV, but Johnson, as we come to know him in the privacy and intensity of his own suffering, takes on the likeness of another Lear, the Lear who cries out in terrible fear and premonition

> O! let me not be mad, not mad, sweet heaven;
> Keep me in temper; I would not be mad!

Soame Jenyns writes fatuously: "I doubt not but there is some truth in that rant of a mad poet, that there is a pleasure in being mad, which none but madmen know." And Johnson replies heavily:

> On the happiness of madmen, as the case is not very frequent, it is not necessary to raise a disquisition, but I cannot forbear to observe, that I never yet knew disorders of mind encrease felicity: every madman is either arrogant and irascible, or gloomy and suspicious, or possessed by some passion or notion destructive to his quiet. He has always discontent in his look, and malignity in his bosom. And, if we had the power of choice, he would soon repent who should resign his reason to secure his peace.[24]

We may even see shadows of Johnson's anxiety in a place as unlikely as his Dictionary. So often that great achievement is spoken of casually: an outdated monument to Johnson's genius. Yet to the student of Johnson's life a feeling persists that author and book in this case enjoy a special compatibility. Many, perhaps most, of Johnson's other works, like the *Lives of the Poets*, he came to write by accident, as booksellers or poverty suggested projects. But the Dictionary he sought out himself and clung to over eight long, difficult years, from his humiliation in Lord Chesterfield's waiting rooms in 1747 to triumphant publication in 1755. "When I survey the Plan which I have laid before you," he wrote Chesterfield, "I cannot, my Lord, but confess, that I am frightened at its extent, and, like the soldiers of Caesar, look on Britain as a new world, which it is almost madness to invade."[25] It says much to us about Johnson's reverence for the faculties of reason—and his fear of their opposite—that he should have struggled so many years to organize, systematize, and reduce the language. In the preface to the Dictionary he dwells on the "exuberance" of what he has attempted to tame, its wildness and "extravagance." English, he remarks, has been

> hitherto neglected; suffered to spread, under the direction of chance, into wild exuberance; resigned to the tyranny of time and fashion; and exposed to the corruptions of ignorance, and caprices of innovation.
>
> When I took the first survey of my undertaking, I found our speech copious without order, and energetick without rules: wherever I turned my view, there was perplexity to be disentangled, and confusion to be regulated; choice was to be made out of boundless variety, without any established principle of selection; adulterations were to be detected, without a settled test of purity; and modes of expression to be rejected or received, without the suffrages of any writers of classical reputation or acknowledged authority.[26]

Of English spelling he complains: "caprice has long wantoned without control"; of certain classes of verbs: "the signification is so loose and general, the use so vague and indeterminate, and the senses distorted so widely from the first idea, that it is hard to trace them through the maze of variation, to catch them on the brink of utter inanity, to circumscribe them by any limitations, or interpret them by any words of distinct and settled meaning." These clashes between ordering reason and exuberant imagination, between chaos and moral regulation, belong to the continuing battle that all his life Johnson fought in his own mind. But it was with a sense of inevitable failure that he regarded the finished work—more than modesty prompted so many declarations of fallibility and certain error—and much of the pessimism of the preface must spring from his recognition of the intractability of the forces of unreason. Then too, time had already altered the language he was attempting to fix into place, and time had altered the author and his audience. From "this gloom of solitude," in an uncharacteristic gesture of personal weariness and detachment, he dismisses his work "with frigid tranquility."

CHAPTER FIVE

Madness at Mid-Century: Melancholy and the Sublime

By the late 1740s in England a general dissatisfaction with the premises of Augustan literature existed. Formalist, neoclassic writing had proved somehow to be inadequate, the feeling ran; it had failed somehow to touch fully or rightly the emotions literature aims for; and so in the mid-century decades literary England can be seen turning restlessly first in one direction, then another, searching for more satisfactory styles and approaches. Immediate evidence of this discontent lies simply in the jumble of movements that make up the standard literary history of the period: sentimentalism; the rise of primitivism; melancholy poetry; the new bardic poetry of Collins and Gray; the cult of genius, including primitive geniuses like Stephen Duck, the Thresher Poet, a notable farmboy turned writer; the new critical writing; and finally the aesthetics of the Sublime. The explanations for this discontent and for the remarkable trends and reactions it produced are naturally various. Yet one explanation recently offered seems broadly applicable. "Whatever else can be said of the spate of critical writing that suddenly begins in the middle of the eighteenth century in England," asserts W. J. Bate, "we can describe it as an attempt, however confused at first, to reground the entire thinking about poetry in the light of one overwhelming fact: the obviously superior originality, and the at least apparently greater immediacy and universality of subject and appeal, of the poetry of earlier periods."[1] Certainly the then widespread belief in the decline of the arts contributed heavily to the changes I am describing. Beginning in the late seventeenth century English writers, led by Dryden, had begun self-consciously to measure their achievements against those of the ancients and of "the giants before the flood": Shakespeare, Jonson, Chaucer, Milton. And the undoubted inferiority of the modern achievement had thrown many writers into a kind of elegant despair. "Mr. Walsh," said Pope, ". . . used to tell me that there was *one way left of excelling;* for though we had several great poets, we never had any one great poet that was *correct;* and he desired me to make that my study and aim."[2] Some poets, of course, looked philosophically upon the art of maturity: "Whatever be the reason," says Imlac calmly, "it is commonly observed that the early writers are in possession of nature, and their followers of art: that the first excel in strength and invention, and the latter in elegance and refinement."[3] But to others refinement, decorum, and propriety were growing intolerably insufficient; some wilder song was wanted.

In its search for new forms and themes with which to match and overmatch previous generations, the age moved consistently, if slowly, to break down the public mode of literature—and here our subject enters. The Augustan reaction against madness had been a severe denial of the claims of the merely private in human affairs and also an affirmation of the moral interdependence of every member of the community. The powers of fantasy and inventiveness so evident in *Gulliver's Travels* or *The Dunciad* are held in check by public contexts and public decorum, directed by the necessarily public purposes of their satire. If the literature that emerged at mid-century now seems to us more "imaginative," it is because its uses of the imagination are more private. *Tristram Shandy,* to take a famous example, the first great work of the new imagination, celebrates just those private claims and moments that the Augustans repress. The Shandean family is forever flying apart from a nonexistent center, each member piloting a separate course, each hobbyhorse racing a different track. Time falls to pieces in Tristram's world (the novel begins with a joke about a forgotten clock) and every other *form* is similarly forgotten or fragmented. Each character perceives the life around him through a narrowly subjective filter; nothing is related, nothing communicated. Indeed, in their relentless eccentricity the inhabitants of Shandy Hall inevitably remind us of the Bedlam inmates that Pope or Swift or Ned Ward pictures, whose ruling passions also distort reality and encase their victims in selfhood and illusion. But if Shandy Hall is only a greater Bedlam, the spirit in which we visit it is different. We are asked to laugh at its craziness, and to laugh happily, not satirically or angrily as we laughed at Swift's "Digression" or Pope's Dunces. Nor do we feel pity, as a Richardsonian heroine might. The selfish disorder of Tristram's world—chaos is not too strong a word—is neither apocalyptic nor immoral: it is simply the nature of things, the true nature of the subjective, insistently individual reality—according to Sterne—which everyone perceives. Like all madhouses, Shandy Hall in some sense serves as a mirror.

For all its popular success *Tristram Shandy* did not by itself constitute a literary movement, at least not one that bears directly on our subject. Johnson has already bodied forth for us the emerging contradictions of the mid-century period, the stern rejection of unreason and at the same time the disposition to regard it sympathetically, curiously. In this chapter I want to discuss two closely related literary movements that illuminate more steadily the new uses of imagination in English culture: melancholy and the Sublime. They will draw us unavoidably outwards toward social and medical developments as well—toward discursive considerations of madness and cities, for example, and the insanity of King George III—but the enlargement of scale should only confirm the conclusiveness of the change we are marking. The mid-eighteenth century discloses fully for the first time those voices and themes that we now recognize as distinctly modern; and the profound changes that came over the English conception of madness are part of this immensely greater change in Western consciousness. The latter half of the eighteenth century was to be shaken by political revolutions, signaling a new order of things. By contrast, intellectual revolutions are rarely so dramatic, but the new order of mind established during the cumulative intellectual revolutions of the eighteenth and early nineteenth centuries has proved at least as enduring as the political one. Since the Renaissance and Augustan worlds, moreover, some of our ideas about the nature of human beings have changed, our feeling for the interaction of consciousness and irrationality and the value of each. We think we are lonelier and madder in the twentieth century.

Despite so sweeping a backdrop, however, our scope here is necessarily confined to a few kinds of change: every perspective focuses. Clearly sentimentalism in its largest sense—a passion for passions, a fascination with feeling simply for its own sake and without regard to context—begins the march from neoclassic to Romantic English literature. In two related aspects of sentimentalism, the histories of melancholy and sublimity at mid-century, we can see how the new age came to create literature deliberately out of the irrational parts of the human self that the Augustans had regarded as anarchic and insane, for melancholy and sublimity are two openly irrational experiences that transform men (temporarily) into good likenesses of madmen, into good likenesses of Cibber's manic and depressive brothers in fact. Such transformations were despised and contested by the great Augustans, but increasingly modern writers seek them out; they resemble those ecstatic moments of madness that Plato describes with so much approval; they seem not life-denying now, but life-enhancing, just as the inspiration of the gods formerly did. But one difference separates this ecstasy from the Platonic one: whatever madness comes about now, the modern tendency is to locate its source within the human personality, not outside it. Melancholy and sublimity are good examples of this new order emerging, indirect but unmistakable statements of change. In them we see the beginning of the dissolution of the Augustan fear of madness, and the modern embracing of it.

I

The first of these movements is the rise of *melancholia* in the mid-century decades, that strange state of vague, obsessive discontent that all men suffer from time to time. Professor Klibansky and his colleagues have clarified the changing terms of the relationship between madness and melancholy from the Greeks to the Renaissance, but the relationship itself has remained almost axiomatic: melancholy is traditionally the first stage of madness. The gloom and withdrawal—the morose, brooding abstraction of the melancholy man—resemble the more complete withdrawal from reality that madness means, and the resemblance implies identification. The man racked by religious melancholy may soon become a raving enthusiast, and the melancholy lover may collapse into the stylized insanity of a Don Quixote over his Dulcinea. "Melancholy madness" is a phrase too natural to English ears to be much insisted upon here: the malcontent manifestly totters on the edge of abnormality. And the causes and meanings of melancholy therefore will be to some extent the causes and meanings of madness as well.

We have only to think of Robert Burton's great mid-seventeenth-century *Anatomy of Melancholy* to feel the tug of the connection:

> Folly, melancholy, madness, are but one disease, delirium is a common name to all.

> . . . to omit all impertinent digressions, to say no more of such as are improperly melancholy, or metaphorically mad, lightly mad, or in disposition, as stupid, angry, drunken, silly, sottish, sullen, proud, vainglorious, ridiculous, beastly, peevish, obstinate, impudent, extravagant, dry, doting, dull, desperate, harebrain, etc., mad, frantic, foolish, heteroclites, which no new hospital can hold, no physic help: my purpose and endeavor is, in the following discourse to anatomize this humour of melancholy.

> . . . this being granted, that all the world is melancholy, or mad, dotes, and every member of it, I have ended my task.[4]

In a vast, gently satiric vision Burton makes melancholy madness a metaphor for all of human life—it is one of the points of similarity between him and Johnson. Fear and sorrow are common to all melancholy, he says. Madness is simply melancholy turned violent, "full of anger and clamour, horrible looks, actions, gestures, troubling the patients with far greater vehemency both of body and mind, without all fear and sorrow, with such impetuous force and boldness that sometimes three or four men cannot hold them." A more precise, less excited description of the relationship comes from Thomas Willis's influential textbook, *An Essay of the Pathology of the Brain and Nervous Stock* (1672):

> After Melancholy, Madness is next to be treated of, both
> which are so much akin, that these Distempers often
> change, and pass from one into the other . . . And indeed, if
> in Melancholy the Brain and Animal Spirits are said to be
> darkened with fume, and a thick obscurity; In Madness they
> seem to be all as it were of an open burning or flame. . . .
> Three things are almost common to all: *viz.* First, That their
> Phantasies or Imaginations are perpetually busied with a
> storm of impetuous thoughts. . . . Secondly, that their
> Notions or conceptions are either incongruous or
> represented to them under a false or erroneous image.
> Thirdly, To their Delirium is most often joyned
> Audaciousness and Fury.[5]

Like most observers, Willis does not name the point at which one
passes into the other: they seem as a rule, in fact, not to be
interested in it. Melancholy is a Cumaean portal through which
one passes hurriedly into an underworld of fantasies and delirium.
It is defined most often in terms of its own extreme, insanity;
sharp discrimination between the two defeats the nebulous
purposes to which, in the eighteenth century at least, melancholy
is being put. To talk about melancholy is an indirect way of
talking about madness; to create a new literature of melancholy is
to move deviously but surely toward the private voices and
private visions formerly called madness, to exchange the
Augustan balance for shifting, burning storms of imagination. Yet
before we come to the literature the phenomenon itself must be
dealt with. What exactly, besides first cousin to madness, is this
melancholia?

A synonym for madness in some classical cultures, melancholy,
says Klibansky, became "a synonym for 'sadness without cause' "
at the end of the Middle Ages. It "lost the meaning of a quality
and acquired instead the meaning of a 'mood.' " This mood in
early seventeenth-century England, which carried a rich
encrustation of motif and association, he describes simply as "a
double-edged feeling constantly providing its own nourishment,
in which the soul enjoys its loneliness, but by this very pleasure
becomes again more conscious of its solitude. . . . This modern
melancholy is essentially an enhanced self-awareness, since the
ego is the pivot round which the sphere of joy and grief
revolves."[6] It was a fact as well as a feeling, I might add, a

genuine physical evil, for the causes of melancholy were understood in the seventeenth century according to the widely accepted medical theory of humors, those four fluids in the human body thought to determine temperaments and moods. Besides phlegm, Burton explains, "Melancholy, cold and dry, thick, black, and sour, begotten of the more feculent part of nourishment, and purged from the spleen, is a bridle to the other two hot humours, blood and choler, preserving them in the blood, and nourishing the bones. These four humours have some analogy with the four elements, and to the four ages in man."[7] The external causes of melancholy, moreover, were chills, fogs, wet weather, its internal fumes and obscurity anatomical parallels to this dank outer blackness. Symptoms and causes thus mirror each other, fused in the seventeenth-century manner, appearance and explanation not yet dissociated, but creating and reinforcing each other.

By the early eighteenth century melancholy had become in England (though not elsewhere in Europe) a convention as well as a disease. It was called other names besides melancholy, as Nicholas Robinson recounts in his *New System of the Spleen* (1729), but the broad characteristics were identical:

> When I first dabbled in this art, the old distemper call'd *Melancholy* was exchang'd for *Vapours*, and afterwards for the *Hypp*, and at last took up the now current appelation of the *Spleen*, which it still retains, tho' a learned doctor of the west, in a little tract he hath written, divides the *Spleen* and *Vapours*, not only into the *Hypp*, the *Hyppos*, and the *Hyppocons*; but subdivides these divisions into the *Markambles*, the *Moonpalls*, the *Strong-Fiacs*, and the *Hockogrogles*.[8]

The very blurring of nomenclature, however, points toward a new imprecision, a severing of the psychological connection between symptoms and causes. John Hill gives an unforgettable account in *Hypochondriasis* (1766):

> The pulse becomes low, weak, and unequal; and there are frequent palpitations of the heart, a little dark-coloured urine is voided at some times; and a flood of colourless and insipid at others. . . .

> The lips turn pale, the eyes loose their brightness and by
> degrees the white grows as it were greenish, the gums want
> their due firmness, with their proper colour; and an
> unpleasing foulness grows upon the teeth: the inside of the
> mouth is pale and furred, and the throat dry and husky: the
> colour of the skin is pale (though there are periods when the
> face is florid) and as the obstruction gathers ground, and
> more affects the liver, the whole body becomes yellow,
> tawny, greenish, and at length of that deep and dusky hue,
> to which men of swift imagination have given the name of
> blackness.[9]

The characteristics could hardly be broader! *Anything* serves as a
symptom—any color, any discomfort. In Hill's recital we see that
melancholy has become a nervous condition, not a specific
ailment. And when we look beyond Hill we see that it had
become the *aristocratic condition of life*. Renaissance views of
melancholia placed relatively little stress on the highborn
character of the disease—Burton's *Anatomy* only proves that the
whole world is mad—but the Augustan age firmly yoked one to
the other, though every satirist mocked the affectation. (We may
think of Pope's Cave of Spleen or of Gulliver's ironic observation
that even the Yahoos are periodically afflicted by it.) "Fashion
has long influenced the great and opulent in the choice of their
physicians," wrote Dr. James Makittrick Adair with a certain
amiable cynicism later in the century, "but it is not so obvious
how it has influenced them also in the choice of their diseases."[10]
He attributes the prevalence of spleen among the quality to royal
example: "The Princess, afterwards Queen Anne, often chagrined
and insulted in her former station, and perplexed in the latter was
frequently subject to depression of spirits. . . . This circumstance
was sufficient to transfer both the disease and the remedy to all
who had the least pretensions to rank." Dr. George Cheyne offers
a fuller account in *The English Malady* (1733):

> The Title I have chosen for this Treatise, is a Reproach
> universally thrown on this island by Foreigners, and all our
> Neighbours on the Continent, by whom nervous
> Distempers, Spleen, Vapours, and Lowness of Spirits, are in
> Derision, called the ENGLISH MALADY. And I wish there
> were not so good Grounds for this Reflection. The moisture
> of our Air, the Variableness of our Weather, (from our

Situation amidst the Ocean), the Rankness and Fertility of our Soil, the Richness and Heaviness of our Food, the Wealth and Abundance of the Inhabitants (from their universal Trade), the Inactivity and Sedentary Occupations of the better Sort (among whom this Evil mostly rages) and the Humour of living in great, populous and consequently unhealthy Towns, have brought forth a Class and Set of Distempers, with atrocious and frightful Symptoms, scarce known to our Ancestors, and never rising to such fatal Heights, nor afflicting such Numbers in any other known Nation. These nervous Disorders being computed to make almost one third of the Complaints of the People of Condition in England.[11]

He adds that he might never have published his book if his friends had not entreated him and if he had not become alarmed by the "late Frequency and daily Encrease of wanton and uncommon self-murderers, produc'd mostly by this Distemper." He hopes "to put a Stop to so universal a Lunacy and Madness."[12] In Cheyne the perils of spleen beset the aristocratic, but we can also discern a whole set of other associations that Englishmen by now attach to an original heightened self-awareness: the English climate, the hectic quality of urban life, national prosperity, suicide. The only point omitted is the special susceptibility of women to nervous maladies, something we touched on in chapter 3. The fate of Fielding's Amelia reminds us:

"These fatigues, added to the uneasiness of her mind, over-powered her weak spirits, and threw her into one of the worst disorders that can possibly attend a woman; a disorder very common among the ladies, and our physicians have not agreed upon its name. Some call it fever on the spirits, some a nervous fever, some the vapours, and some the hysterics."

"O say no more," cries Miss Matthews; "I pity you, I pity you from my soul. A man had better be plagued with all the curses of Egypt than with a vapourish wife."

"Pity me! madam," answered Booth; "pity rather that dear creature who, from her love and care of my unworthy self, contracted a distemper, the horrors of which are scarce to be imagined. It is, indeed, a sort of complication of all diseases together, with almost madness added to them."

[*Amelia*, Book III, chapter 7]

It is fair to add that Cheyne himself was considered a crank in his own lifetime because of his insistence that melancholy was no more than a "bodily Distemper" like smallpox;[13] proper diet, he claimed, would remedy it. His theories were ridiculed in part because of pride in English beef and ale (Pierre Grosley, a French visitor to England later in the century, lists among the causes of English melancholy meat and beer, fog, and a taste for science; as a cure he proposes they drink French wine[14]). Cheyne was also called a crank because, as he said, nervous distempers are kept "under some Kind of Disgrace and Imputation, in the Opinion of the Vulgar and Unlearned; they pass among the Multitude, for a lower Degree of Lunacy, and the first step towards a distemper'd Brain." "If I said it was Vapours, Hysterick or Hypochondriacal Disorders, they thought I call'd them Mad or Fanatical." But significantly he declined to offer prescriptions in his book for the cure of madness, "being satisfied that the Methods here laid down are sufficient, and the most effectual for these Distempers."[15]

II

"No characteristic of English poetry in the mid-eighteenth century is more familiar to students of the period," says Professor Cecil A. Moore, "than the perpetual reference to melancholy. . . . Whatever one's opinion of this versified melancholy or of its genuineness as an expression of personal feeling, there can be no dispute over the quantity. Statistically, this deserves to be called the Age of Melancholy."[16] This remarkable tide of *melancholia,* unprecedented in its intensity and concentration, began to rise in the 1740s with the publication of a number of poems like "The Ruins of Rome," "The Enthusiast," "The Pleasures of Imagination," "The Pleasures of Melancholy," and particularly Edward Young's introspective epic *Night Thoughts* (1742–45). The title alone of Young's poem suggests how rays of darkness were beginning to streak the Augustan light, and its extraordinary popular success indicates new eagerness to follow poets into the realm of what the age called "gloomth." Most of the classic themes persisted[17]—visions of death, decay, and solitude—but a new ecstatic melancholy like that painted by Milton in "Il Penseroso" came dramatically forward. Over and over the poet retires to an evocative setting and there awaits "mystic visions" or communion with the "shad'wy tribes of *Mind*":

> O lead me, queen sublime, to solemn glooms
> Congenial with my soul; to cheerless shades,
> To ruin'd seats, to twilight cells and bow'rs,
> Where thoughtful Melancholy loves to muse,
> Her fav'rite midnight haunts.
> [Thomas Warton, Jr., "The Pleasures of Melancholy"]

Where the Renaissance melancholic tends to isolate himself only to bemoan an unrequited love, betraying the Italian origins of Renaissance melancholy,[18] his eighteenth-century counterpart transforms himself into a dreamlike figure, one prepared by time and place to receive visitations; he becomes a solitary creature living at the limits of his sensibility, a prophet, a hermit, an enthusiast. He has not yet become a kind of medium for other voices.

In this connection we may remark how much the poets of melancholy depend upon stage trappings (Martin Price speaks of their "theatre of the mind"). The ecstasies of melancholy occur only when a number of formulae have been followed, when the poet has retreated imaginatively in time or space to ruins of a forest or a cave, when he has called on some personified spirit or idea, when he has renounced the pleasures of sunlight and society. The rewards of melancholy depend, in other words, upon external forces. The ruins and solitude and so forth themselves bring about the desired effect, and they bestow upon the supplicant whatever he seeks. The religious atmosphere is deliberate, and it may well put us in mind of those other external religious forces that in earlier periods brought the curse or blessing of madness. The melancholy poets seem struggling to re-establish that personal relationship with higher powers that the Augustans had relinquished. The internal physical causes of melancholy are fast vanishing—no recluse calls on his sour spleen for visions—but the ritualized external forces are gaining in potency and reality. In this changeover we see the clustered, connected world of Burton's *Anatomy* giving way to an automatic inspiration, one whose causes and effects the mind can, in the beginning at least, control.

The Age of Melancholy has its nonliterary side, too; during this period in the culture at large certain features of melancholy received renewed emphasis, with important implications for a new approach to madness. The spectacle of suicides, for example, a cause of concern early in the century, grew to what in contemporary minds seemed an epidemic. Long before Cheyne wrote *The English Malady* other observers had voiced distress. William Congreve and John Dennis, replying to Jeremy Collier's indictment of the stage, had justified theatrical comedy in this lugubrious way: "Are we [the English] not of all people the most unfit to be alone, and most unsafe to be trusted with ourselves? Are there not more self-murders and melancholic lunatics in England, heard of in one year, than in a great part of Europe besides?"[19] By the early 1740s suicide seemed worse than ever, and for the next two decades it constituted a national scandal. Young cries out in *Night Thoughts*:

> O Britain, infamous for suicide!
> An island in thy manners! far disjoin'd
> From the whole world of rationals beside!
> In ambient waves plunge thy polluted head,
> Wash the dire stain nor shock the Continent.
>
> [V. 442–46]

Spectator 387 cites England's growing notoriety by pointing to the first sentence of a new French novel: "*In the gloomy month of* November, *when the People of England hang and drown themselves.* . . ." The peak came, according to Professor Moore, in 1755, when on New Year's Day Lord Mountford inaugurated the season, followed swiftly by his friend Sir John Bland; one company went so far as to offer insurance against suicide.[20]

The English climate, long blamed for the English malady by natives and foreigners alike, was also increasingly regarded with despair. "Is there in the world a climate more uncertain than our own?" ask Congreve and Dennis. "And, which is a natural consequence, is there anywhere a people more unsteady, more apt to discontent, more saturnine, dark and melancholic than ourselves?"[21] Throughout the century a gloomy national eye was fixed on that uncertain climate, frequently personalized as the East Wind, the wind that blows forever in Pope's Cave of Spleen, a wind wicked enough, as Voltaire learned, to set Englishmen to cutting their throats or to send Sterne's friend John Hall-Stevenson to bed for its duration. (During George III's madness in 1788 prayers were sent up for a westerly.) Indeed, the East Wind has found a place in popular lore as far away as Boston, where old-timers speak of it in the same miserable tones as Mr. Jarndyce does in *Bleak House*. Goldsmith, surely with Pope in mind, remarks good-humoredly that, "It is impossible to describe what a variety of transmutations an east wind shall produce; it has been known to change a lady of fashion into a parlour couch; an Alderman into a plate of custards, and a dispenser of justice into a rat trap. Even philosophers themselves are not exempt from its influence; it has often converted a Poet into a coral and bells, and a patriot Senator into a dumb waiter."[22] Johnson speaks in the "Life of Addison" of the "variable weather of the mind, the flying vapours of incipient madness, which from time to time cloud reason, without eclipsing it."

This habitual association of melancholy and cold, wet weather had its origin, of course, in the melancholy humor, the most chilling and vaporish of the four fluids. But we may also be reminded of that other link between madness and water, in which water appears both to inaugurate and to absolve the curse of madness, just as the storm does in *King Lear*. Why else, as Foucault asks, are madmen sent across the ocean in a ship of fools? Water denotes, however vaguely, some sacred character in madness, and here in mid-century melancholy we also find the special if unspecified blessings of a distemper that wetness causes—and cures. The importance of water as medical treatment was never greater than in mid-eighteenth-century England, and with more insight than perhaps they imagined the world of fashion fussed unceasingly about the purity of what they drank and toured regularly a circuit of medicinal spas like Bath and Scarborough, soothing the symptoms of spleen. (Though Bath was a place, Horace Walpole remarked, where people of fashion went in good health and came away even better.)

Other aspects of melancholy seem also to have gained in intensity during the 1740s and '50s. Cheyne names the quality of modern English life as a cause. At the end of the seventeenth century Swift's mentor, Sir William Temple, had made the same point in observing the absence of spleen among the Dutch: "this is a disease too refined for this country and people, who are well, when they are not ill; and pleased, when they are not troubled; are content, because they think little of it; and seek their happiness in the common eases and commodities of life, or the increase of riches; not amusing themselves with the more speculative contrivances of passion, or refinements of pleasure."[23] Sir William's tone compliments neither the splenetic English at whom he glances obliquely nor the phlegmatic Dutch. Thinking the spleen "to be the disease of people that are idle . . . and attribute every fit of dull humour, or imagination, to a formal disease, which they have found this name for," he aligns himself solidly with Augustans of the old school.[24] But his concession that spleen or melancholy was a refined disease would recur with greater and greater elaboration throughout the eighteenth century. Refinement in such a connection, however, can have at least two meanings. On the one hand it may mean aristocratic refinement, as it usually did in the early part of the century: indolence, wealth, luxury. This is not the laziness that produces poverty, the enervating laziness of *The Dunciad*, but the laziness of a leisured class. Johnson attacks such refinement, holding that hardship prevents madness. Cheyne says much the same thing, prescribing exercise and austere diet for nervous maladies. And Edmund Burke remarks that in the languid, inactive state of indolence, "the nerves are more liable to the most horrid convulsions, than when they are sufficiently braced and strengthened. Melancholy, dejection, despair, and often self-murder, is the consequence of the gloomy view we take of things in this relaxed state of body. The best remedy for all these evils is exercise or *labour*."[25] John Brown in a remarkably popular mid-century blast against the English spirit (*An Estimate of the Manners and Principles of the Times*) contends, "Our effeminate and unmanly Life, working along with our Island-Climate, hath notoriously produced an Increase of *low Spirits* and *nervous, Disorders*."[26] A bit later Dr. Thomas Arnold explains the prevalence of insanity in England by the nation's "*excess of wealth and luxury*" (making the Johnsonian point that "In Scotland, where the inhabitants in general are neither opulent nor luxurious, Insanity, as I am informed, is very rare").[27] The

American colonials at this time, largely for their own reasons, publicized England as a country sinking rapidly into effeminacy, laziness, and corruption.[28] By the end of the century one doctor declares quite seriously that "it is easier to meet with a mad, than a healthy woman of fashion."[29]

The second meaning of refinement has far more positive connotations: it may mean special acuteness or education or creativity. Even the hard-headed Cheyne says, not without a spirit of flattery for his wealthy patients, that nervous disorders strike mainly "those of the liveliest and quickest natural Parts, whose Faculties are the brightest and most spiritual, and whose Genius is most keen and penetrating. . . . So equally are the good and bad Things of this mortal State distributed!"[30] This meaning of refinement comprises a restatement—or resurrection—of Aristotle's Problem XXX: why is the melancholy man a man of genius? We hear frequently in the Renaissance of melancholy's parts: Jaques's mordant intellect in *As You Like It*, the miseries of scholars in Burton, the Knight of the Mournful Countenance in Cervantes. But the Augustans deny the connection: "I never was hippish in my whole life," Pope declared proudly on his deathbed; Swift was a "perfect stranger to the Spleen." At mid-century, however, the self-induced sensitivity of the melancholy poets pointed the way for the coffeehouse crowds to follow; and though they no longer wore the ostentatious black hat and cloak of the Elizabethan melancholic, every would-be wit or critic nonetheless assumed the symptoms of creative unhappiness. Spleen was no longer a female failing exclusively, as it had often seemed to Pope and Swift; men everywhere spoke easily and vainly of their "hyps" and "vapours." Johnson of course is an exception. To Mrs. Thrale, who had warned him against melancholy, he replies: "The black Dog I hope always to resist, and in time to drive though I am deprived of almost all those that used to help me. . . . When I rise my breakfast is solitary, the black dog waits to share it, from breakfast to dinner he continues barking."[31] In the Dictionary he calls it "A kind of madness, in which the mind is always fixed on one object" and also "a gloomy, pensive, discontented temper." Speaking of Cheyne, he growls to Boswell: "Do not let him teach you a foolish notion that melancholy is a proof of acuteness."

Boswell cannot quite agree: " . . . Dr. Johnson and I had a
serious conversation by ourselves on melancholy and madness;
which he was, I always thought, erroneously inclined to confound
together. Melancholy, like 'great wit,' may be near allied to
madness; but there is, in my opinion, a distinct separation
between them."[32] As always Boswell speaks for the fashion:
melancholy is something other than, better than, madness, which
remains an undeniable evil (Boswell's brother John was insane
intermittently all his life). By mid-century melancholy, like great
wit, had become a sign of deeper life; *poseurs* of all kinds claimed
a compensated wound like Philoctetes'.

III

In these developments something startling and immensely
important for the later history of madness came to pass. The
individual traits of melancholy were transformed first into
aristocratic traits (class traits) *and thence into national traits.*
Writing about spleen in 1725 Sir Richard Blackmore reaches a
modestly patriotic conclusion: "The temper of the Native of
Britain is most various, which proceeds from the Spleen, an
Ingredient of their Constitution, which is almost peculiar, at least
in the Degree of it, to this Island. Hence arises the Diversity of
Genius and Disposition, of which this Sort is so fertile."[33] We
meet such claims continually in the mid-eighteenth century and
after. Englishmen swell with satisfaction at their achievements in
the arts, in government, in science; and their congenital
melancholy both signifies and makes possible their national
genius. Bishop Percy puzzles over the large number of English
songs and ballads about madness; a later observer offers a widely
accepted explanation. "The last century," writes Thomas Trotter
in 1807, "has been remarkable for the increase of a class of
diseases, but little known in former times. . . . Sydenham at the
conclusion of the seventeenth century computed fevers to
constitute two thirds of the diseases of mankind. But, at the
beginning of the nineteenth century, we do not hesitate to affirm,
that *nervous disorders* have now taken the place of fevers, and
may be justly reckoned two third of the whole, with which
civilized society is afflicted." Trotter goes on to point out that
politeness has lost its monopoly on spleen: "nervous ailments are

no longer confined to the better ranks in life, but rapidly extending to the poorer classes. . . . It is probable the other countries of Europe do not exhibit such general examples of these diseases; as many of their causes are to be traced to the peculiar situation of Britain; its insular varieties of climate and atmosphere; its political institutions and free government; and above every thing, its vast wealth, so diffused among all ranks of people."[34] Even those foreigners like Voltaire who mock the English malady acknowledge its strange conjunction with great accomplishments and the preservation of liberty, its standing as a national creative principle.[35]

As the century progresses, however, melancholy trails its chauvinistic banners, and men begin to see it not merely as a British peculiarity but as the inevitable attendant of civilization itself. Nervous disorders and higher civilization march in locked step forward. William Rowley summarizes the new dogma:

> In proportion as the arts, sciences, and luxury increase, so do vices and madness. In countries where the fewest wants and desires are experienced, there are the smallest number of mad persons; in those kingdoms where the greatest luxuries, refinements, wealth, and unrestrained liberty abound, are the most numerous instances of madness. England, according to its size and number of inhabitants, produces and contains more insane than any other country in Europe, and suicide is more common. In other nations mankind are obedient under either military or religious despotism, and are educated from infants in implicit submission and non-resistance; in Britain everyone thinks and acts as he pleases; this produces all that variety and originality in the English character, and causes arts, sciences, and inventions to flourish. The agitations of passions, this liberty of thinking and acting with less restraint than in other nations, force a great quantity of blood to the head, and produce greater varieties of madness in this country, than is observed in others. Religious and civil toleration are productive of political and religious madness; but where no such toleration exists, no such insanity appears.[36]

Restraint and madness, we notice in Rowley, are still inseparable; madness is still a force that bursts loose and forces free. Other observers, perhaps closer to the problem, blame tea drinking; and a bewildering number find novel-reading a cause of lunacy in young ladies. As an article of faith the equation of madness and civilization (and to a lesser degree the equation of madness and liberty) has proved wonderfully tenacious and self-serving. An American writer named George Beard describes the remarkable symptoms of American nervousness in the nineteenth century, declaring that "All this is modern, and originally American; and no age, no country, and no form of civilization, not Greece, nor Rome, nor Spain, nor the Netherlands, in the early days of their glory, possessed such maladies."[37] But long before Beard, mid-eighteenth-century England had found comfort and congratulation in its advanced distempers. It is not surprising that Robert Burton, whose popularity had waned during the early part of the eighteenth century, began to attract new readers in great numbers in the middle years; the Romantic era was to take him as one of its heroes.

Every age believes that madness is increasing—the early eighteenth century says it with terrified intensity—but the mid-century period bolsters the modern claim by referring over and over to a new cause of madness: the stress of urban life. Between 1700 and 1800 the population of London nearly doubled, growing to better than a million people, and all the frustrations of crime, sanitation, transportation, and anonymity so familiar to us now grew with it.[38] Moreover, the very real problem of gin-drinking, which ravaged the working classes through the mid-century, placed further strain on London stability: Hogarth's Dantesque prints of *Gin Lane* and *Beer Street* exaggerated nothing. In the early part of the century particularly, London life was disorderly and crime-ridden, and a concomitant, pervasive sense of uncertainty did much to harden writers like Swift and Pope against the claims of disorder. The dangers of simply moving about safely in the gang-infested London night helped shape the nightmare of *The Dunciad* (there was no regular police force in the city until 1792). The threat of financial ruin, spectacularly but not uniquely shown in the collapse of the South Sea Bubble, also runs, as Dorothy George says, all through eighteenth-century literature, contributing to its preoccupation with instability. Yet stresses like these were not openly recognized as causes of madness in the early eighteenth century. It was only when reform had begun, when social organization and stability were improving that the melancholy complaint began that modern life is maddening. The mid-eighteenth century then sounded the theme (we may think it our own) that as a man's life grows more and more complex, he loses touch with what is natural in it. He no longer lives, to take a common example, by the natural sequence of day and night. He sleeps and wakes according to artificial cycles; unlike his ancestors and his rural contemporaries he quakes amid the violence and corruption of the city; he works and lives in the confinement and darkness of offices and shops; he sees the sun only on holidays, and even then through the smoky London sky. By cutting himself off from nature thus, a man disorders his senses and invites "nervous disorders." The image of madness begins to bring the city itself within the range of its meanings. "Rambling, riding, rolling, rushing, justling, mixing, bouncing, cracking, and crashing in one vile ferment of stupidity and corruption," Smollett's Matt Bramble says of Londoners. "All is tumult and hurry; one would imagine they were impelled by some disorder of the brain, that will not suffer them to be at rest. . . . How can I help supposing they are actually possessed by a spirit, more absurd and pernicious than any thing we meet with in the precincts of Bedlam?"[39]

The emergence of the city as Bedlam is all the more striking when we recall that in earlier literature madness is usually identified with the forest—Euripides' *The Bacchae* and *A Midsummer Night's Dream* are representative—in part because the forest is dark, seemingly disordered and dreamlike; in part, too, because there dwell the supernatural spirits who cause madness. In the forest man easily becomes an animal. (King Lear goes out of the castle into the heath in a variation.) But by mid-century the city, not the forest, had become the site of madness; and to the Romantic generations the forest was to be attractive, safe, magnetic. Stirrings of this change are evident in the early part of the century, of course. In Swift's "A City Shower" parallels and allusions to the falls of other great cities are camouflaged in the commonplace details of London sanitation: The evils of the city, previously understood by pastoral poets as the polite evils of the Court, had become as concrete and inescapable as the sewage ditch that flowed through the center of its streets. Johnson said the man who is tired of London is tired of life, but the melancholy poets who swarmed to their fields and cottages spoke more to the moment. In France Jean-Jacques Rousseau was beginning to give eloquent voice to the pleasures of primitivism. In America the absence of cities was taken as evidence of superiority to Old World culture. Even Johnson's "London" and Blake's "London" are related in substance if not style.

In this context of growing fascination with primitive society and growing rejection of the city the fear of madness is still present, just as it was for the Augustans; but it is a different fear, not posited on the inhumanity of madness, but rather on its complex promise of achievement and defeat. Madness slowly becomes explicable. In the earlier part of the century it had been the badge of folly, a reprehensible condition brought about, the satirists thought, almost by an act of will; in the latter half of the century it was becoming the inevitable consequence of progress, the price paid by the sensitive and vulnerable for refinement. Small wonder that the poetry of the next age would retreat in panic from the city to the country, would attempt to reverse the progress of civilizing and return to the garden. And small wonder, too, that the growth of historical sensibility that characterizes this period would be fed by dissatisfaction with the present and a deep nostalgia for the imagined past.

IV

What we have seen thus far is a survey, however abrupt, of the ways in which *melancholia* worked in the mid-eighteenth century to tear down the public modes of Augustanism. It turned men away, for example, from the physical symbols of their community like the city. At the same time its heightened self-awareness led mid-century Englishmen to explore and to exploit theatrically those aspects of self that the Augustans rejected because they were frighteningly inexplicable and because they fostered a dark, destructive individualism. Dreams, enthusiasm, and madness are fellow travelers of melancholy.

We can look now still more briefly at some of the developments in the last quarter of the century that accelerated earlier trends.

Medical science made no great actual headway in treating nervous disorders in the eighteenth century; indeed, its progress was really rather insignificant. But the number of books and pamphlets on the subject grew steadily, and that quantity alone made for a kind of public education on the physical nature of mental illness. No matter how laughable theories of corpuscular mental vibrations or of Ideal vs. Original Insanity now seem to us, in their times their elaborate scientific guise served to dispel much of the mystery. (Are we any less gullible today?) Discussions of the East Wind, the English diet, and so on were only laymen's halting attempts to frame this new conception of nervous disease in common, logical language. Even while melancholy poets were invoking their own irrationality, medicine was reducing madness to an illness. Anger and impatience, for example, at the treatment accorded lunatics in Bedlam led to the establishment in 1750 of St. Luke's Hospital, which, under the supervision of the redoubtable Dr. Battie, dealt with the insane in a more humane and straightforward way (see plate 6); new routines and reforms were instituted, and the hospital significantly abolished the practice of opening its door to sightseers. Other hospitals founded on the same principles came soon after, notably in Manchester in 1763 and Newcastle-upon-Tyne in 1764. The scandalous discoveries of the Parliamentary committee investigating private madhouses in the mid-sixties also roused public opinion on the side of the victimized mad.

If we look ahead as far as the eighties we see these trends solidifying into established truths. Three developments in that decade particularly advanced scientific conceptions of madness. One was the phenomenal popularity (and subsequent debunking) of Franz Mesmer's "mesmerism," a fascinating hypnotic spectacle put forward as medical treatment. Another was the publication in 1783 of William Cullen's *First Lines of the Practice of Physic*, a book largely devoted to nervous diseases, in which the term "neurosis" first appeared. And the third was the madness of King George III in 1788. When the king's incapacitating fevers and convulsions were at last pronounced after several weeks of delay to be mental derangement, secret midnight confrontations and intrigue took place between Pitt's government and the Prince of Wales's slightly inept opposition; a regency was arranged and

voted, though the king recovered before it could be put into
effect. These rather frantic political maneuverings took place
against a backdrop of general panic, as the nation tried to
interpret the daily bulletins of the squabbling doctors (matters
were complicated by royal protocol: even the doctors could not
address the mad king unless he first spoke to them). Stocks
plunged with every report of the king's incoherence or violent
behavior, and rumors continually surfaced concerning his
wholesale accusations of treachery or his amorous ravings toward
Lady Elizabeth Pembroke—the story is told fully by Ida
MacAlpine and Richard Hunter in *George III and the Mad-
Business*. Yet out of the midst of the panic emerged an unlikely
medical hero, the Reverend Dr. Francis Willis, known as the
"Duplicate Doctor." Willis had run a private madhouse
successfully for many years; and he was called to the king's
sickroom when all other efforts had failed. An adherent of the
school of mechanical rather than moral management, Willis did
not hesitate to treat the king like any other patient (though he
permitted him to read *King Lear*!). He went so far as to place the
king in a straitjacket, a step for which the queen, he said, never
forgave him. When a fiery Edmund Burke demanded whether he
could have controlled the king without his restraining apparatus,
Willis showed another side of his mastery of madness:

> "Place the candles between us, Mr. Burke," replied the
> Doctor, in an . . . authoritative tone—"and I'll give you
> an answer. There, Sir! by the EYE! I should have looked at
> him *thus*, Sir—*thus*!
> Burke instantaneously averted his head, and, making no
> reply, evidently acknowledged this basiliskan authority.[40]

But Willis will be remembered for something more than his
arresting eye. He claimed that insanity was curable—he himself,
he declared, cured nine out of ten patients—and cure the king he
did, though MacAlpine and Hunter argue persuasively that the
king's illness was porphyria, which appeared and disappeared on
its own. The king's madness, however, was an event with
extraordinary impact in medical history:

George III's first attack of derangement, played out in a blaze of publicity such as has probably never before or since been accorded the illness even of a monarch . . . brought with it a fundamental change of attitudes. No longer could insanity be equated with ignorance or sin or superstition. If it was possible for the highest in the land to be struck down after an utterly blameless life of devotion to duty, to country and to family, to have all the confidences of his sickroom revealed to the world, to make a remarkable recovery and have the courage to resume his dignities and station, surely such an illness could not be anything but natural, demanding of sympathy and amenable to medicine as any other? The lesson was quickly learnt. Much of what had gone for knowledge was revealed as idle speculation. No longer could the sufferer be blamed for succumbing to weakness or acceding to unbridled passion. Insanity ceased to be a matter of shame or blame. Furthermore, as Willis had proclaimed, it could be cured, and 'insanity proved curable' became the slogan which attracted doctors to the specialty and patients to doctors.[41]

Not surprisingly, the number of patients admitted to madhouses rose dramatically after the king's madness, and a brief wave of fear crested.

It is awkward and frustrating to speak so generally of these developments, but the medical history of the period has been written more than once and its details in fact bear very little relevance to our main theme. No single work or person in England stands out as decisive in rescuing madness from its Augustan immurement. In France the end of the century saw another great breakthrough, when Pinel, acting in the spirit of the Revolution, set free the shackled inmates at Bicêtre. What I have been sketching here is the movement of "melancholy" toward modern "mental illness." And this movement of melancholy did break ground and prepare the way for madness itself to follow, for "madhouses" to give way to "asylums" and then to "mental hospitals." The condition associated in Augustan minds with crime and confinement was now spoken of in terms of creativity and freedom; what had once been linked to poverty was now understood as the consequence of civilized riches.

V

Melancholy and the Sublime form a kind of continuum of irrationality in the eighteenth century. Together they complete the transformation of Augustan madness into something more nearly resembling the classical madness of inspiration by gods and devils. But while melancholy as a word remains meaningful to us now, the Sublime describes a more recondite state of mind. At mid-century it was a name given to almost any transcendent experience, any sight or sound that overwhelmed the spectator or gave, in Edmund Burke's definition, a feeling of terror without real danger.[42] John Dennis had said earlier in the century that to read a sublime poem "ravishes and transports us, and produces in us a certain Admiration, mingled with Astonishment and with Surprize, which is quite another thing than the barely pleasing . . . [;] it gives a noble Vigour to a Discourse, an invincible Force, which commits a pleasing Rape upon the very Soul of the Reader . . . [;] it thunders, blazes, and strikes at once, and shews all the united Force of a Writer."[43] Others found the same noble force in great vistas of ocean or mountains; Americans in the nineteenth century were to say that the easiest way to see what was meant by the Sublime was to stand and gaze at Niagara Falls. From our vantage point what the emergence of the Sublime at mid-century represents is another of those indirect, eyes-averted embracings of madness that help to mark the end of the Augustan world. Increasingly during this period sublime transcendence is compared to flights of madness—James Usher's outburst is typical: "In the poet's language it flies, it soars, it pursues a beauty in the madness of rapture, that words or description cannot contain; and if these expressions be extravagant and improper in the ordinary commerce of life, they yet exactly describe the intellectual and real state of the mind at the presence of the sublime."[44] More important than such comparisons, however, is that sublimity calls forth the same buried parts of the human self that melancholy draws on and finds this buried life, not bestial or chaotic, but rapturous and ennobling. The Sublime therefore seems to bear upon the history of madness and literature in two broad ways, and we can proceed with these in turn. First, as an aesthetic doctrine the Sublime appropriated positively most of the ideas and values that the

Augustans had associated negatively with madness. And second, it helped to spread a new anti-Lockean conception of the human mind and its powers.

The first of these points almost springs from the pages of any mid-century treatise—sublimity is irregular, enthusiastic, terrifying, wild: the sublime writer will

> Rise in Disorder to a glorious Height:
> And with Contempt of just, tho' vulgar Arts,
> Rear up illustrious, incoherent Parts.[45]

Here disorder and incoherence, prime Augustan vices, are sublime. Elsewhere terror, which we learned from Swift and Johnson to feel when we approach a Bedlamite, appears as a sublime *frisson*; the storm scenes of *King Lear* are regarded as sublime because of their "judicious horror." Moreover the Sublime requires surrender of that self-control so central to the Augustan style, so personally important to Johnson; self-rape, not self-control, describes its mysterious, eruptive power. And enthusiasm, pervasive eighteenth-century synonym for insanity, now belongs to the genius of the sublime poet. William Duff notes that the word is

> almost universally taken in a bad sense; and, being conceived to proceed from an overheated and distempered imagination, is supposed to imply weakness, superstition, and madness. ENTHUSIASM, in this modern sense, is in no respect a qualification of a Poet; in the ancient sense, which implied a kind of divine INSPIRATION, or an ardor of Fancy wrought up to Transport, we not only admit, but deem it an essential one.[46]

Little elaboration is needed. All those qualities that necessarily enter into a thundering, blazing, astonishing experience clearly work against Augustan values. Sublimity bursts bonds, overruns boundaries, shatters restraints, cannot be contained—nothing in it serves the Augustan sense of community or of moral passion; everything about it destroys them. The Sublime is neither a public nor a moral moment, but rather a private, solitary, somehow insane one.

The second point, the way in which the Sublime helps to disseminate a new conception of mind, is less obvious. Like melancholy, sublimity requires certain stage properties. Its devotee moves, as the melancholy poet does, to special settings, to ruins or mountains or the ocean; and these natural objects by themselves are able to excite feelings of sublimity; they constitute a kind of external explanation for the emotions that follow. But feelings of sublimity are also made possible by innate powers of the human mind, and no one does more to call attention to those powers than the youthful Edmund Burke in *A Philosophical Enquiry into the Origin of Our Ideas of the Sublime and Beautiful* (first published in 1757 but written considerably earlier). Burke undertakes to discover the *origins* of our ideas of the Sublime and its lesser partner the Beautiful—undertakes, that is, to describe the operations of our minds and to answer the question: by what means do we respond to the Sublime? In most instances, he concludes, we respond to a physical stimulus; we receive an item of sensory information and through the mechanism of association we experience a deep emotional response to it, an emotion of terror without real peril. Now plainly Burke assumes a Lockean model of the mind: he sees an apparatus fueled by sensation, a mind essentially passive before the objective natural world. He quibbles occasionally, but in its outlines he accepts uncritically the mind as *tabula*; his own mind shows clearly Locke's stamp. And yet his concentration on emotions drives him away from Lockean values: to give oneself up to sublime ravages, after all, is far different from giving oneself up to the impressions of objects in a dark closet. Where Locke stresses the mind's limitations, Burke finds himself turning toward its powers. Where Locke dwells with gloom on the errors of association, Burke (and other mid-century philosophers like David Hartley) sees it as a means whereby the mind releases a surge of unconscious forces.

Beneath the surface, then, is an internal explanation to complement the rather mechanical external ones. The poet who stands dwarfed before a sublime range of mountains takes up inevitably an attitude of worship toward them; earlier writers on the Sublime, Shaftesbury for example, speak impressively of the religious character of the experience, the relationship it reveals between man and the divine power that overawes him. But whereas the early eighteenth century perceives the *otherness* of the sublime force, its separation and superiority, the mid-century sees a significant change in this relationship. When the sublime poet reaches his special setting, he begins to call up Presences—the Passions, the Poetical Character, Liberty, Duty, Fancy, Fear—and these Presences, Martin Price observes, "are frankly states or faculties of the poet, and his evocation of them is a release of their power within himself." The movement from public to private mode has reached its farthest point. "The sense of otherness remains, of course, as do the ritual of prayer or invocation and the myth of the sacred place. But the otherness has been displaced into a vision of the *other self*, the self at last controlled by powers that have been submerged by culture, the self either mastering the familiar world or annihilating it."[47] Some buried self, which the Augustans condemned as destructive and disordering, has now come forth not only to respond to the Sublime but in the end to embody it.

The buried self that the Sublime sets free is a far more vigorous creation than the one set free by melancholy. We feel something of its power in the Satanic villains of Gothic novels (which originated in the 1760s), textbook examples of terror without peril: in them the device of the Double Life brings into the light the demonic energy within themselves that civilized men deny, the savage passions concealed, as Mrs. Radcliffe might say, behind the bland physiognomy of a Schedoni, the incestuous satisfactions of the monk Ambrosio. The ceaselessly swooning heroines of these novels remind us of mediums, Northrop Frye suggests, broadcasting the presence of some greater power.[48]

The Gothic novel, however, with all its interest in madness and incarceration reached its peak only in the last decade of the century, thus lying outside our subject here. We see just as clearly the vigor of the second self in the cult of genius that flowered in the 1760s. For in this period the idea of genius took on a new strength, referring not merely to one's spirit but specifically to those human prodigies of intellect that remain nonetheless representative. Natural geniuses were turned up everywhere, like fairer flowers, and a whole literature of genius arose. While Burke seems to have been solving by what means we respond to the

Sublime, others at mid-century turned to a related question: by what means do we create sublime art? And their overwhelming answer was—by our own genius: the power for which we serve as medium is our own. In Carlyle's phrase, it is a "natural supernaturalism." Here is Alexander Gerard on genius: " . . . the fire of genius, like a divine impulse, raises the mind above itself, and by the natural influence of imagination actuates it as if it were supernaturally inspired."[49] And William Duff, who claims that genius in poetry is distinguished by "an IRREGULAR GREATNESS, WILDNESS, and ENTHUSIASM. . . . By the vigorous effort of a creative Imagination, he calls shadowy substances and unreal objects into existence. They are present to his view and glide, like spectres, in silent, sullen majesty, before his astonished and intranced sight."[50] James Usher in *Clio; or, A Discourse on Taste* rejects Lockean epistemology because "There appeared in that philosophy but one common first motive, or source of determination and action to man and brute; and the human divine mind was only considered, as endued with a greater capacity, or with a superiority in degree, but not in kind." The poet, he says, "feels, with all the certainty of intuition, the presence of the universal genius."[51] "The human divine mind" and "the certainty of intuition"—these are phrases not likely to have been spoken by Swift or Pope, but they convey perfectly the new sense of power the Sublime brought to the eighteenth century. The human mind that creates sublime poetry was seen now (as sometimes in the Renaissance) in analogy to the divine mind that creates the mountains and the seas; the word "creative," with all its religious resonance, was more and more applied to the human artist, the human genius. Shadowy substances, William Duff implies, parade obediently before him much as they paraded before an earlier, still greater Artist.

The discovery, so to speak, of original genius in the late sixties completed the process of explanation begun two decades earlier with the rise of melancholy. The eighteenth-century mind could now explain its own unpredictableness, its own contradictions, and sudden impulses; the inspiration that former ages attributed to gods and devils (and which medicine could not fathom) was now internalized, the voice of the inner "divine" self speaking through the outer man. And explanation and acceptance quickly brought about a number of specific aesthetic changes. The sublime experience, in the first place, reverses the standings of reason and imagination: our unconscious godlike imagination is what responds to a sublime idea, and reason has a decidedly inconspicuous role. "The judgment," Burke argues, "is for the greater part employed in throwing stumbling blocks in the way of the imagination, in dissipating the scenes of its enchantment, and in tying us down to the disagreeable yoke of our reason" (though without its control, as Alexander Gerard says, Pindar "would have produced, not wild sublimity, but madness and frenzy").[52] In this view the poet becomes less and less a moral figure, as he was for Pope, and more a prophetic, bardic genius. Satire wanes. Genius likewise, says Gerard, is marked by a "restless activity of imagination"; and we may think of Swift's contrasting image of the swarming restlessness of the mind, and of Johnson's image of the mind in constant unproductive motion. Moreover, this imagination so essential to genius *creates order*—reversing the Augustan dictum: "THUS imagination is no unskillful architect," Gerard says; "it collects and chuses the materials; and though they may at first lie in a rude and indigested chaos, it in great measure, by its own force, by means of its associating power, after repeated attempts and transpositions, designs a regular and well-proportioned edifice." Even where Augustan standards appear most tenacious, as in that concluding phrase, a difference is felt. Gerard takes a familiar metaphor: "A horse of high mettle ranging at liberty, will run with great swiftness and spirit, but in an irregular track and without any fixt direction: a skillful rider makes him move straight in the road, with equal spirit and swiftness." But what a distance from Swift's version! In *A Tale of a Tub* we were fearful of the horse, fearful of his throwing the rider or running away with him, fearful of madness. Gerard feels no fear at all of the inner self and its primitive force, only confidence and a certain curiosity.

Burke's *Enquiry* offers two concluding, concrete examples of the changes brought about at mid-century by melancholy and the Sublime. In Part II of the book he lists the various attributes of an object, like vastness or difficulty, that can produce the effect of the Sublime. One such quality is *darkness*. Surely we have only to

look back to the conclusion of *The Dunciad* to measure how far
we have come. "Mere light," he writes in a phrase to make
Augustans shiver, "mere light is too common a thing to make a
strong impression on the mind, and without a strong impression
nothing can be sublime." The sun, he allows, "is a very great
idea. . . . But darkness is more productive of sublime ideas than
light." He acknowledges that Locke's theories "stand in the way
of our general principle" here, yet he stands by his principle,
asserting that darkness causes ideas of terror to arise in us, and
these alone evoke the sublime; hence darkness is more affective
than light.[53] In the concluding section of the book Burke looks at
another side of darkness. Arguing that "WORDS may affect
without raising Images,"[54] he offers as proof two blind men, the
poet Thomas Blacklock and the mathematician Nicholas
Saunderson, who were perfectly able to describe colors and other
visual phenomena, although they could have no real Lockean
idea of them. Burke is satisfied that these blind men understand
and may be affected by what they do not see. And he goes
further: we are *all* thus affected by what we do not "see." The
subversiveness of Burke's speculations is apparent when we recall
Locke's own blind man, who furnished exactly the opposite proof,
that experience or sensation is necessary for understanding the
names of simple ideas. And we have already seen in our
considerations of Augustan madness a number of other
examples—Swift's professor in the Grand Academy is an
instance—of the blind man who, like the madman, cannot
understand.[55]

This topsy-turvy posture toward the meaning of blindness leads
us to our second point about Burke's *Enquiry*. After describing
the powers of Blacklock and Saunderson, he goes on to show that
a similar operation takes place in all of us. Poetry, he claims, does
not always raise images in our minds of what it describes, but
nonetheless we are affected. Burke quotes a few lines from the
Aeneid, then remarks: "This seems to me admirably sublime; yet
if we attend coolly to the kind of sensible image which a
combination of ideas of this sort must form, the chimeras of
madmen cannot appear more wild and absurd than such a
picture."[56] Following so closely upon a discussion of blindness
that sees and illogical poetry that is sublime, Burke's argument

pushes forward irresistibly toward new ideas of what is and what is not real.[57] Certainly he grants to language a force greater than he can easily understand; our minds respond so completely to a systematic set of abstractions that hesitantly he ascribes to language an essential being of its own. Poetry, he writes, is not an imitative art like painting: "*descriptive* poetry operates chiefly by *substitution*; by the means of sounds, which by custom have the effect of realities."[58] Words have extraordinary dominion over our passions, more so than the other arts and sometimes more than nature itself. "There are many things of a very affecting nature, which can seldom occur in the reality, but the words which represent them often do; and thus they have an opportunity of making a deep impression and taking root in the mind, whilst the idea of the reality was transient."[59] Subtly the emotional and intellectual realities grow more important than prosaic Lockean reality; the reality of words may even be set above other realities.

It is the idea of some other reality that we have been coming to. Burke expresses it only tentatively, but as the walls of the eighteenth century began to crack we see through to new dimensions. Johnson is never more Augustan than when he dismisses the reality of what is not empirical, when he kicks the solid stone that Berkeley calls merely mental: "I know not any thing more pleasant or more instructive than to compare experience with expectation, or to register from time to time the difference between Idea and Reality."[60] The usurpation of reason by imagination and the consequent loss of the sense of reality are the beginnings of madness, both for Pertinax and for the astronomer. The Augustan view is perfectly expressed in *Adventurer* 88:

> In lunacy, as in dreams, ideas are conceived which material objects do not excite; and which the force of imagination, exerted by a voluntary effort, cannot form: but the mind of the lunatic, besides being impressed with the images of things that do not fall under the cognizance of his sense, is prevented from receiving corresponding images from those that do. When the visionary monarch looks round upon his clothes which he has decorated with the spoils of his bed, his mind does not conceive the ideas of rags and straw, but of velvet, embroidery, and gold.

Swift too, in the sections of *A Tale of a Tub* I have discussed, accepts the world as he receives it; even the relativism of the fantasy of *Gulliver's Travels* is offset by its verisimilitude, by the unstinting conformity of its complex ideas to the realities of simple ones. And Johnson's most deeply felt praise of Shakespeare was that he "holds up to his readers a faithful mirrour of manners and of life." But one of the great radical shifts of the eighteenth century, as M. H. Abrams has shown, is the shift from the mind as mirror (Locke's term) to the mind as lamp, creating its own light and its own reality: Rasselas is succeeded by Kubla Khan. Neoclassic literature uses metaphor mainly to enrich or encrust an objective subject. But the new language emerging at mid-century enables metaphor to *identify* (that is, give an identity to) its subject independently; it permits creation of a new reality. In a fine passage Paul Fussell describes precisely the phenomenon we are considering.

> To the humanist, metaphor, which operates like rapid or almost instantaneous simile, does not actually assert that 'a *is* b'; instead it suggests that 'a is *like* b.' Tenor and vehicle are never thought to interfuse; regardless of closeness of resemblance, the two terms in a comparison remain ultimately distinct. This distrust of the 'reality' of metaphor underlies Johnson's point when he tells Boswell: 'I do not approve of figurative expressions in addressing the Supreme Being; and I never use them. Taylor gives a very good advice: "Never lie in your prayers . . ." ' (BLJ, IV, 294—5). But within the monistic rhetorical world all the way from Shelley to Wallace Stevens the metaphor is so far from being a 'lie' that instead it becomes the avenue, and often the sole avenue, to reality: the two terms of a figure actually fuse and thus generate a more 'real' third thing.[61]

New realities, creativity—these are the delusions of madmen, fevers of the poetic fit. In the mid-eighteenth century the chains and shackles around madness have been quietly unlocked. Now a few prisoners step forward to speak.

CHAPTER SIX

Cowper and Blake

The authentic voice of the madman, drowned out by the belligerent sanity of the Augustan era, is heard everywhere in the "age of sensibility." The phrase is Northrop Frye's, and he uses it in a provocative essay to describe the period extending roughly from 1760 to 1800, what other scholars sometimes call slightingly the "pre-Romantic period."[1] It is a truism that the best poets of the age of sensibility were mad—Collins, Smart, Cowper, Blake, Chatterton, Burns; these are the men, as Frye says, who give a special, elusive literary character to their time, and in most instances their madness (or melancholy) subsumes or stands for their special quality. (Indeed, A. E. Housman once claimed that the only *true* poets of the eighteenth century were those late mad ones.[2]) Frye himself characterizes this poetry as oracular, repetitious, unconventional, primitive in certain ways. "It expresses itself as an imaginative animism, or treating everything in nature as though it had human feelings or qualities." In such an age the poet himself becomes a very different figure from, say, a public moralist-satirist like Pope.

> The poetry of process is oracular, and the medium of the oracle is often in an ecstatic or trance-like state: autonomous voices seem to speak through him. . . . The free association of words, in which sound is prior to sense, is often a literary way of representing insanity. In Rimbaud's terrifyingly accurate phrase, poetry of the associative or oracular type

> requires a "dérèglement de tous les sens." Hence the
> qualities that make a man an oracular poet are often the
> qualities that work against, and sometimes destroy, his social
> personality. Far more than the time of Rimbaud and
> Verlaine is this period of literature a period of the *poète
> maudit*. The list of poets over whom the shadows of mental
> breakdown fell is far too long to be coincidence.[3]

Finally, he remarks that the poetry of process, as he terms it, tends to regard metaphor and image not as resemblance but as reality.

Christopher Smart is a famous example of what Frye has in mind: a poet whose best work is enigmatic and superficially formless, supposedly written while Smart was confined to a madhouse because of his obsessive public praying. (He would drop suddenly to his knees at any time and require everyone to join him. Johnson saw nothing wrong in this and remarked that he would "as lief pray with Kit Smart as any one else."[4]) Yet Smart's poems have nothing to say about madness, though they may well have grown out of it. Nor do they shed much light on late eighteenth-century England's changing attitudes toward irrationality. The general response of readers in the 1760s to Smart's confinement and the subsequent publication of *Song to David*, in fact, was crushingly negative: "Peace be to the manes of his departed muse," wrote the *Critical Review* (July 1763); "I have seen his *Song of David* and from thence conclude him as mad as ever," William Mason told Thomas Gray. One critic worked a new version of the Augustan metaphor of blindness:

> Wrapt in a Vision, he presumed to sing
> The attributes of Heaven's Eternal King:
> But O! approaching towards the Throne of Light,
> Its flashing splendors overpowered his sight.
> Hence blind on Earth, behold him sadly stray;
> 'Tis we must cheer the horrors of his way.

Even his poem with the promising title "Reason and Imagination" proves to be only a conventional fable of reconciliation and judgment. What Smart and the other mad poets share is a style, not a subject. Their styles seem in every case to exist as extensions of their personalities, private and energetic, frequently indifferent to conventional forms. Often, in fact, their style serves as costume or mask for them; it extends some buried or repressed aspect of the poet's personality, as in the case of Chatterton, and makes it articulate. Yet these mad poets of the age of sensibility can hardly be taken in the profounder sense that Wordsworth uses to describe the poet's vatic task:

> Some call'd it madness—such, indeed it was. . . .
> If prophesy be madness; if things viewed
> By poets of old time, and higher up
> By the first men, earth's first inhabitants,
> May in these tutored days no more be seen
> With undisorder'd sight.
>
> [*The Prelude*, 1805, III.149, 153–59]

Their private use of the oracular, ecstatic stance strikes us now as an overreaction, arising directly out of the mid-eighteenth century's increasing fascination with feelings for their own sake, not as shared values or beliefs. The age of sensibility presents stirrings, but not a movement.

From our point of view the period offers two major examples of the directions madness and literature took after the watershed decades of the 1750s and '60s. In both cases the attitudes toward madness expressed by victims and, so to speak, by audience were regressive, but only partially so. The Augustan fear and hatred had largely vanished—we have been tracing their dissolution in the two preceding chapters—and traditional ideas about the redemptive or divine powers of madness had returned. They returned, but not altogether in their ancient forms, not in the forms we examined in *King Lear*. They had been modified necessarily by the experience of three generations, more particularly by the growing importance of the scientific investigation of madness. The sheer accumulation of medical—that is to say, materialistic, rational—discussion of mental illness was formidable by the end of the period we speak of, and its approaches and content were absorbed almost as a habit of speech and thought. Pervasive, authoritative, in some sense it weighed down the English imagination.

In counterpoise we see reappearing at the end of the century a mythic turn of poetic imagination. (By *mythic* I mean only a dramatic representation of states of the human mind.) We have already remarked how the gods and devils who once caused madness can be understood as externalizations of inner states: Athena embodies Achilles' prudence. This symbolic external representation of the mind tends to disappear from the literature of the Augustan Age, though Pope's Dulness and Cave of Spleen are notable exceptions; things are simply *there*, like objects in Robbe-Grillet's novels. In the age of sensibility, however, when mythological poetry began again to proliferate, we can see through Collins's personifications and Gray's Celts toward the great mythmaking of the Romantics. Blake's mythic figures are undeniably externalizations of the human mind; Shelley's drama of Prometheus similarly shows various facets of self; to Wordsworth nature itself sometimes takes on such a role, as when in the famous scene in Book I of *The Prelude* the mountain looms like conscience over the boy and his stolen boat. These secular gods, moreover, like their holier predecessors, are perpetually in combat. Los and Urizen, Asia and Demogorgon—all such dramatizations of parts of the mind sway back and forth for mastery of the whole, just as reason and imagination do for the Augustans. Yet where the Augustans feared such combat and would end it if they could, the emerging Romantics rejoice in it. Only through such conflict, they say, can the splintered, civilized soul of modern man be reunited on a higher plane: or as Blake puts it, "Without Contraries is no progression." Schiller writing in 1788 sums up succinctly the new fearlessness: "In the case of a creative mind, it seems to me, the intellect has withdrawn its watchers from the gates, and the ideas rush in pell-mell, and only then does it review and inspect the multitude. You worthy critics . . . are ashamed or afraid of the momentary and passing madness which is found in all real creators, the longer or shorter duration of which distinguishes the thinking artist from the dreamer."[5] The image is Augustan. Madness is a mob, an army besieging a walled city, a battle. But the fear has vanished, and a certain eager dialectic has replaced it.

   In the light of what has so far been said it appears unnecessary to trace in any detail the reversals the Romantic era made of eighteenth-century attitudes toward madness. The Augustan suspicion of sleep, for example, was overturned altogether by the Romantic interest in its creative possibilities: Keats in "Sleep and Poetry" or the headnote to Coleridge's "Kubla Khan" suggests how far we have moved from Dulness's yawn. The criminality that the Augustans so significantly lump with madness gave way to a fascination with Cain, the Ancient Mariner, and Faust. The moon that had driven Dunces to true lunacy now mesmerized Endymion. The blindness in Swift's madmen became the "triple sight in blindness keen" that Keats discovers in Homer. And the solitary focus of these kinds of madness—their isolation and alienation—served as a wedge to split apart Augustan community. Yet the Romantic image of madness, whether applied to the poet himself or used by him, is still no more than an image enlisted in the service of a literary goal, just as the satiric image of madness had been. If we believe along with Geoffrey Hartman that one large element of nineteenth-century Romanticism is the diffused presence of the ancient "quest-romance," it becomes easier to see that creative madness for poets like Wordsworth, Byron, or Coleridge actually stands for that self-renewing retreat from ordinary reality (often to the underworld) which figures so prominently in the romance cycle. Where Pope and Swift turned to the image of madness to express the extent and the danger of a destructive dullness, the Romantic writers use the same image to communicate a sense of frustrated human possibilities— possibilities often frustrated in their view by exactly those Augustan pressures of community. These contradictory meanings of a single idea, each with its claims and truths, correspond roughly of course to the ancient theories of benevolent or demonic madness. Yet madness exists in Romantic literature, too, it ought to be emphasized, only as a metaphor for inspiriting power. No more than the Augustans are these later writers confronting the actual phenomenon of insanity. Our concern, however, is with the eighteenth-century experience rather than the Romantic. In this chapter I want only to point out the major paths leading out of the eighteenth-century world, not to guess at their ultimate destinations.

I

Unlike Blake, William Cowper was unquestionably insane; at

least three times in his life, possibly more, he required professional care, and he was once confined for something over two years in a private madhouse outside London—not, we should add, an inhumane and squalid prison like those madhouses Defoe campaigned against at the beginning of the century. Such places still existed in England in the late eighteenth century, and in numbers, as a Parliamentary committee had recently discovered. But Cowper was placed initially in the hands of Dr. Nathaniel Cotton, a man of great kindness (and a fellow poet); later when his illness recurred he found friends who devoted themselves sympathetically to his welfare.

Cowper himself regarded his madness far more severely than his contemporaries ever did. In his letters and frequently in his poems we catch the Augustan tone. Like Johnson he speaks of madness with all the authority of personal experience, and for him too there is nothing redemptive, nothing creative, nothing divine in madness. Unlike Johnson, however, he writes publicly about what he has endured, and, as these lines from "The Shrubbery" show, Augustan severity does not exclude an occasional note of self-pity:

> Oh, happy shades—to me unblest!
>   Friendly to peace, but not to me!
> How ill the scene that offers rest,
>   And heart that cannot rest, agree!
>
> This glassy stream, that spreading pine,
>   Those alders quiv'ring to the breeze,
> Might soothe a soul less hurt than mine,
>   And please, if any thing could please.
>
> But fix'd unalterable care
>   Foregoes not what she feels within,
> Shows the same sadness ev'ry where,
>   And slights the season and the scene.[6]

Cowper's sense of exclusion predominates here, his forlorn estrangement not only from other humans but even from natural life. His "fix'd unalterable care," the source of his madness, is the conviction that God has damned him to everlasting Hell, and the obscure, irreparable guilt in this conviction paralyzes him. In

1763, between the time he first attempted to commit suicide and the time he was committed, he described his state in "Lines Written During a Period of Insanity":

> Hatred and vengeance, my eternal portion,
> Scarce can endure delay of execution,
> Wait, with impatient readiness, to seize my
> Soul in a moment.
>
> Damn'd below Judas: more abhorr'd than he was,
> Who for a few pence sold his holy Master.
> Twice betrayed Jesus me, the last delinquent,
> Deems me the profanest.

Later he wrote a short account of his madness and recovery—conversion is a more appropriate word—in "A Song of Mercy and Judgment," a poem not published until 1890.

> Me thro' waves of deep affliction,
> Dearest Savior! thou has brought,
> Fiery deeps of sharp conviction
> Hard to bear and passing thought.
> Sweet the sound of Grace Divine,
> Sweet the grace which makes me thine.
>
> From the cheerful beams of morning
> Sad I turn'd my eyes away:
> And the shades of night returning
> Fill'd my soul with new dismay.
> Grace Divine, &c.
>
> Bound and watch'd, lest life abhorring
> I should my own death procure,
> For to me the Pit of Roaring
> Seem'd more easy to endure.
> Grace Divine, &c.
>
> Fear of Thee, with gloomy sadness,
> Overwhelm'd thy guilty worm,
> Till reduc'd to moping madness
> Reason sank beneath the storm.
> Sweet the sound, &c.
>
> Then what soul-distressing noises

> Seem'd to reach me from below,
> Visionary scenes and voices,
>   Flames of Hell and screams of woe.
>   Grace Divine, &c.
>
> But at length a word of healing
> Sweeter than an angel's note,
>   From the Savior's lips distilling
>   Chas'd despair and chang'd my lot.
>   Sweet the sound, &c.

By no means are we in the presence of a visionary madman; fear,
not ecstasy, shakes him. More than once in his poetry, in fact,
Cowper uses the word "overwhelmed" to describe his madness,
here and powerfully at the conclusion of "The Castaway":

> We perish'd, each alone:
> But I beneath a rougher sea,
> And whelm'd in deeper gulphs than he.

His helplessness and his blind terror at the forces set against him
seem to us less irrational than the fantasies and obsessions of other
madmen we have considered. Not fancying himself a king or a
bottle, he seems less ridiculous to us, and if his imagination is at
fault, we nevertheless respond not so much to his delusion as to
his genuine suffering. (John Clare's poem "Badger" has a similar
effect.) We tend to perceive him in the same way Harley
perceives the mad young woman of Bedlam, and we hear his
voice not with amusement, but with a deep, miserable understanding. His story, moreover, may in its outline remind us of
King Lear: the plunge downward to the "Pit of Roaring," the
storm that reason sinks beneath, above all the religious meanings
of rescue and healing. But Cowper describes his salvation in
unmistakable eighteenth-century accents:

> All at once my chains were broken,
> From my feet my fetters fell,
> And that word in pity spoken,
>   Snatched me from the gates of Hell.

And ultimately whatever Lear he plays is a pathetic, not a

sublime character. No titanic rage or willfulness exalts his madness; the scale is smaller and far more human.

The sad truth is that the recovery Cowper celebrates was not permanent; periodically his madness reasserted itself throughout his life, and although as time went on he wrote less openly of his own experience, his descriptions of madness remained much the same. In the didactic poem "Retirement," written about 1781, we find another, more elaborate picture of the melancholy madman (Cowper's comments on madness, like Johnson's, are nearly all commentary on his own case):

> Look where he comes—in this embow'r'd alcove—
> Stand close conceal'd, and see a statue move:
> Lips busy, and eyes fixt, foot falling slow,
> Arms hanging idly down, hands clasp'd below,
> Interpret to the marking eye distress,
> Such as its symptoms can alone express.
> That tongue is silent now; that silent tongue
> Could argue once, could jest or join the song,
> Could give advice, could censure or commend,
> Or charm the sorrows of a drooping friend.
>
> [283–92]

He anticipates and censures the laughter that such a figure might inspire—certainly *did* inspire a generation earlier:

> This, of all maladies that man infest,
> Claims most compassion, and receives the least.
>
> But, with a soul that ever felt the sting
> Of sorrow, sorrow is a sacred thing:
> Not to molest, or irritate, or raise
> A laugh at his expense, is slender praise;
>
> 'Tis not, as heads that never ache suppose,
> Forg'ry of fancy, and a dream of woes;
> Man is an harp whose chords elude the sight,
> Each yielding harmony dispos'd aright;
> The screws revers'd, (a task which if he please
> God in a moment executes with ease)
> Ten thousand thousand strings at once go loose,
> Lost, till he tune them, all their pow'r and use.
>
> [301 ff.]

Here man is clearly a Coleridgean harp, not a machine, and
Cowper is painfully sensitive to the way great forces sweep over
it, tuning or untuning it at will. He conceives of madness as
almost primitive, viewing it as a supernatural malady, "sacred,"
turned on and off by an inscrutable divinity.

To the rendering of madness as sorrow, which is the staple of
his poetic accounts, Cowper adds another dimension, one hinted
at in the lines just quoted, in his *Memoir of the Early Life of
William Cowper, Esq., Written by Himself*. This extraordinary
piece of autobiography retells the story we have already heard in
the "Song of Mercy and Judgment," Cowper's first attack of
madness at the age of 31. Just when the *Memoir* was written we
cannot say, although a date in the late 1760s seems likely, for at
that time Cowper had recovered and was enjoying for the first
time the reflective peace of his new home in Olney. In any case,
although it was not published until 1816, some years after the
poet's death, its contents were known earlier through Southey's
and Hayley's biographies. Because Cowper was by then so closely
identified with the Evangelical faction of English religion and
because the *Memoir* tells the concurrent stories of his madness
and his conversion, the real interest and importance of the book
were instantly obscured by the religious quarrels that started up
around it. The editions and the reviews that followed took up
constantly the question of whether Cowper's suicidal insanity was
the result of spurious and degrading Evangelical enthusiasm, or
whether indeed Evangelical passion alone had saved him from a
lifetime of madness. It is a question that ran in a general form
throughout the eighteenth century—we glanced at the American
Great Awakening of 1740 in chapter 2—and it stirred combative
energies on both sides difficult for us in our secular twilight to
appreciate.

Cowper's *Memoir* belongs ostensibly to that typical Evangelical subgenre, the personal history, exemplified best in such
documents as John Wesley's *Journal* or Jonathan Edwards's
Personal Narrative, and like them it tells in direct fashion the
basically simple story of a sinner's conversion. From our point of
view, however, Cowper also tells in the same direct way the story
of his madness:

> At eleven o'clock, my brother called upon me, and in

about an hour after his arrival, that distemper of mind, which I had so ardently wished for, actually seized me. While I traversed the apartment in the most horrible dismay of soul, expecting every moment that the earth would open and swallow me up; my conscience scaring me, the avenger of blood pursuing me, and the city of refuge out of reach and out of sight; a strange and horrible darkness fell upon me. If it were possible, that a heavy blow could light on the brain, without touching the skull, such was the sensation I felt. I clapped my hand to my forehead, and cried aloud through the pain it gave me. At every stroke, my thoughts and expressions became more wild and incoherent; all that remained clear was the sense of sin, and the expectation of punishment. These kept undisturbed possession all through my illness, without interruption or abatement.[7]

After so many pages covering so many years, how astonishing that here at last is our first account of the experience of madness! Whatever reservations one might hold about Cowper's tone of voice or the nature of his delusions, surely we come here to a new moment, when the madman speaks to us—and we can hear and understand him. That dialogue with insanity—what Foucault calls Freud's major contribution to psychiatry—took place before when we listened to Lear's madness with all possible attention, but now in Cowper's words we encounter, not imagined madness, but undeniably madness itself, the voice of a human being speaking across some mysterious, still-dark divide.

And yet as the excitement of such a meeting fades, how deflating it is in truth, how unmysterious. For Cowper speaks calmly, almost monotonously. He tells us flatly the time of day, the place, the symptoms; even his recital of fears—"expecting every moment that the earth would open and swallow me up"—somehow lacks energy. We remember that Cowper is here consciously holding himself stiffly at a distance from his experience, naturally fearful of falling back into it. But so intimate a passage still should not come to us so placidly. Our minds may go back to a similar point in *The English Malady*, where George Cheyne launches into the story of his own melancholy crisis, its symptoms and treatment, complete in such homey matters as his diet and regularity. Cheyne too approaches madness in a way that might be called reductive: difficult of cure, a creation of manifold circumstances, but controllable, an "illness" as Cowper soberly says. Both Cheyne and Cowper are writing propaganda of a certain kind, exemplary case histories, and necessarily they engage our sympathies. But both men are detached; our sympathies are not their primary objectives. Cheyne's narrative is deliberately cool because it claims to be scientific, factual rather than emotional. Cowper's account reads like a paragraph from Richardson (an uninspired one): "I screamed, and ran to the bed, and Mrs. Jervis screamed too; and he said, I'll do you no harm, if you forbear this noise; but otherwise take what follows." It belongs to Frye's category of the literature of process, re-creating the moment-to-moment life of a mind. Possibly we see only the undoubted superiority of art to life in Cowper's awkwardness, but possibly too he was pointing even more eagerly than Richardson toward a moral.

The moral basis of Cowper's madness is, in fact, established immediately in the *Memoir*. Once he has described the coming on of madness, Cowper draws up short (just at the moment, perhaps, when an Augustan might only begin): "It will be proper to draw a veil over the secrets of my prison-house; let it suffice to say, that the low state of body and mind, to which I was reduced, was perfectly well calculated to humble the natural vainglory and pride of my heart."[8] Intimations of this moralistic perception of his madness are present, as we have said, in the "Song of Mercy and Judgment," but Cowper's next sentences declare it plainly: "These are the efficacious means which Infinite Wisdom thought meet to make use of for that purpose." "All that passed in this long interval of eight months, may be classed under two heads: conviction of sin, and despair of mercy. But blessed be the God of my salvation for every sigh I drew, for every tear I shed; since thus it pleased him to judge me here, that I might not be judged hereafter." God punishes him for his sins with madness, and thereby redeems him. It is just these lines, naturally, that set divines of the early nineteenth century off against one another. From our more secular perspective, however, we may be struck that the ancient notion of madness as punishment from the gods has reappeared, but in its milder Christian guise as suffering inflicted upon a chosen victim not to destroy but ultimately to save him. This is the movement upward, stripped of doctrine, that we find at the end of *King Lear*. And yet, stripped of doctrine, the conviction that one is a chosen victim also brings with it a tragic modulation. "Whom the gods would destroy," the Greeks said, "they first make mad." In Cowper's time, and ever more intensely thereafter, the alienated man attached to himself this heightened fatalism; and regularly the alienated man—it is an old-fashioned term for madness—would be the articulate, superior man, the melancholy man refined in the *poète maudit*.

> I thought of Chatterton, the marvellous Boy,
> The sleepless Soul that perished in his pride;
> Of Him who walked in glory and in joy
> Following his plough, along the mountain-side:
> By our own spirits are we deified:
> We Poets in our youth begin in gladness;
> But thereof come in the end despondency and madness.
>   ["Resolution and Independence"]

Wordsworth's lines could never have been written by the great Augustans (though they might have been written about them). The sense of a man deified by his poetic gift is too strong for Swift or Pope. And the destructiveness of the gift is likewise incomprehensible. If the poet is a marked man, as indeed Pope sometimes thought he was, it is because, on the surface at least, the world is filled with madmen, not otherwise.

II

It is tempting to see in the tragic aspect of Cowper's madness the beginnings of that stock Romantic figure, the poet haunted by his own genius, and Cowper's biographers and friends have contributed to such an impression. William Hayley observes that the calamity of madness strikes human beings "perhaps in proportion as they have received from nature those delightful, but dangerous gifts, a heart of exquisite tenderness, and a mind of creative energy."[9] An anonymous commentator sighs that the "uncontrollable force" of Cowper's imagination "during periods of despondency may make a plain man thankful that his judgment has not been perverted, or his self-command destroyed by the dear-bought distinctions of genius."[10] Yet the *Memoir* itself gives not the slightest sign that its author is a poet (and

Cowper had not in fact turned seriously to writing yet). Futhermore, his critics, when not pursuing religious issues, frequently offer another line of comment. It is possible, after all, to consider the poet's madness in a sympathetic, even a tragic light and at the same time ponder coolly its medical side. Hayley, for example, declares his opinion that Cowper's "mental disorder arose from a scorbutic habit, which, when his perspiration was obstructed, occasioned an unsearchable obstruction in the freer parts of his frame."[11] More fancifully, he also speculates that "Thwarted in love, the native fire of his temperament turned impetuously into the kindred channel of devotion. The smothered flames of desire uniting with the vapours of constitutional melancholy, and the fervency of religious zeal, produced altogether that irregularity of corporeal sensation, and of mental health."[12] The publisher of the *Memoir* contributed a preface in which he emphasizes Cowper's "constitutional tendency towards derangement."[13] Perhaps the most remarkable of these scientific explanations is presented by R. R. Madden (fittingly named) in a little book called *Infirmities of Genius*. For him Cowper is one of many examples of the ways in which literary geniuses aggravate their inherent physical weaknesses: "The most frequent disorders of literary men are dyspepsia and hypochondria, and in extreme cases, the termination of these maladies is in some cerebral disorder, either mania, epilepsy, or paralysis."[14] In the case of Cowper in particular Madden discusses symptoms in a clinical but not unsympathetic manner and concludes complacently "That, under happier circumstances"—he alludes to Cowper's Evangelical friends—"and with due attention to the digestive organs, Cowper might have been rescued from the misery he endured through life."[15]

These pseudo-medical investigations might appear to us now as so much quackery or whimsy, depending on our tempers; but above the details of diagnosis, I think, we can discern a general trend of more importance. Madden complains that Cowper's religiously oriented admirers "have looked upon his gloom as a supernatural visitation and not a human infirmity, which was explicable on any known principle of science." And he goes further to say: "*We have endeavored to divest his malady of the obscurity and mystery in which it has been involved.*"[16] Surely a new age was dawning when all the mystery of madness, the very heart of the ancient reverence for it, was being scrubbed away by medical science, when all the primitive possibilities of demonic possession or of supernatural visitation were disappearing in the full, clear light of common sense and science. If we consider the patient's diet and his nerves, the circumstances of his life and so forth, we may also consider fearlessly the patient himself; we may talk with him and, denying him the reality of his delusions and reinterpreting his language according to our ordinary standards, we may consider him less tragic than scorbutic. It is by now a familiar approach to madness. We have looked earlier at the growth of medical literature on mental illness and of medical practice, rising in a curve through the eighteenth century; at the spread of melancholy through every part of society; and at the impact of celebrated cases of madness like that of King George III on the English mind. Now at the beginning of the nineteenth century we find that the tide had swelled faster and farther than we may have imagined. It had brought with it a certain diminished view of madness, but also, since mental illness is now leveled with physical illness, it had brought with it the chance for cure and restoration.

Benjamin Rush, the great American physician, is representative:

> After the history that has been given of the distresses, despair, and voluntary death, which are induced by that partial derangement which has been described [i.e., melancholy], I should lay down my pen and bedew my paper with my tears, did I not know that the science of medicine has furnished a remedy for it, and that hundreds are now alive, and happy, who were once afflicted with it. Blessed science! which thus extends its friendly empire, not only over the evils of the bodies, but over those of the minds of the children of men.[17]

Rush acknowledges that madness or melancholy sometimes sharpens the wits of its victims and discovers new talents in them—he compares it to an earthquake that throws upon the surface new fossils from the soil—but such occasions are only curiosities. His real interests lie elsewhere, as this extract shows:

In reviewing the slender and inadequate means that have
been employed for ameliorating the condition of mad
people, we are led further to lament the slower progress of
humanity in its efforts to relieve them, than any other class
of the afflicted children of men. For many centuries they
have been treated like criminals, or shunned like beasts of
prey; or, if visited, it has been only for the purposes of
inhuman curiosity and amusement. Even the ties of
consanguinity have been dissolved by the walls of a madhouse, and sons and brothers have sometimes languished or
sauntered away their lives within them, without once
hearing the accents of a kindred voice. Happily these times
of cruelty to this class of our fellow creatures, and
insensibility to their sufferings, are now passing away. In
Great Britain, a human revolution, dictated by modern
improvements in the science of the mind, as well as of
medicine, has taken place in the receptacles of mad people.
. . . The clanking of chains, and the noise of the whip, are no
longer heard in their cells. They now taste of the blessings of
air, and light, and motion, in pleasant and shaded walks in
summer, and in spacious entries, warmed by stoves, in
winter, in both of which the sexes are separated, and alike
protected from the eye of the visitors of the hospital. In
consequence of these advantages, they have recovered the
human figure, and, with it, their long forgotten relationship
to their friends and the public.[18]

For all its humaneness and all its truth, all its revolutionary
goodness, this particular response to madness may still seem to us
deficient in some indistinct way. Every reform that our hearts
could have wished for the early eighteenth century is present and
established in Rush's account, yet uncomfortably, ungratefully,
we may feel it to be lacking some dimension of spirit even so. The
"human figure" that these patients recover is a familiar one,
indeed a thoroughly conventional one; cure is restoration, cure is
also conformity to some "long forgotten relationship" inflexible
in its normality. Quite possibly the scientific approach may seem
to us as reductive in the end as the Augustan hatred. "At
bottom," observes Jung, "we discover nothing new and unknown
in the mentally ill; rather, we encounter the substratum of our
own natures."[19] In his madness King Lear, in Maynard Mack's

phrase, "suffers his own nature." It is the nature of our own natures that something in Rush seems to deny.

III

On the surface it might easily seem that William Cowper and William Blake had little more in common than the friendship of William Hayley, biographer of the first and patron of the second.[20] Certainly two poets could hardly be more dissimilar. Blake in particular we might have expected to scorn Cowper's style of mind and poetry as timid, unimaginative, conventional. Yet strangely enough Blake in his later years appears to have thought often of Cowper and even in a tentative way to have identified their forsaken situations. In his notebook for the years 1808–11 he writes this poem, entitled "William Cowper, Esq[re]":

> For this is being a Friend just in the nick,
> Not when he's well, but waiting till he's sick.
> He calls you to his help: be you not mov'd
> Untill, by being Sick, his wants are prov'd.
>
> You see him spend his Soul in Prophecy.
> Do you believe it a confounded lie
> Till some Bookseller & the Public Fame
> Proves there is truth in his extravagant claim.
>
> For 'tis atrocious in a Friend you love
> To tell you any thing that he can't prove,
> And 'tis most wicked in a Christian Nation
> For any Man to pretend to Inspiration.[21]

And in about 1819 he made this note in the margin of Spurzheim's *Observations on the Deranged Manifestations of the Mind, or Insanity:*

> Cowper came to me and said: "O that I were insane always. I will never rest. Can you not make me truly insane? I will never rest till I am so. O that in the bosom of God I was hid. You retain health and yet are as mad as any of us all—over us all—mad as a refuge from unbelief—from Bacon, Newton and Locke."

[p. 772]

Madness is clearly the basis for Blake's friendliness, the common ground he thinks they meet on. Blake, of course, was not mad in any medical sense, as Cowper was, yet he was called madman so often that he sometimes ironically took up the role. As these dialogues with Cowper suggest, there are two special meanings that Blake brought to madness: the belief that the inspired man is always called mad in this world; and the belief, profoundly ironic, that in such a world insanity is healthy. These are not ideas that Cowper could have shared—one thinks of his conviction that his madness was punishment, an instance of divine mercy and wrath, or of his description of the madman as a motionless, passive, terrified, and suffering being. In these characteristic attitudes of Cowper we see little that Blake could have regarded patiently. The single point where their sympathies meet is in the alienation that madness brought to each of them, Cowper the stricken deer, Blake the dishonored prophet. But Cowper plays the outcast for its pathos; his response is meekness itself and self-hating depression. Blake turns his anger outward, and his "madness" blazes with defiance and with a superb, unwavering confidence.

The reason for Blake's confidence is to be found in the kind of madman he was, or people thought he was. Admirers of Blake are always expressing surprise that he should have been called mad by anyone—"The legends of Blake's 'madness' never seem to cease, despite all scholarly rebuttal," complains Harold Bloom.[22] Such puzzlement is unrealistic. The legends of Blake's madness persist because he wrote poetry that describes Milton entering his left foot, because he claimed to speak daily and hourly with the spirit of his dead brother and with other spirits, because he wrote long incomprehensible poems about unheard-of beings with names like Enitharmon and Golgonooza. In almost any age of human history such a man would have seemed insane. It is, in fact, surprising to hear critics maintaining that earlier ages would have understood and appreciated Blake, while his own mocked and neglected him. The fields of the past are strewn with the names of madmen or prophets who were neglected, misunderstood, even trampled by their ordinary fellows. What is striking in a way about Blake's career is not that so many people considered him insane but that so many people did not; and that, moreover, so many people listened attentively to what Crabb Robinson called Blake's "interesting insanities."

Cowper's madness was more comprehensible; the receptivity of science and of the culture itself to his kind of illness was growing steadily. But Blake was no melancholic. He was a visionary who rejoiced in his madness, who published and proclaimed it, and who fought back vigorously at times against what passed elsewhere for sanity. His first biographer, Alexander Gilchrist, writing in the mid-nineteenth century, observes sadly that attitudes toward madness have changed. "It is *only* within the last century and a half," he notes, that "the faculty of seeing visions could have been one to bring a man's sanity into question."[23] A madness like Cowper's, which is tending, even yearning, to return to sanity, can be understood and compassionated. A madness like Blake's, which rejects sanity and celebrates itself, threatens a rational people. And once the possibilities of its being a divine madness, even in the sense that Cowper's was, have faded, society's responses become quite limited: if the patient *will* not be helped, one determines only whether he is harmless. Robert Hunt's famous review of Blake's paintings in *The Examiner* (No. 90, 17 September 1809) hits chiefly at Blake's patrons. Blake himself is "an unfortunate lunatic, whose personal inoffensiveness secures him from confinement, and, consequently, of whom no public notice would have been taken, if he was not forced on the notice and animadversion of The EXAMINER, in having been held up to public admiration by many esteemed amateurs and professors as a genius in some respect original and legitimate."[24]

There is no guarantee that Blake would not have forced himself upon the public attention anyway. A great part of his madness consisted of anger at those who clung to what he regarded as insanities, and in the privacy of his poems he struck back. At John Flaxman, an artist and former friend, he scoffs in his notebook:

> "Madman" I have been call'd: "Fool" they call thee.
> I wonder which they Envy, Thee or Me?
>
> I mock thee not, tho' I by thee am Mocked.
> Thou call'st me Madman, but I call thee Blockhead.

[pp. 538, 539]

Flaxman, however, bears nothing like the brunt of Blake's anger. That falls, as the Spurzheim note declares, on his unholy trinity of Bacon, Newton, and Locke, augmented at times by supporting characters like Sir Joshua Reynolds or Voltaire. Again and again he lashes these symbols of rationalism; again and again he denounces the order and propriety they stand for. "Burke's Treatise on the Sublime & Beautiful," he asserts in his annotations to Reynolds's *Discourses*, "is founded on the Opinions of Newton & Locke; on this Treatise Reynolds has grounded many of his assertions in all his Discourses. I read Burke's Treatise when very Young; at the same time I read Locke on Human Understanding & Bacon's Advancement of Learning; on Every one of these Books I wrote my Opinions, & on looking them over find that my Notes on Reynolds in this Book are exactly Similar. I felt the same Contempt & Abhorrence then that I do now. They mock Inspiration & Vision. Inspiration & Vision was then, & now is, & I hope will always Remain, my Element, my Eternal Dwelling place; how can I then hear it Contemned without returning Scorn for Scorn?" (Pp. 476—77.) The extent of Blake's anger is frequently passed over, yet apart from the famous lyrics of Innocence and Experience, his poetry is filled with violence and "mental Fight," and the contest is always the same, between reason and imagination:

> "I must Create a System or be enslav'd by another Man's.
> I will not Reason & Compare: my business is to Create."
> [p. 629]

To Blake the character of the creating imagination is radically different from, and greater than, the faculty understood by the Augustans as fancy or the power of bringing images to mind; fundamentally different from Johnson's sense of it as obsessive hope or fear. In a 1799 letter he sets out his conception of imagination, in a framework that may remind us of my earlier discussions of blindness and vision.

> I feel that a Man may be happy in This World. And I know that This World Is a World of Imagination & Vision. I see Every thing I paint In This World, but Every body does not see alike. To the Eyes of a Miser a Guinea is more beautiful

than the Sun, & a bag worn with the Use of Money has more beautiful proportions than a Vine filled with Grapes. The tree which moves some to tears of joy is in the Eyes of others only a Green thing that stands in the way. Some See Nature all Ridicule & Deformity, & by these I shall not regulate my proportions; & Some Scarce see Nature at all. But to the Eyes of the Man of Imagination, Nature is Imagination itself. As a Man is, So he Sees. As the Eye is formed, such are its Powers. You certainly Mistake, when you say that the Visions of Fancy are not to be found in This World. To Me This World is all One continued Vision of Fancy or Imagination.[25]

It is the whole Augustan view of the mind that Blake is rejecting, the view that leads Johnson to define "visionary" as "imaginary; not real." The emphasis of Locke, as I have said before, falls heavily on the mind's limitations, its liabilities and weaknesses; and the emphases of Newton and Bacon, as Blake read them, fall on facts, memory, and analysis, especially on a perception of nature as objective and without spiritual life. "It is not in Terms that Reynolds & I disagree," Blake says. "Two Contrary Opinions can never by any Language be made alike. I say, Taste & Genius are Not Teachable or Acquirable, but are born with us. Reynolds says the Contrary" (p. 474). Blake means born with *all* of us. His view of the mind begins with its powers, its powers of imagination, and these are creative powers that affirm the holiness of every man. Like Keats, Blake is sublimely uninterested in certainties of logic. Willingly he gives himself up to his inspiration and sets down in art and poetry the dictates of his visions. "It is Evident that Reynolds Wish'd none but Fools to be in the Arts & in order to this, he calls all others Vague Enthusiasts or Madmen. What has Reasoning to do with the Art of Painting?" (P. 458.)

The anger that pervades so much of Blake's poetry was fueled in part by his exclusion from the established orthodoxy symbolized by Reynolds and the rationalists. "The Enquiry in England," he remarks, "is not whether a Man has Talents & Genius, But whether he is Passive & Polite & a Virtuous Ass & Obedient to Noblemen's Opinions in Art & Science. If he is, he is a Good Man. If Not, he must be Starved" (pp. 452–53). Or, as he puts it in *Milton*, the task is

To cast off Bacon, Locke & Newton from Albion's covering,
To take off his filthy garments & clothe him with Imagination,
To cast aside from Poetry all that is not Inspiration,
That it no longer shall dare to mock with the aspersion of Madness
Cast on the Inspired by the tame high finisher of paltry Blots
Indefinite. . . .

[p. 533]

The poem "Mary" from the Pickering Manuscripts, in itself a slight effort, re-creates the dilemma of a truly good person (a poet-prophet) in Reynolds's world. "Sweet Mary" attends a ball for the first time and is called "beautiful" and an "angel" by all the men and ladies there. Next morning when she arises to go among her new friends,

> Some said she was proud, some call'd her a whore,
> And some, when she passed by, shut to the door;
> A damp cold came o'er her, her blushes all fled,
> Her lillies & roses are blighted & shed.

She bemoans the beauty that sets her apart, and resolves to dress plainly and stay from the ball.

> She went out in Morning attir'd plain & neat;
> "Proud Mary's gone Mad," said the Child in the Street;
> She went out in Morning in plain neat attire,
> And came home in Evening bespatter'd with mire.

[p. 428]

It is what in his more maudlin moments Blake saw happening to himself, as his painting was passed by or laughed at, as his poetry was dismissed as mad. In other moments he could write with wicked relish that he was "delighted with the enjoyments of Genius, which to Angels look like torment and insanity" (p. 150). The unwelcome otherness thus thrust upon him impelled him, as did his doctrine of imagination, to sympathize with all the other visible outcasts in his world—not the kind of sympathy Johnson felt for everything wretched and unhappy in this life, but a sympathy built more obviously on kinship in a common un-deserved fate; not sympathy for the human condition, but fraternal feeling for members of the same oppressed class. Hence we find so many of Blake's poems commiserating with the poor and the victimized, commiserating especially with children, who represented in late eighteenth-century London the most intense symbolic concentration of all these qualities.

The obverse to Blake's sympathy is satire. Recognizing that prosaic men call men of imagination mad, Blake almost cheerfully returns the favor. When he is not accepting the title of madman ("All Pictures that's Painted with Sense & with Thought / Are Painted by Madmen as sure as a Groat"), like Pope he calls his critics lunatics themselves. We have seen instances already, but perhaps the finest stroke is the little poem from *Poetical Sketches* "Mad Song." Here a madman, one like Tom o' Bedlam, sings in the nighttime wilderness and runs terrified from the dawn:

> Like a fiend in a cloud,
>   With howling woe,
> After night I do croud,
>   And with night will go;
> I turn my back to the east,
> From whence comforts have increas'd;
> For light doth seize my brain
> With frantic pain.
>
> [p. 9]

The madman foreshadows Urizen and all Blake's other specters of reason, turning foolishly from the Christian light of the east, from the saving grace of imagination. Like this poor benighted figure and like the sterile angels of *The Marriage of Heaven and Hell*, Blake says, the world enslaved to another man's system harbors true madness; and the madness of that world is fruitless, uncreative, uninspired. In the Augustan Age one means of describing this conflict between madness and reason was to call it a conflict between light and darkness, sight and blindness. Blake uses the same idiom when he calls men blind, although understandably an artist employs "blind" to mean "insightful" infrequently: for him the conflict is between two visions; in *The Marriage of Heaven and Hell* between the way the Devil sees the Monster and the way the Angel sees it. In both cases, however, when Blake calls the "sane" world "mad," he is exercising a rhetoric fundamentally different from that of the Augustans, who were also given, as we have seen, to calling life mad. When Swift declares all the world to be like the inhabitants of Bedlam or Hogarth nails a shilling on the wall of Bedlam to show that Britannia shares the Rake's folly, the idea expressed is one of simple equation between Bedlam and outside society: both are dismissed as equal and as equally absurd. Just as the lunatic is obsessed by his vision, so is the general or the merchant or the dunce; except for the circumstance of confinement they are alike. But for Blake the ordinary sane man is not like the poet-madman. There is no equation. The ordinary man is fallen, enslaved by reason, unable to use his imagination, afraid of the frantic pain of light. Only the "madman" is free and fulfilled.

In Blake's hands this reversal of meaning is often presented satirically, as in the "Mad Song," and indeed it is one of the measures of his real sanity (in the ordinary sense) that he responds to abuse with such wry, confident irony. The *Songs of Innocence and Experience* together constitute a kind of satiric comparison of things as they are and as they should be.[26] Another work, *The Marriage of Heaven and Hell*, satirizes the doctrines of Swedenborg, which Blake had recently turned against; but in its exuberance the *Marriage* touches any number of Blake's other enemies in a chaotic procession that reminds us of nothing else in literature. Swedenborg early ceases to serve as Blake's primary target (for pages he forgets him entirely) while the contrast between sane angels and mad devils captures his imagination. The "Proverbs of Hell" are sardonic gnomisms, as full of energy as their devilish creator:

> Damn braces: Bless relaxes.
> You never know what is enough unless you know what is more
>   than enough.
> The cistern contains: the fountain overflows.

The "Memorable Fancies" are comic episodes or encounters between the forces of containment and those of imagination. He writes in mock-formality:

> An Angel came to me and said: "O pitiable foolish young
> man! O horrible! O dreadful state! consider the hot burning

dungeon thou art preparing for thyself to all eternity, to
which thou art going in such career."

I said: "Perhaps you will be willing to shew me my eternal
lot, & we will contemplate together upon it, and see
whether your lot or mine is most desirable."

[p. 155]

Blake's fantasy overwhelms the Angel, and at the end he adds
"Note: This Angel, who is now become a Devil, is my particular
friend; we often read the Bible together in its infernal or
diabolical sense, which the world shall have if they behave well"
(p. 158). He talks with the prophet Isaiah too and asks: "does a
firm perswasion that a thing is so, make it so?" Isaiah replies: "All
poets believe that it does, & in ages of imagination this firm
perswasion removed mountains" (p. 153). It is the same point
Blake makes sarcastically in his poem to Cowper:

> For 'tis atrocious in a Friend you love
> To tell you any thing that he can't prove.

We may be reminded of the astronomer in *Rasselas*, who cannot
prove that he controls the weather: "It is sufficient that I feel this
power."

IV

What I have been calling Blake's satirical mode is plainly his
sense of mission, his single-minded determination to name and
publish the moral errors of his generation. For him as well as for
Swift and Pope the times are out of joint. His perception of moral
error reverses the Augustan one, of course: where Pope denounces the prevalence of madness, Blake despises the prevalence of
reason; where *The Dunciad* shows a world destroyed by
irrationality, *Milton* shows a world redeemed by it. Yet it is useful
to keep in mind Blake's ties to Augustan literature, even if those
ties are merely points of rebellion. If he reminds us at all of the
great satirists of the early eighteenth century, in fact, he probably
reminds us of Swift (though it may be worth noting that the
greatest unread poems of the century are *The Dunciad* and
Blake's prophecies). Swift and Blake share the same sustaining
anger, and the younger Swift at least shares Blake's confidence in

the correctness of his own standards. They have in common too a certain clarity almost too powerful for their purposes. In Blake, outside certain *Songs of Experience*, we hear that voice most sharply in the early prose satiric piece "An Island in the Moon," written about 1784–85 and directed against a circle of Blake's pretentiously intellectual friends. Almost the whole of chapter 6, for example, recalls Swift's investigations into surface and anatomy in the digression on madness:

> "Ah!" said Sipsop, "I only wish Jack Tearguts had had the cutting of Plutarch. He understands anatomy better than any of the Ancients. He'll plunge his knife up to the hilt in a single drive, and thrust his fist in, and all in the space of a Quarter of an hour. He does not mind their crying, tho' they cry ever so."
>
> > [p. 50]

Then the Cynic sings a similarly surgical ditty, which includes such stanzas as these:

> And when the child began to swell,
>   He shouted out aloud,
> "I've found the dropsy out, & soon
>   Shall do the world more good."
>
> He took up fever by the neck
>   And cut out all its spots,
> And thro' the holes which he had made
>   He first discover'd guts.
>
> > [p. 51]

Sipsop concludes with a remark disturbingly analogous to Swift's on the woman flayed: "There was a woman having her cancer cut, & she shriek'd so that I was quite sick." Besides such thumps at human obtuseness, Blake also indulges in a variety of excremental joking (we see this frequently in his notebooks); and he gives vent to a cynical misogynism that recalls the tirades of Swift and Lear:

> Hail Matrimony, made of Love,
> To thy wide gates how great a drove

On purpose to be yok'd do come!
Widows & maids & youths also,
That lightly trip on beauty's toe,
    Or sit on beauty's bum.

For if a Damsel's blind or lame,
Or Nature's hand has crooked her frame,
    Or if she's deaf, or is wall eyed,
Yet if her heart is well inclined,
Some tender lover she shall find
    That panteth for a Bride.

[p. 56]

We see the Augustan side of Blake in many of the themes he takes up, satirically or not. His treatment is typically a reaction against the Augustan expression of them, but that reaction underscores the extent to which the new age of the late eighteenth century rejected the immediate past on that past's own terms. We have mentioned, for example, Blake's deep sympathy for children, a sympathy that symbolically embraces all deviants from the adult standards of sanity and reason. Locke in the *Essay on Human Understanding* (or "An Easy of Humming Understanding," as Blake calls it) characteristically illustrates the negative side of the human mind by turning naturally to examples of children, idiots, and madmen. Like every Augustan he looks at childhood not in the Romantic way as a magical time of life, but as a time of thwarted powers. The Augustan interest is in the adult, rational mind, as Johnson says, between the "ignorance of infancy, or imbecility of age."[27] In contrast Blake observes,

I am happy to find a Great Majority of Fellow Mortals who can Elucidate my Visions, & Particularly they have been Elucidated by Children, who have taken a greater delight in contemplating my Pictures than I even hoped. Neither Youth nor Childhood is Folly or Incapacity. Some children are Fools & so are some Old Men. But There is a vast Majority on the side of Imagination or Spiritual Sensation.[28]

Again, he says: "Jesus supposes every Thing to be Evident to the Child & to the Poor and Unlearned. Such is the Gospel" (p. 774).

For Blake children and childhood mean more than merely an alternative to Augustan adulthood; they typify that sought-for state of innocence in which imagination unhorses reason. Swift or Johnson might well comment sourly on the similarity between Bedlam and the nursery, but the parallel would delight Blake rather than daunt him.

Children are also closely bound in his mind with another Augustan theme that we have touched on, that of poverty. "The Child, the Poor, the Unlearned": the *Songs of Innocence and Experience* contain the most moving of Blake's attacks on the inhumanity of an age that impoverished children for profit. When we recall how poverty was so frequently used as an image of dullness by Pope and Swift, we see how far Blake carries his sympathy; and we see that he looks forward no more than a handful of years to Wordsworth's equally sympathetic and sometimes reverential contemplation of the childish, the poor, the idiotic.

We may also believe, though the point is stretching, that Blake's frequent use of animals as symbols of positive meanings—of energy, like the tiger; of innocence, like the lamb—is in part a reaction to the brutalizing view of the animal world assumed by the Augustans. Ned Ward's leopard that pisses like a madman or Pope's dying pheasant belongs to another world than that of the tiger, the Ancient Mariner's albatross, or even Smart's cat Jeoffrey. Blake's world is a world charged with significance; in it "all sensible objects" (p. 153) are animated by our imaginations; in the Augustan world such objects and animals exist merely as objects, unrelated to human meanings, lifeless links in a chain of being.

One final theme—properly speaking, an image—is common to Blake and to the Augustans. We have remarked before how Johnson so often speaks of the chains and shackles of the human condition, how he applies the image to the madness of uncontrolled imagination. Blake too speaks of the "mind forg'd Manacles." But his meaning is precisely the reverse of Johnson's. "Note: The Reason Milton wrote in fetters when he wrote of Angels & God, and at liberty when of Devils & Hell, is because he was a true Poet and of the Devil's party without knowing it" (p. 150). "The Giants who formed this world into its sensual existence and now seem to live in it in chains, are in truth the causes of its life & the sources of all activity; but the chains are the cunning of weak and tame minds which have power to resist energy; according to the proverb, the weak in courage is strong in cunning" (p. 155). The Augustan fear was well founded, for this is the language of revolution. The man of imagination, whom the world calls mad, must cast off his chains, burst free. He must be free, Blake says, to live as he pleases in the only reality that matters, the reality he creates, the reality of his imagination.

> I assert for My Self that I do not behold the outward Creation & that to me it is hindrance & not Action; it is as the Dirt upon my feet, No part of Me. "What," it will be Question'd, "When the Sun rises, do you not see a round disk of fire somewhat like a Guinea?" O no, no, I see an Innumerable company of the Heavenly host crying, 'Holy, Holy, Holy is the Lord God Almighty.' I question not my Corporeal or Vegetative Eye any more than I would Question a Window concerning a Sight. I look thro' it & not with it.
>
> [p. 617]

The literal chains have already been lifted from the madman at the end of the eighteenth century. Blake cries out to release us from those chains we are blind to.

V

There is one further image by which we can take the measure of where we have arrived. In all that we have said *King Lear* has been present as an embodiment of traditional ideas about madness and also as a medium through which the eighteenth century sometimes confronted madness.[29] In *King Lear* the Augustans, like every succeeding age, witnessed the terrifying phenomenon of a mind utterly and forcibly removed from the world of ordinary reality; and their response, apart from a few men like Burke and Johnson, seems to our modern minds curiously inadequate, a response of puzzlement, disapproval, perhaps even obtuseness. They make no acknowledgment that Lear's madness may resemble the madness of Plato's poet or lover, which unites madman and truth in a kind of transcendent ecstasy. The meaning of a violent transport like Lear's madness—its *truth*—they simply deny, for by all their instincts such a path to truth is treacherous and uncertain, its outcome obscure. And Lear's truths, as I have said, are only satirical. The age of Pope and Swift is not likely to be impressed that madness was necessary to teach an old man how this world goes.

In the age Blake introduces, *King Lear* comes to stand at the head of Shakespeare's creations. The eighteenth century, which had doubted Lear's sanity from the beginning of the play and had seen nothing redemptive in his madness, would hardly recognize the Lear of Shelley or Hazlitt or Lamb or Keats. "The greatness of Lear," according to Lamb, who believed that the play was too profound to be acted, "is not in corporal dimension, but in intellectual: the explosions of his passion are terrible as a volcano: they are storms turning up and disclosing to the bottom that sea, his mind, with all its vast riches. It is his mind which is laid bare" ("On the Tragedies of Shakespeare"). "The mind of Lear," argues Hazlitt,

> staggering between the weight of attachment and the hurried movements of passion, is like a tall ship driven about by the winds, buffeted by the furious waves, but that still rides above the storm, having its anchor fixed in the bottom of the sea; or it is like the sharp rock circled by the eddying whirlpool that foams and beats against it, or like the solid promontory pushed from its basis by the force of an earthquake.
>
> [*Characters of Shakespeare's Plays*]

These are splendid images; if we recall Burke strictly, they are *sublime* images.[30] But the sublime madman is not an idea that the eighteenth century could have taken seriously, even in its most determined Gothic moments. To the Augustans, what strengths the mind possesses are snatched from us by madness, not created by it: could Locke have spoken of the vast riches of the human mind? When Boswell compares Johnson's mind to a gladiator driving back the beasts of unreason and fear that attack him, we see what the eighteenth century understood as the strengths of the mind, for it is Johnson's courageous reason alone that sustains him, and the battle itself is perpetual and dangerous.[31] But when

Hazlitt and Lamb describe Lear's mind, they ask us to admire not only his courage but also his passions; in the Romantic spectacle both elements are equal, the fixed anchor of his mind and also the sea that threatens it. Boswell imagines a single human being, a Roman, bounded by the walls of the Coliseum. We are to respect and fear the beasts of unreason, but not to admire them. If we remember Swift's description of the brain as "a Crowd of little Animals, but with Teeth and Claws extremely sharp, . . . or like Bees in perpendicular swarm upon a Tree, or like a Carrion corrupted into Vermin,"[32] the habitual eighteenth-century association of madness and bestiality seems more than ever comprehensible; the animals in the arena of Johnson's mind are not to be mistaken for Blake's tiger.

What Boswell shows us—the theme runs through all that we have been saying about the eighteenth century—is a mind in control of itself. What the Romantics show is a mind going out of control, a mind whose horizons are boundless but whose fate is uncertain. The two poets we have been considering here suggest the fates in store for such a mind. Cowper prefigures the poet whose madness is merely medical—the tender, alienated writer who succumbs periodically to the larger Bedlam that the modern city in particular and society in general is becoming. Blake represents an attempt to return to the bardic role, to the creative madness of inspiration and divinity; yet he too remains alienated, as the ancient poet never was, from his own world. Unlike Lawrence's artist Loerke, who believes art should interpret industrialism, Blake struggles still to interpret the spirit to a distracted or indifferent audience. But the high hopefulness with which the Romantic period opened slights these for other possibilities. The eighteenth century had constricted the "soul's immensity" of Lear; in Nahum Tate's version they acted out a drama in which sinful, willful madness was punished but reformed, a drama of reassurance for an age of distrust. The Romantics surrendered to the opposite temptation. They leapt into Lear's madness as if into the sea, believing that those forces that carry us out of "Reality's dark coil," as Coleridge calls it, may yet carry us nearer a life that both reason and imagination can grasp as partners.

Notes

NOTES TO THE PREFACE

1. Cicero, *De Natura Deorum*, II.167.
2. Seneca, *De Tranquilitate Animi*, XVII.10.
3. *Phaedrus, The Dialogues of Plato*, trans. Benjamin Jowett, 3rd ed. (Oxford, 1892), I, 449–50.
4. *Ibid.*, 450–51.
5. Aristotle, *Problems*, XXX.1. I use the text in the Loeb Classical Library, trans. W. S. Hett (London, 1936). Klibansky *et al.* (see note 6 immediately below) argue that in all probability Aristotle is not the author of this problem. They discuss "melancholy" and "mad" as synonyms on page 40.
6. Raymond Klibansky, Erwin Panofsky, and Fritz Saxl, *Saturn and Melancholy* (London, 1964), p. 67. A shorter survey of some of the same material is Rudolf and Margot Wittkower, *Born Under Saturn* (New York, 1963), chapter 5.
7. Edward Young, *Conjectures on Original Composition* (London, 1759), p. 27.

NOTES TO CHAPTER ONE

1. *King Lear*, ed. Kenneth Muir, The Arden Shakespeare (London, 1952), IV.vi.172–73. All citations from *King Lear* are to this edition.
2. Enid Welsford, *The Fool: His Social and Literary History* (London, 1935); Walter Kaiser, *Praisers of Folly* (Cambridge, Mass., 1963).
3. Edward Ward, *The London Spy* (1698–1709; rpt. London, 1964), p. 65. Italics omitted.
4. Herman Melville, "Hawthorne and His Mosses," in *Major American Writers*, ed. Perry Miller (New York, 1962), I, 894.
5. G. Wilson Knight, "*King Lear* and the Comedy of the Grotesque," in *Shakespeare's Tragedies*, ed. Laurence Lerner (London, 1963), p. 139.
6. Jonathan Swift, *A Tale of a Tub*, ed. A. C. Guthkelch and D. Nichol Smith, 2nd ed. (Oxford, 1958), p. 173.
7. See Robert C. Elliott, *The Power of Satire* (Princeton, 1960), chapters 1 and 2. Timon, Thersites, and Jaques are other such figures in Shakespeare.
8. Maynard Mack, "The Muse of Satire," *Yale Review*, 41, No. 1 (1951), 85.
9. See, for example, Maynard Mack, "The Jacobean Shakespeare: Some Observations on the Construction of the Tragedies," most readily available in the Signet Shakespeare *Othello*, ed. Alvin

Kernan (New York, 1963), pp. 208—44. See also Harold Clurman, *The Nation*, 25 November 1968, p. 574.

10. William Richardson, *Essays on Shakespeare's Dramatic Characters* (London, 1784), pp. 73 ff.

11. Thomas Davies, *Dramatic Miscellanies* (London, 1783), III, 315. The final quotation in this paragraph is from II, 320. See also Charlotte Lennox, *Shakespeare Illustrated* (London, 1753), III, 287, and *The Adventurer*, No. 122, 5 January 1754. For somewhat more general comments see the epilogue to Horace Walpole's *The Mysterious Mother* (London, 1781).

NOTES TO CHAPTER TWO

1. All quotations from Pope's poetry are taken from *Poetical Works*, ed. Herbert Davis (Oxford, 1966). I refer to the 1743 *Dunciad* throughout.

2. *Aeneid*, VI.100.

3. *Dunciad*, note to I.16. W. B. Yeats, "An Acre of Grass," in *The Collected Poems* (New York, 1956), p. 299.

4. Samuel Johnson, "Pope," *Lives of the Poets*, ed. G. B. Hill (Oxford, 1905), III, 242.

5. *The Prose Works of Alexander Pope, 1711—1720*, ed. Norman Ault (Oxford, 1936), p. 276. See also pp. 155—68, 259—66, 275—85.

6. *Epistle to Dr. Arbuthnot*, 154—56, and *Imitations of Horace*, Book II, Epistle I, 420.

7. Edward Ward, *The London Spy*, p. 65.

8. Note to II.258. See George Williamson, "The Restoration Revolt Against Enthusiasm," *Studies in Philology*, 30 (October 1933).

9. Charles Chauncy, *Enthusiasm Described and Cautioned Against*, in *American Thought and Writing*, ed. Russell B. Nye and Norman S. Grabo (Boston, 1965), 1, 371—72.

10. *Dunciad*, note to IV.478.

11. *Ibid.*, note to II.338. For the origins of the conception of the mad poet see E. R. Dodds, *The Greeks and the Irrational* (Berkeley, 1968), chapter 3. A related study is a history of epilepsy by O. Temkin, *The Falling Sickness* (Baltimore, 1945).

12. *Remarks on Prince Arthur*, in *The Critical Works*, ed. E. N. Hooker (Baltimore, 1939), I, 46. The following description of Dennis from *Memoirs of the Life of Scriblerus*, in Swift, *Satires and Personal Writings*, ed. W. A. Eddy (Oxford, 1932), pp. 150—51, is irresistible if not relevant. "It happen'd unluckily about this Time that Tim fell

sick of a Fever that settled in his Head, and he would run up and down in Alleys and Corners affronting every Body: In this Mood a Friend of mine met him one Day, and Tim accosted him with an great Oath, Z——ds. Sir, Don't you know me? Not I indeed, Sir, quoth my Friend, very civilly. No, Sir, I am J——n D——s Sir the only Man alive that has a true Taste of the Sublime. Sir, your most humble Servant, says my Friend, then you are not the Man I took you for. To convince you that I am, quoth Tim, stooping down to the Kennel, take that, and throws a great Handful of Mud all over his Cloaths. . . . In these Reveries he continued a good while, till Somebody put him into a Course of Physick, and recovered him perfectly."

13. "Of Poetry," in *Critical Essays of the Seventeenth Century*, ed. J. E. Spingarn (Oxford, 1908–9), III, 75.
14. John Locke, *An Essay Concerning Human Understanding*, ed. A. C. Fraser (New York, 1959), I, 135. For the preceding point cf. the article by Tony Tanner cited in note 23 below, p. 153. See also *A Tale of a Tub*, p. 209.
15. *A Treatise of Dreams and Visions*, in *Three Hundred Years of Psychiatry*, ed. Richard Hunter and Ida MacAlpine (Oxford, 1963), p. 233. Cf. David Hartley, *Observations on Man* (London, 1749), I, 389.
16. Pope, *Poetical Works*, p. 457.
17. See Arthur O. Lovejoy, " 'Pride' in Eighteenth-Century Thought," in *Essays in the History of Ideas* (Baltimore, 1948).
18. Ward, *The London Spy*, pp. 62–63.
19. Note to II.282. See also Emrys Jones, "Pope and Dulness," in *Pope: A Collection of Critical Essays*, ed. J. V. Guerinot (Englewood Cliffs, N.J., 1972), p. 140.
20. Pope, *Prose Works*, pp. 158–59.
21. *Ibid.*, p. 158.
22. Note to I.15.
23. Martin Price, *To the Palace of Wisdom* (New York, 1965), pp. 434–36. For an excellent essay on this general aspect of *The Dunciad* see Tony Tanner, "Reason and the Grotesque: Pope's *The Dunciad*," *The Critical Quarterly*, 7, No. 2 (1965).
24. I am paraphrasing his remarks in *The Century of Revolution* (London, 1961), pp. 4–5.
25. An important study of the economics and politics of the period is Isaac Kramnick, *Bolingbroke and His Circle* (Cambridge, Mass., 1968).
26. Ed. A. W. Secord (New York, 1938), III, 365. Cf. pp. 393–97.
27. Price, *Palace of Wisdom*, p. 153.

28. Reuben A. Brower, *Alexander Pope: The Poetry of Allusion* (Oxford, 1959), p. 342.

29. For more on this point see Marjorie H. Nicholson, *Newton Demands the Muse* (Princeton, 1946).

30. *Dunciad*, note to IV.11,12.

31. Samuel Butler, "Wit and Folly," *Characters and Passages from the Notebooks*, ed. A. R. Waller (London, 1908). For discussion of the Christian allusions of the poem see the final chapter of Aubrey L. Williams, *Pope's "Dunciad"* (Baton Rouge, 1955).

32. Trans. Richard Howard (New York, 1965). The subsequent reference to Ophelia and the Lorelei occurs on page 13.

33. See, for example, E. G. O'Donoghue, *The Story of Bethlehem Hospital* (London, 1914). Other interesting texts describing aspects of Bedlam include Roger L'Estrange, "Bethlehem's Beauty, London's Charity, and the City's Glory" (London, 1677); Thomas Brown, *Works Serious and Comical* (London, 1715), III, 32—34; Abraham Cowley, "Several Discourses," in *Complete Works*, ed. A. B. Grossart (London, 1881), II, 335 ff.; anon., "Bedlam" (London, 1776); Edward Ward, "A Letter from Tom O' Bedlam" (London, 1717); and Samuel Garth, *The Dispensary* (London, 1699), canto iv. Other relevant references are in *Three Hundred Years of Psychiatry* and in the following notes to this chapter.

34. Foucault, *Madness and Civilization*, pp. 166 ff.

35. This and many similar cases are documented in *Three Hundred Years of Psychiatry*.

36. Quoted in Ida MacAlpine and Richard Hunter, *George III and the Mad-Business* (New York, 1969), p. 338.

37. Quoted in Foucault, *Madness and Civilization*, p. 68.

38. *A Tour of London*, trans. T. Nugent (London, 1772), I, 242 ff.

39. (London, 1752), pp. 85, 11.

40. Defoe, *Augusta Triumphans; or, The Way to Make London the Most Flourishing City in the Universe* (London, 1728), p. 30. Hunter and MacAlpine in *Three Hundred Years of Psychiatry* discuss this question, p. 154. See also Defoe's list in Letter 5 of *A Tour Through the Whole Island of Great Britain* (London, 1724—26).

41. Alexander Cruden, *The London-Citizen Exceedingly Injured . . .* (London, 1739), p. 12. The Story of Cruden's imprisonment is also told in his *The Adventures of Alexander the Corrector* (London, 1754). The quotations following are from *The London-Citizen*, pp. 8—9, 16. Cruden made up a significant name for his tormentors: The "Blind Bench."

42. Tobias Smollett, *Sir Launcelot Greaves* (London, 1774), chapter 23. For more on reform see Kathleen Jones, *Lunacy, Law, and*

Conscience, 1744–1845 (London, 1955). Smollett returns to the theme in chapter 64 of *Roderick Random*.

43. Anon., *Proposals for Redressing Some Grievances Which Greatly Affect the Whole Nation* (London, 1740), in *Three Hundred Years of Psychiatry*; p. 366.

44. Sir William Fownes to Swift, 9 September 1732, in *The Correspondence of Jonathan Swift, D.D.*, ed. F. Elrington Ball (London, 1910–14), IV, 345.

45. This second Defoe quotation is from *Augusta Triumphans*, p. 36. The first quotation is taken from the *Review*, III, 279.

46. Christopher Hill, "Clarissa Harlowe and Her Times," in *Puritanism and Revolution* (London, 1962). It was not always women who fell victim to money. In Eliza Haywood's *The Female Spectator*, 2nd ed. (London, 1748), I, 128–29, we hear the story of Adulphus, who dreamed of finding money, spent it, and went to Bedlam, "a sad example of indulging prospects which are merely speculative." In *The Midnight Rambler*, anon., undated, we hear familiar phrasing: a young man gains a lucky inheritance, and "possessed of a considerable sum, his brain now maddened at the thought. . . ."

47. Quoted in Daniel H. Tuke, *Chapters in the History of the Insane in the British Isles* (Amsterdam, 1968) pp. 98–99. This is a reprint of the London edition of 1882.

48. Foucault, *Madness and Civilization*, p. 39.

49. Ward, *The London Spy*, p. 311.

50. *Ibid.*, p. 84.

51. *Leviathan*, ed. Michael Oakeshott (Oxford, 1946), p. 47. Book I, chapter 8.

52. *Ibid.*, p. 51.

53. Entry for 21 April 1657. James Carkesse, a madman kept in Bedlam and author of *Lucida Intervalla* (London, 1679), was told by the authorities that he could not be released until he stopped writing poetry.

54. Quoted in Louis I. Bredvold, *The Intellectual Milieu of John Dryden* (Ann Arbor, 1934), p. 9. See also two important articles by Donald F. Bond, " 'Distrust' of Imagination in English Neoclassicism," *Philological Quarterly*, 14 (1935), 54–69, and "The Neo-Classical Psychology of the Imagination," *English Literary History*, 4 (1937), 245–64.

55. Ward, *The London Spy*, pp. 234–35.

56. Pope, *Peri Bathos*, chapter 3. Cf. chapter 9: "as the main end and principal effect of the Bathos is to produce *Tranquility of Mind*, (and sure it is a better design to promote sleep than madness) we have little to say on this subject."

57. George Granville, *An Essay upon Unnatural Flights in Poetry* (1701) in Spingarn, *Critical Essays*, III, 294.
58. Robert Wolseley, "Preface to Valentinian," *ibid.*, 12.
59. Quoted in the introduction to *Eighteenth Century English Literature*, eds. Geoffrey Tillotson, Paul Fussell, Jr., Marshall Waingrow, and Brewster Rogerson (New York, 1969), p. 3.
60. Note to IV.99,100.
61. Edmund Burke, *A Philosophical Enquiry into the Origin of Our Ideas of the Sublime and Beautiful*, ed. J. T. Boulton (New York, 1958), p. 143.
62. I, 209.
63. Foucault, *Madness and Civilization*, p. 95.
64. Locke, *Essay*, I, 212.
65. *Ibid.*, 528.
66. Peter (7th Baron) King, *The Life of John Locke with Extracts from His Correspondence, Journals, and Commonplace Books* (London, 1830), II, 172–73. The comparison occurs in an essay on memory. Other references to madness in the same essay repeat Locke's better-known positions.
67. Locke, *Essay*, I, 402. Cf. II, 213. Note again in this passage how blindness is equated with ignorance. Locke speaks elsewhere of *"intuitive knowledge"* as "being the highest of all human certainty" (II, 407), but he means knowledge "which nobody has any doubt about," not intuition in our present sense.
68. *Errand into the Wilderness* (Cambridge, Mass., 1956), p. 168.
69. C. S. Lewis, *The Allegory of Love* (Oxford, 1938), p. 11.
70. Cruden, *Alexander the Corrector*, pp. 29–30.
71. Pope, *Correspondence*, ed. George Sherburn (Oxford, 1956), III, 3.

NOTES TO CHAPTER THREE

1. Samuel Johnson, "The Vanity of Human Wishes," line 318; James Joyce, *Ulysses* (New York, 1961), p. 39; W. B. Yeats's translation of *Ubi Saeva Indignatio / Ulterius / Cor Lacerare Nequit*.
2. See particularly Irvin Ehrenpreis, *The Personality of Jonathan Swift* (London, 1958), for Swift's medical history.
3. Quotations of Swift's poetry are taken from *Poetical Works*, ed. Herbert Davis (Oxford, 1967). Whenever convenient, line numbers are enclosed in brackets after the quotation.
4. (Lawrence, Kansas, 1958), chapter 2.
5. In *Prose Works*, ed. Herbert Davis (Oxford, 1939–67), IV, 49. The following quotation from *The Adventurer*, No. 88 (8 September

1753), reveals a similar distrust and also a hostility toward madness not uncommon in the period: "A LUNATIC is, indeed, sometimes merry, but the merry lunatic is never kind; his sport is always mischief; and mischief is rather aggravated than atoned by wantonness; his disposition is always evil in proportion to the height of his phrenzy; and upon this occasion it may be remarked, that if every approach to madness is a deviation to ill, every deviation to ill may be considered as an approach to madness."

6. "Hints Towards an Essay on Conversation," *Prose Works*, IV, 93—94.
7. *A Tale of a Tub*, ed. Guthkelch and Smith, p. 157. All quotations are from this edition (see note 6 to chapter 1).
8. *Ibid.*, p. 171.
9. *Ibid.*, p. 180.
10. VI.77 ff.
11. Sigmund Freud, *New Introductory Lectures on Psychoanalysis*, trans. James Strachey (New York, 1965), p. 77. Cf. Wassily Kandinsky, "Reminiscences," in *Modern Artists on Art*, ed. Robert L. Herbert (Englewood Cliffs, N. J., 1964), p. 33.
12. "A Serious and Useful Scheme to Make an Hospital for Incurables," in *Works*, ed. T. Scott (London, 1897—1908), VII, 294.
13. See especially "Verses on the Death of Dr. Swift" and "Part of the Seventh Epistle of the First Book of Horace Imitated." See also Irvin Ehrenpreis, "The Pattern of Swift's Women," *PMLA*, 70, No. 4 (1955).
14. Kathleen Williams, " 'Animal Rationis Capax,' " in *Fair Liberty Was All His Cry*, ed. A. N. Jeffares (New York, 1967), pp. 133—34.
15. Lines 162—63. The phrase "Blind and thoughtless Croud" appears in the "Ode to the Athenian Society," *Poetical Works,* p. 11.
16. *Poetical Works*, p. 617.
17. *Prose Works*, IV, 252.
18. *Poetical Works*, p. 40.
19. Lines 234—35 and 63 ff.
20. "To Mr. Congreve," *Poetical Works*, p. 32.
21. Bernard (De) Mandeville, *A Treatise of the Hypochondriack and Hysteric Passions* (London, 1711), p. 199.
22. *Ibid.*, p. 177.
23. John Arbuthnot, *The History of John Bull*, Part II, chapter 8; in *Life and Works*, ed. G. A. Aitken (London, 1892).
24. "Cassinus and Peter," *Poetical Works*, p. 531.
25. "The Journal of a Modern Lady," *Poetical Works*, p. 379.
26. "Part of the Seventh Epistle of the First Book of Horace Imitated," *Poetical Works*, p. 108.
27. *Tale*, pp. 114—15. Whenever possible, page references will be given

in the text in parentheses. I have relied on two useful treatments of the subject: C. M. Webster, "Swift's *Tale of a Tub* and Earlier Attacks on Puritanism," *PMLA*, 47, No. 1 (1932), and W. P. Holden, *Anti-Puritan Satire, 1572–1642* (New Haven, 1954).

28. Denis Leigh, *The Historical Development of British Psychiatry* (London, 1961), I, 66.

29. David Hume, "Of Superstition and Enthusiasm," in *Of the Standard of Taste and Other Essays*, ed. John W. Lenz (New York, 1965), p. 147.

30. Pope, *Imitations of Horace*, Book II, Satire I, 97–100. The famous lines in the *Epistle to Arbuthnot*, by their antibaptismal imagery and their elaborate protests of filial obedience, further betray this sense of danger:

> Why did I write? what sin to me unknown
> Dipt me in ink, my parents', or my own?
> As yet a child, nor yet a fool to fame,
> I lisp'd in numbers, for the numbers came.
> I left no calling for this idle trade,
> No duty broke, no father disobey'd.
>
> [125–30]

31. Norman O. Brown, *Life Against Death* (Middletown, Conn., 1959), chapter 13.

32. "Swift: The Metamorphosis of Irony," in *Discussions of Swift*, ed. J. Traugott (Boston, 1962), p. 46.

33. "Speaker and Satiric Vision in Swift's *Tale of a Tub*," *Eighteenth Century Studies*, 3, No. 2 (Winter 1969) 175–99.

34. "Legion Club," *Poetical Works*, p. 604, and "A Simile," p. 286.

35. Concluding line to the poem *Somnia quae mentes ludunt volitantibus umbris*.

36. *Love and Death in the American Novel*, rev. ed. (New York, 1966), pp. 32–33.

37. "The Imaginative and the Imaginary," in *Fables of Identity* (New York, 1963), p. 163.

38. See Ronald Paulson, *The Fictions of Satire* (Baltimore, 1967), p. 144. A good example of the mad world theme is *Tatler* 125.

39. In *Poetical Works*, ed. Gladys I. Wade (London, 1932), p. 228.

40. Gardner D. Stout, Jr., "Speaker and Satiric Vision," p. 189.

41. Swift, *A Letter of Advice to a Young Poet*, in *Prose Works*, IX, 342.

42. *Wayward Puritans: A Study in the Sociology of Deviance* (New York, 1966), p. 20.

43. *Ibid.*, p. 22.

44. Swift to Arbuthnot, July 1714, in *Correspondence*, ed. Ball, II, 190–91.

45. *Poetical Works*, pp. 601–8. The poem is anticipated by "Traulus," p. 425:

> I own, his Madness is a Jest,
> If that were all. But he's possess't:
> Incarnate with a thousand Imps,
> To work whose Ends, his Madness pimps.
> Who o'er each String and Wire preside,
> Fill ev'ry Pipe, each Motion guide.
> Directing ev'ry Vice we find
> In Scripture, to the Dev'l assign'd:
> Sent from the Dark Infernal Region
> In him they lodge, and make him *Legion*.

46. Introduction to "*Gulliver's Travels*" *and Other Writings* (Boston, 1960), pp. xxv-xxvi. For more on the sense of decline in English life see James William Johnson, *The Formation of English Neo-Classical Thought* (Princeton, 1967), pp. 60–68.
47. "A Voyage to Laputa," chapter 8. Quotations are from *Prose Works*, XI.
48. *Swift: The Man and His Works* (London, 1962), I, 218.
49. *Prose Works*, XII, 111–12.
50. Ernst Cassirer, *The Philosophy of the Enlightenment*, trans. Fritz C. A. Koelln and James P. Pettegrove (Boston, 1955), pp. 115–16.

NOTES TO CHAPTER FOUR

1. "Apothegms, Sentiments, Opinions & Occasional Reflections of Samuel Johnson," in *Johnsonian Miscellanies*, ed. G. B. Hill (New York, 1966), II, 8. This is a reprint of the Clarendon Press edition of 1897. Hereinafter cited as JM.
2. JM, I, 296.
3. *Familiar Letters on Important Occasions*, ed. Brian W. Downs (London, 1928).
4. Henry MacKenzie, *The Man of Feeling*, ed. Brian Vickers (Oxford, 1967).
5. *Boswell's Life of Johnson*, ed. G. B. Hill, revised by L. F. Powell (Oxford, 1934–50), II, 374–75; IV, 208–9. Hereinafter cited as BLJ. *Rasselas* is quoted from the edition by Bertrand Bronson, *Rasselas, Poems, and Selected Prose* (New York, 1952).
6. JM, I, 219.
7. From *Diaries, Prayers, and Annals*, ed. E. L. McAdam, Jr., with Donald and Mary Hyde (New Haven, 1958). The first quotation is from Easter Eve, 1757; the second from 21 April 1764.

8. *Passionate Intelligence* (Baltimore, 1967), pp. 58–59.
9. Bertrand Bronson, "Johnson Agonistes," in *Johnson Agonistes and Other Essays* (Berkeley, 1965).
10. BLJ, I, 471.
11. Lionel Trilling, "Mansfield Park," in *The Opposing Self* (New York, 1959), p. 218.
12. In *The Age of Johnson*, ed. F. W. Hilles (New Haven, 1949), pp. 10–11.
13. *Rambler* 117.
14. *The Achievement of Samuel Johnson* (Oxford, 1955). See especially chapter 5. Johnson was not always so sympathetic, as the story of the packthread man shows (JM, I, 300–301).
15. JM, I, 251.
16. *Adventurer* 131.
17. "Collins," *Lives of the Poets*, III, 340.
18. *Achievement*, p. 162.
19. BLJ, V, 215; JM, I, 199. Johnson also wrote on 18 September 1768: "This day it came into my mind to write the history of my melancholy. On this I purpose to deliberate. I know not whether it may not too much disturb me."
20. JM, I, 199.
21. JM, I, 234.
22. "Johnson's 'Vile Melancholy, ' " p. 13.
23. See Paul Fussell, *Samuel Johnson and the Life of Writing* (New York, 1971), p. 226.
24. "A Review of Soame Jenyns' *A Free Enquiry into the Nature and Origin of Evil*," in *Works* (Oxford, 1825), VI, 56.
25. "Plan of an English Dictionary," *ibid.*, V, 21.
26. *Ibid.*, pp. 23–24.

NOTES TO CHAPTER FIVE

1. *The English Poet and the Burden of the Past* (Cambridge, Mass., 1970), p. 48.
2. Quoted *ibid.*, p. 31.
3. *Rasselas*, chapter 10.
4. Burton, *Anatomy of Melancholy* (London, 1964), I, 39, 120. For the subsequent quotation see I, 140.
5. In *Three Hundred Years of Psychiatry*, p. 191.
6. Klibansky, Panofsky, and Saxl, *Saturn and Melancholy*, p. 231.
7. *Anatomy of Melancholy*, I, 148.
8. Quoted by G. S. Rousseau in his introduction to John Hill,

Hypochondriasis, The Augustan Reprint Society (Los Angeles, 1969), p. i.

9. *Ibid.*, p. 13.
10. Quoted in MacAlpine and Hunter, *George III and the Mad-Business*, p. 287.
11. (London, 1733), pp. i–ii.
12. *Ibid.*, p. iii.
13. *Ibid.*, p. 262.
14. Grosley, "Fools and Lunatics," *A Tour of London*, I, 246–48.
15. Cheyne, *English Malady*, pp. 260–61, 255.
16. "The English Malady," in *Backgrounds of English Literature, 1700–1760* (Minneapolis, 1953), p. 179.
17. See Amy Reed, *The Background of Gray's Elegy* (New York, 1924), pp. 125–26.
18. See Lawrence Babb, *The Elizabethan Malady: A Study of Melancholia in English Literature from 1580 to 1642* (East Lansing, Mich., 1951).
19. Quoted in *Boswell's Hypochondriack*, ed. Margery Bailey, (Stanford, 1928), I, 77.
20. Moore, "The English Malady." Moore lists many other such developments in great detail.
21. *Boswell's Hypochondriack*, I, 77.
22. *The Citizen of the World*, Letter XC, in *Collected Works*, ed. Arthur Friedman (Oxford, 1966), II, 365.
23. *Observations upon the United Provinces*, in *Works* (London, 1757), I, 170.
24. *Ibid.*, 169.
25. *A Philosophical Enquiry into the Origin of Our Ideas of the Sublime and Beautiful*, p. 135.
26. Seventh ed. (London, 1758), I, 88–90.
27. *Observations . . . on Insanity* (Leicester, 1782), I, 25–27.
28. For more on this point see Bernard Bailyn, *The Ideological Origins of the American Revolution* (Cambridge, Mass., 1967), especially chapter 3.
29. William Pargeter, quoted in Denis Leigh, *Historical Development of British Psychiatry*, I, 64.
30. *English Malady*, p. 262.
31. 28 June 1783, in *The Letters of Samuel Johnson*, ed. R. W. Chapman (Oxford, 1952), III, 41.
32. BLJ, III, 87, 175.
33. "A Treatise of the Spleen and Vapours," quoted by Leigh, *Historical Development of British Psychiatry*, I, 30.
34. *A View of the Nervous Temperament* (Newcastle, 1807), pp. xv–xviii.

35. See, for example, Montesquieu, *L'Esprit des lois* (Paris, 1749), I, 249.
36. Quoted in Leigh, *Historical Development of British Psychiatry*, I, 40.
37. *American Nervousness* (New York, 1881), pp. vii–viii. See also "Age of Melancholy," *Medical Times*, 10 January 1885.
38. For an excellent description of these problems see M. Dorothy George, *London Life in the Eighteenth Century* (London, 1925), especially chapter 1. George Rosen, *Madness in Society* (Chicago, 1968) is also useful.
39. Tobias Smollett, *The Expedition of Humphrey Clinker*, letter of 29 May.
40. *George III and the Mad-Business*, p. 272.
41. *Ibid.*, p. 291.
42. I refer throughout to the edition by J. T. Boulton cited in note 61 to chapter 2.
43. Quoted in Samuel H. Monk, *The Sublime* (Ann Arbor, 1960), p. 53.
44. *Clio; or, A Discourse on Taste*, 4th ed. (Dublin, 1778), p. 104.
45. Quoted in Monk, *The Sublime*, p. 67. The phrase "judicious horror" which follows was used by Longinus's translator William Smith (1739) to describe the mad scenes of *King Lear*.
46. *An Essay on Original Genius*, ed. John L. Mahoney (Gainesville, Fla., 1964), pp. 170–71.
47. "The Sublime Poem: Pictures and Powers," *Yale Review*, 58 (Winter 1969), pp. 201–2.
48. *A Study of English Romanticism* (New York, 1968), p. 29.
49. *An Essay on Genius*, ed. Bernhard Fabian (Munich, 1966), p. 68.
50. *Essay on Original Genius*, pp. 162, 177.
51. Pp. iii–iv, 118.
52. Burke, *Philosophical Enquiry*, p. 25; Gerard, *Essay on Genius*, p. 74. The next quotations from Gerard are on pp. 58, 65, and 71.
53. Burke, *Philosophical Enquiry*, pp. 80, 143.
54. *Ibid.*, pp. 167 ff.
55. James Usher (*Clio*, p. 121) discusses enthusiastic orators and the passions they raise in their listeners: "if they were not there before, the preacher could no more raise them than he could give a man born blind the idea of colours."
56. Burke, *Philosophical Enquiry*, p. 171.
57. It is hard not to suspect that Burke had in mind as he wrote Locke's distinction, toward the end of the *Essay*, between "real" and "chimerical" ideas: "by *real ideas*, I mean such as have a foundation in nature; such as have a conformity with the real being and existence of things, or with their archetypes. *Fantastical* or *chimerical*, I call such as have no foundation in nature, nor have any conformity with that reality of being to which they are tacitly

referred, as to their archetypes" (I, 497). Simple ideas originate in sensation and their reality is empirical and primary; complex ideas depend for their reality on their consistency with what is possible in existence. Language does not appear to have the power to achieve reality independently.

58. Burke, *Philosophical Enquiry*, p. 173.
59. *Ibid.*
60. Johnson to Bennet Langton, 27 June 1758, in *Letters*, I, 110.
61. *The Rhetorical World of Augustan Humanism* (Oxford, 1965), p. 120. The preceding reference is to M. H. Abrams, *The Mirror and the Lamp* (New York, 1953). Johnson is quoted from *Preface to Shakespeare*, in *Johnson on Shakespeare*, ed. Arthur Sherbo (New Haven, 1968), I, 62.

NOTES TO CHAPTER SIX

1. "Towards Defining an Age of Sensibility," in *Fables of Identity* (New York, 1963).
2. "The Name and Nature of Poetry," in *The Creative Process*, ed. Brewster Ghiselin (Berkeley and Los Angeles, 1952).
3. Frye, "Age of Sensibility," p. 136.
4. BLJ, I, 397. The poem quoted in the same paragraph is taken from Christopher Devlin, *Poor Kit Smart* (London, 1961), p. 103. Ironically Smart himself describes several fictitious visits to Bedlam in *The Midwife; or, The Old Woman's Magazine*, 1 (1750), 176 ff. These stories are typical of the new sentimentalism: Mary Midnight, the heroine, frequently bursts into tears; she also sees a woman whose husband committed her and took her money.
5. The Blake quotation is from *The Marriage of Heaven and Hell* (see note 21 below). J. C. Schiller, quoted in Sigmund Freud, *The Interpretation of Dreams*, in *The Basic Writings of Sigmund Freud*, trans. A. A. Brill (New York, 1938), p. 191. The relevant essay by Hartman in the next paragraph is "Romanticism and Anti-Self-Consciousness," in *Beyond Formalism* (New Haven, 1970).
6. I quote from the Everyman's Library edition of Cowper's poems, edited by Hugh I'Anson Fausset (London, 1931).
7. *Memoir of the Early Life of William Cowper*, 2nd American ed. (Newburgh, 1817), p. 51.
8. *Ibid.*, p. 52.
9. *Life of Cowper* (London, 1803), I, 26.
10. *Essays on the Lives of Cowper, Newton, and Herber* (London, 1830), p. 10.
11. *Life of Cowper*, II, 211.

12. *Ibid.*, 222.
13. P. v.
14. (Philadelphia, 1833), p. 5.
15. *Ibid.*, p. 201.
16. *Ibid.*, p. 199.
17. *Medical Inquiries and Observations upon the Diseases of the Mind* (Philadelphia, 1833), p. 95.
18. *Ibid.*, pp. 241–42.
19. C. G. Jung, *Memories, Dreams, Reflections,* ed. Aniela Jaffe, trans. Richard and Clara Winston (New York, 1963), p. 127.
20. Hayley seems to have been fascinated by mad poets. His own poem "The Triumphs of Temper," in Volume V of *Poems and Plays* (London, 1785), deals obliquely with the question of madness. See also Morton D. Paley, "Cowper as Blake's Spectre," *Eighteenth Century Studies*, 1, No. 3 (Spring 1968), 236–52.
21. William Blake, *Complete Writings,* ed. Geoffrey Keynes, rev. ed. (Oxford, 1966), p. 551. All quotations of Blake's poetry have been taken from this edition, with the page numbers cited in the text.
22. *Blake's Apocalypse* (London, 1963), p. 442. For a time in the nineteenth century a legend persisted that Blake had been confined to Bedlam for several years.
23. *Life of William Blake,* rev. Ruthven Todd (London, 1945), p. 324.
24. Keats was also called a madman who had been exploited by friends in many of the early reviews of *Endymion.*
25. *The Letters of William Blake,* ed. Geoffrey Keynes (London, 1968), pp. 35–36.
26. I adapt several points from Martin Price's brilliant discussion of Blake's satire in *To the Palace of Wisdom,* pp. 390–445.
27. *Rasselas,* chapter 4.
28. *Letters,* p. 36. The whole question of children in the eighteenth century is an interesting one. Locke, Hartley, and most rationalistic philosophers of the early part of the century tended to class children, idiots, and madmen together as inadequate human beings. But slowly the century did see the rise of children's literature. And the moral treatment that characterizes late-eighteenth-century psychiatry was founded on a view of patients as simply overgrown children who would listen to reason if forced to. But the child's life, especially his freedom and his innocence, grew obviously more important as a symbol to Romantic writers. Childishness seems also to have been somehow connected with the rise of pornography in the latter half of the century.
29. Conceivably one could trace a similar career for *Don Quixote* in the eighteenth century.

30. "Throughout all the play is there not sublimity felt amidst the continual presence of all kinds of disorder and confusion in the natural and moral world,—a continual consciousness of eternal order, law and good? This it is that so exalts it in our eyes. There is more justness of intellect in Lear's madness than in his right senses, as if the indestructible divinity of the spirit gleamed at times more brightly through the ruins of its earthly tabernacle." *Blackwood's Magazine,* 5 (May 1819), 228.

31. BLJ, II, 106.

32. Cf. *The Memoirs of Martinus Scriblerus,* chapter 8.

Index